ASSESSING THE
GEORGE W. BUSH PRESIDENCY

# ASSESSING THE GEORGE W. BUSH PRESIDENCY

## A Tale of Two Terms

Edited by Andrew Wroe and Jon Herbert

Edinburgh University Press

To Amanda, Albert and Alice – AW
To Camille Herbert – JH



Edinburgh University Press Ltd
22 George Square, Edinburgh
www.euppublishing.com

Typeset in Palatino Light by
Norman Tilley Graphics Ltd, Northampton,
and printed and bound in Great Britain by
CPI Antony Rowe, Chippenham and Eastbourne

A CIP record for this book is available from
the British Library

ISBN 978 0 7486 2740 0 (hardback)
ISBN 978 0 7486 2741 7 (paperback)

# CONTENTS


Notes on the Contributors vii

1 Introduction: A Tale of Two Terms 1
*Andrew Wroe and Jon Herbert*

Part I: Institutions and Structures

2 George W. Bush and the US Congress 13
*Robert Singh*

3 George W. Bush as Chief Executive 29
*James P. Pfiffner*

4 George W. Bush and the US Supreme Court 44
*Emma Long*

5 Federalism in the Bush Era 59
*M. J. C. Vile*

Part II: Foreign Policy Leadership

6 To Usher in a New Paradigm? President Bush's Foreign Policy Legacy 77
*Jason Ralph*

7 Reforming the National Security Apparatus 100
*Steven Hurst*

8 Bush and Europe 115
*David Patrick Houghton*

9 International Trade Policy under George W. Bush 129
*Nitsan Chorev*

Part III: Domestic Policy Leadership

10 President Bush and the Economy 149
*Graham Wilson*

11 The Politics of Aging 166
*Alex Waddan*

12 No Child Left Behind: The Politics and Policy of Education Reform 182
*Jonathan Parker*

13 The Bush Administration and the Politics of Sexual Morality 199
*Edward Ashbee*

14 Communications Strategies in the Bush White House 216
*John Anthony Maltese*

15 A Lasting Republican Majority? George W. Bush's Electoral Strategy 239
*Kevin Fullam and Alan R. Gitelson*

16 Conclusion: The Legacy of George W. Bush 258
*Jon Herbert and Andrew Wroe*

Index 277

# NOTES ON THE CONTRIBUTORS

Edward Ashbee is an associate professor at Copenhagen Business School's International Center for Business and Politics. He is author of *The Bush Administration, Sex and the Moral Agenda* (Manchester University Press, 2007) and co-editor of *The Politics, Economics, and Culture of Mexican–US Migration: Both Sides of the Border* (Palgrave Macmillan, 2008).

Nitsan Chorev is assistant professor of sociology at Brown University. She is author of *Remaking U.S. Trade Policy: from Protectionism to Globalization* (Cornell University Press, 2007), which explores the transformation of US trade policies from the 1930s to the present.

Kevin Fullam is an adjunct lecturer at Loyola University. His teaching interests involve the depiction of American government in film and television. Fullam also covers the intersection of politics, sociology and popular culture as the host of *Under Surveillance* on Chicago's WLUW-FM.

Alan Gitelson is professor of political science at Loyola University, Chicago. His books include *American Political Parties: Stability and Change* (Houghton Mifflin), *American Government* (Wadsworth/Cengage Publishers, 2009), *Public Policy and Economic Institutions* (JAI Press) and *American Elections: The Rules Matter* (Longman Pearson Publishers, 2002).

Jon Herbert is a lecturer in American politics at Keele University. His primary research interest is the United States presidency. His research focuses on the relationship between presidential policymaking, presidential agendas and political strategy.

David Patrick Houghton is an associate professor of political science and has taught at the University of Central Florida since 2003. He has also held positions at the Ohio State University, Essex University and the University of Pittsburgh. His most recent book is *Political Psychology: Situations, Individuals and Cases* (Routledge, 2009).

Steven Hurst is a senior lecturer in the Department of Politics and Philosophy, Manchester Metropolitan University. He is the author of *Cold War US Foreign Policy* (2005) and *The United States and Iraq since 1979* (2009), both published by Edinburgh University Press.

Emma Long teaches American history at the University of Kent. Her research interests include US constitutional and legal history, the history of the Supreme Court, post-World War II US history and, in particular, the legal, political and social history of church–state relations. She is currently completing a manuscript on the Court and the establishment clause.

John Anthony Maltese is the Albert Berry Saye Professor and chair of the Political Science Department at the University of Georgia. His books include *Spin Control: The White House Office of Communications and the Management of Presidential News, The Selling of Supreme Court Nominees,* and (with Joseph Pika) *The Politics of the Presidency*.

Jonathan Parker is a senior lecturer in American politics in the School of Politics, International Relations and Philosophy at Keele University. He specialises in public policy, particularly education. He has published on American education at the state and local level and on higher education policy.

James P. Pfiffner is University Professor in the School of Public Policy at George Mason University. He has written or edited twelve books on the presidency and American national government, including *Power Play: The Bush Administration and the Constitution* (Brookings, 2008). His book, *Torture as Public Policy,* will be published by Paradigm Publishers in 2009.

Jason Ralph is a senior lecturer in international relations at the University of Leeds. He is author of *Defending the Society of States: Why*

*America Opposes the International Criminal Court and its Vision of World Society* (Oxford University Press, 2007). His current research project "Law, War and the State of the American Exception" is funded by the Economic and Social Research Council.

Robert Singh is a professor of politics at Birkbeck College, University of London. His research interests are in US politics and foreign policy and he is the co-author, with Tim Lynch, of *After Bush: The Case for Continuity in US Foreign Policy* (Cambridge University Press, 2008).

M. J. C. Vile is an emeritus professor of political science at the University of Kent. His interests lie in the areas of federalism, constitutional theory and American politics. The sixth edition of his *Politics in the USA* was published by Routledge in 2007.

Alex Waddan is a senior lecturer in politics and American studies at the University of Leicester. He teaches US politics and US foreign policy and has published widely on the politics of US social policy. He is currently working on a project examining how ideas have influenced US social policy over the last decade.

Graham Wilson is a professor of political science at Boston University. He was previously a professor at the University of Wisconsin–Madison and began his career at the University of Essex. He is the author of many books and articles on American and British politics. His *Handbook Of Business And Government*, co-edited with David Coen and Wyn Grant, will be published by Oxford University Press in 2010.

Andrew Wroe is a lecturer in United States politics at the University of Kent. His most recent book is *The Republican Party and Immigration Politics: From Proposition 187 to George W. Bush* (Palgrave Macmillan, 2008).

*Chapter 1*

# INTRODUCTION: A TALE OF TWO TERMS

Andrew Wroe and Jon Herbert

George W. Bush left office on 20 January 2009. Many, perhaps most, observers thought the country and world inherited by Barack Obama were considerably less safe and prosperous than those Bush had inherited eight years earlier. While most presidents, even two-term ones, leave office with their reputations damaged, they rarely achieve the level of opprobrium that clung to President Bush. Americans, in a multitude of different polls, consistently rated him as one of the country's worst post-war presidents – and not without reason.

## 1. SECOND TERM WOES

Bush started, and failed to end, wars and civil wars in Afghanistan and Iraq, at great human, financial and geopolitical cost. Tens of thousands of lives and hundreds of billions of dollars were expended in a hitherto unsuccessful attempt to rid the world of "terror". Indeed, many commentators and politicians, including Bush's successor in the White House, suggested that the war on terror was itself a primary motivating factor radicalising elements, particularly fundamentalist Islamists, already hostile to the United States, thus making the world a more dangerous and unstable place. Even outside the two main arenas of conflict, the security situation deteriorated in Europe, Asia and the Middle East. The United Kingdom, Spain, Russia and its satellites, Pakistan, India, Indonesia, China and Egypt, among others, experienced large and deadly terrorist attacks after the instigation of the war on terror. The Israel–Palestine conflict, both a cause and consequence of instability and hostility, erupted again in 2008 with great loss of life. During Bush's tenure, governments friendly to the

United States lost power or were threatened by their public's hostility to American actions (Spain, Pakistan, Turkey) while others used that hostility to bolster, or hang on to, power (Iran, Syria, Cuba). Bush's foreign policy woes were not the result of bad luck or military failure, argues Ralph in Chapter 6, but a strategic failure of the Bush doctrine.

The world is now more hazardous, and critics claim Bush is to blame. He is pilloried, too, for economic failures, none more so than the global financial crisis. As Bush left office, government spending, the national debt, budget deficit and balance of trade were at historically high peacetime levels. Unemployment was rising quickly, the economy shrinking, banks failing and the motor industry on the edge of bankruptcy. The economic environment had not looked so perilous since the dark days of the Great Depression in the 1930s, which ushered in several generations of Democratic Party dominance. Moreover, the slumping stock market and falling house prices reduced significantly the value of many Americans' assets and retirement funds. It is unsurprising that at the end of Bush's last year in office, according to Gallup's polling, about 80 per cent of Americans thought the economy was the most important problem facing the country, that about 90 per cent thought it a bad time to find a good job, and that not since Gallup started asking the question in the mid-1970s had so many Americans felt so pessimistic about their current financial situation.

Wilson (Chapter 10), like many economists, is unsure precisely how much Bush is to blame for the crisis which has its roots in the collapse of the sub-prime mortgage market, but argues convincingly that he made matters much worse by cutting taxes, borrowing heavily, running large deficits and failing to invest during good times; by deregulating the financial markets and failing to oversee risky new financial instruments; by rigidly pursuing free-market solutions; and by adopting a style of policymaking that discounted or ignored professional, independent expert advice and discouraged debate over alternative policy solutions.

The irony of the Bush administration's record on economic policy-making is that the eventual outcome was diametrically opposed to the original intention. Over the opposition of many recalcitrant members of his own party in Congress, Bush spent his last months in office overseeing the largest nationalisation programme in American history, as major banks, and mortgage and insurance companies came under government control or majority ownership, at huge cost to the taxpayer. Billions of dollars more were spent buying up toxic loans, injecting liquidity into the financial markets, and propping up ailing financial and industrial giants, including General Motors, Chrysler and Ford. The American people turned against big business, especially its overpaid executives whose remuneration packages and huge bonuses seemed to bear no relation to their own or their companies' performance. The collapse of some of America's great corporate institutions – Fannie Mae, Freddie Mac, Lehman Brothers, Merrill Lynch, AIG – was accompanied by the disintegration of the Washington consensus, the neo-liberal belief in the sanctity of markets and their mechanisms, which had increasingly dominated economic policymaking in the late twentieth and early twenty-first centuries. As Wilson notes, anyone who had suggested prior to 2008 that the United States would witness such a large-scale government intervention in the US economy and the breakdown of the prevailing free-market ideology would have been dismissed as a crank. That it happened on the watch and, to some extent, at the behest of President Bush is even more remarkable. Henry Paulson, Bush's treasury secretary, called such intervention "objectionable", but advocated it anyway in the absence of any realistic alternative. Clinton claimed the era of big government was over; Bush brought it back.

The economic crisis of Bush's last year in office was preceded by a series of failed attempts to reform public policy, most notably in the areas of Social Security and immigration. Waddan (Chapter 11) shows how the Bush administration badly miscalculated the prospects for reform, underestimating the institutional and structural barriers and overestimating its own persuasive talents. This failure early in the second term undermined the administration's political reputation and public prestige. Together with the federal government's wholly inadequate response, both perceived and real, to Hurricane Katrina in August 2005, the debacle over Social Security set the tone for Bush's remaining time in office. Katrina was particularly significant because it symbolised in one photograph – Bush staring down on New Orleans from Air Force One as he returned to Washington from his vacation – the president's alleged detachment from and disinterest in the plight of fellow Americans on the ground. It also symbolised for some their belief that the president was a man unable to empathise with the suffering of others, with people less fortunate than himself.

Remarkably, Bush did not respond to the dramatic diminution in his political capital by reining in his legislative ambitions but, instead, pushed on with so-called "comprehensive" immigration reform. In a grand bargain, the status of up to ten million immigrants illegally resident in the United States would be "regularised" or "legalised" but the border would finally be closed to prevent the entry of any more. To its opponents, the most ferocious being his own previously loyal Republican lieutenants in the House of Representatives and social and cultural conservatives in the country at large, the reform was nothing less than an "amnesty" for lawbreakers. Bush genuinely believed that immigration was part of America's great story, and a significant force for renewal, but this was not the reason he pursued liberal reform in the face of bewildered opposition from his base. Rather, the main impetus to immigration reform was that Bush and his political svengali, Karl Rove, calculated that it would engender an electoral realignment and allow the Republican Party to dominate American politics for at least a generation. That monumental legacy would, they thought, cement Bush's place in history as a great Republican and a great president. The reality is likely to be very different, as we discuss in more detail in Chapter 16.

## 2. FIRST TERM SUCCESSES

The many significant failures of Bush's second term are intriguing from both policy and political perspectives because they follow a number of very important successes in his first term. It is usual for presidents to do better in their first term, and the phenomenon of the second-term lame-duck president is well known. What is notable in George W. Bush's case is the magnitude of the difference. The failures and problems of the second term outlined above contrast sharply against his first term successes, such as two of the three largest tax cuts in American history, the most important education reform in thirty-five years and the largest expansion of health care and most wide-ranging reorganisation of the federal bureaucracy in a generation (see Singh, Chapter 2; Parker, Chapter 12; Hurst, Chapter 7). Such dominance of the legislative agenda in domestic affairs is unusual because presidents often struggle against the institutional advantages of other actors and the established structures of power. Of course, Bush also dominated the agenda on foreign affairs, especially after the terrorist attacks on 11 September 2001, but his dominance in this area is less remarkable than in domestic matters.

Bush's domestic policy triumphs are especially remarkable in part because, as noted above, presidents often struggle to impose their agendas but also because the political environment looked particularly hostile when Bush was sworn in as president on 20 January 2001. Bush did inherit from Bill Clinton a Republican Congress, but he did nothing to enhance its majority during the 2000 cycle, and nor did its GOP members feel they owed their seats to him. Indeed, Bush's electoral coat-tails were actually negative, as the Republicans lost two seats in the House and five in the Senate, yielding a narrow majority in the lower chamber and a 50–50 tie in the upper. Thanks to Vice President Dick Cheney, the President of the Senate, and his deciding vote in the event of a tie, the Republicans gained control of the Senate with an effective majority of one. The situation was particularly problematic given that the majority party usually requires a supermajority (sixty votes) to push legislation to a vote in the Senate, and was made worse when Republican Senator Jim Jeffords (Vermont) resigned the party's whip, declared himself an independent and started to caucus with the Democrats, handing them formal control of the upper chamber. Another seeming impediment to future legislative success was that Bush could not claim, with any seriousness, a mandate for his agenda. He lost the popular vote to Al Gore by some 500,000 votes and sneaked a victory, the closest since 1876, in the electoral college only thanks to the US Supreme Court's controversial decision in *Bush v. Gore* (2000) to award him Florida's electoral college votes. He was in many people's and politicians' eyes an illegitimate or, at best, wounded president who would have to govern from the centre in a bipartisan fashion. That he campaigned as a "uniter, not a divider" and a "compassionate conservative", the right's answer to Clinton's "third way", suggested that he might. He did not.

Moreover, despite the unpromising political environment at the start of his presidency, the first term's significant legislative successes were accompanied by impressive electoral performances in 2002 and 2004. In contrast to most incumbent presidents, who are risk averse and do not want to be associated with electoral defeat, Bush campaigned hard for Republican candidates in the 2002 mid-term congressional elections, putting his authority and prestige on the line to enhance the party's majority in the House and win back the Senate.

On only three occasions in the twentieth century had the pı party won extra congressional seats, but the gamble paid o somely for Bush as Republicans took a further eight seats House and two in the Senate to retake control. The elections were equally satisfying for Republicans. The congressional party enhanced its majorities, to thirty seats in the House and ten in Senate – the first time in seventy years the incumbent presiden party had done so in both chambers. President Bush fought off th challenge of Democratic Senator John Kerry and was re-elected on an improved popular and electoral college vote. Success in 2002 and 2004 helped convince Bush of the efficacy of his electoral and governing strategy, and thus to pursue it with renewed vigour in his second term. History indicates it was the wrong choice, as we explain below.

## 3. CAMPAIGNING TO GOVERN

The same strategy that had brought some impressive election victories would undermine the second half of his presidency; the same strategy that in his first term delivered many important policy successes during a national security crisis created the resentments, tensions and polarisation that precluded success in the second. That strategy was governing by campaigning. On its own, it would have been problematic, but combined with Bush's personal style and belief system, it would prove ruinous (see Singh, Chapter 2; Maltese, Chapter 14; Fullam and Gitelson, Chapter 15). Governing via a permanent campaign requires presidents to present and sell their legislative priorities directly to the American people who, in turn, directly or indirectly pressurise members of Congress to support their passage. Going public in this way is antithetical to the legislative strategies based on persuasion and bargaining long advocated by most respected presidential scholars, because it pressurises, even bullies, members of Congress to support the executive's position.

Another element to governing by campaigning is that it is polarising and frequently partisan. Public policy reform is a complex business because the world is a complex place, but the president's policy solutions must be simplified for an inattentive and ill-informed public. Other interested political actors will also boil down their arguments to readily communicated sound bites as each tries to sell them to the public. Once ideas are in the public domain and become associated with various actors, however, positions become entrenched, and bargaining and compromise become more difficult because shifting or abandoning publicly articulated positions could lead to a loss of reputation and prestige. Just as in an electoral campaign, no side will admit error or acknowledge that the other side may have a good idea. Indeed, positions are often adopted because they are different from, or in opposition to, the other party's or because they present the other party with awkward political decisions. Politics is thus polarised, its partisan nature exacerbated. Campaigning is adversarial while governing is best achieved via collaboration, and therefore the permanent campaign mitigates against effective governance.

Given these problems and the administration's limited political resources initially, it is perhaps surprising that the Bush administration decided to engage in a permanent campaign. It is perhaps even more surprising given that the administration sometimes adopted, at least early in Bush's presidency, a rival approach and often with considerable success. As Singh notes (Chapter 2), the president demonstrated during his first term that he was a relatively skilled congressional operator in terms of knowing which policy changes Congress was capable of delivering, and he could be charming, funny, charismatic and persuasive when meeting in private with members of Congress. Indeed, two historic reforms in education (the No Child Left Behind Act of 2001) and health care (the Medicare Modernization Act of 2003) were products of this bipartisan Bush (see Waddan, Chapter 11; Parker, Chapter 12). The permanent campaign and the partisan polarisation it wrought, then, were not inevitable but a choice the Bush administration made and one that would come to serve it poorly.

The decision to adopt the partisan strategy was probably influenced by four interlinked factors. First, despite the inherent tension between legislative bargaining and going public, all modern administrations and some political scientists believe that presidents must make their case directly to the people in an era in which Congress has atomised, interest groups proliferated and trust declined. Second, Bush was not unique in campaigning to govern but he did it more extensively than any previous president in part because the strategy fitted his personality and style. While he could be engaging and work in a bipartisan fashion as he demonstrated throughout his tenure as governor of Texas and early in his presidency, Bush liked to define himself as "the decider", a man who set the agenda making big decisions, holding steady to them and refusing to countenance doubt. This style lent itself to the simple certainties required by performance in the public arena.

Conversely, he was uncomfortable with policy detail and parsing options which, of course, are central to the alternative, bipartisan approach to lawmaking. Third, governing by campaigning appeared to work, and so was retained. For example, Bush's first significant policy triumph, the 2001 $1.3 trillion tax cut, was the product of a "partisan budgetary strategy" argues Singh. Finally, and perhaps most importantly, the 9/11 terrorist attacks both increased the opportunity for, and enhanced the effectiveness of, governing by campaigning, at least in the short term. Crises centralise power vertically from the states to the federal government and horizontally from the legislature to the executive, and 9/11 was no different in its consequences. Subsequently, Bush deliberately made the war on terror the defining issue of his presidency because of the legislative and electoral advantages it could deliver for him specifically and Republicans generally. The security climate made opposing the president very difficult, even on issues only tangentially related to security. National security trumped all other cards and, of course, the administration worked very hard to make sure that it was defined and controlled by the White House and the Republican Party. Moreover, Bush was equally content to override states' rights arguments and impose the federal government's will when it suited the administration (Vile, Chapter 5). His was not an administration in the conservative, small-government tradition.

The Bush administration's permanent campaign was allied to a sophisticated, professional communications organisation and strategy (Maltese, Chapter 14) and a "fifty-plus-one" electoral and legislative strategy (Fullam and Gitelson, Chapter 15). The aim was to mobilise the party's base, especially culturally conservative Christian voters, to win elections (Ashbee, Chapter 13), and to maintain strong party discipline in Congress to win key votes. It was also allied to an arrogant, perhaps unconstitutional, exercise of executive power (Pfiffner, Chapter 3) that alienated many moderates in Congress. Denying "enemy combatants" in Guantánamo Bay the protection of the international laws of war, spying on American citizens without judicial oversight, and making war in Iraq without reference to expert testimony are a few of the many examples in the following chapters of the Bush administration's dismissive approach to the institutional restraints on the executive branch.

Bush's style and strategy engendered no reservoir of good will when events turned against him, especially when the might of the US armed forces failed to win the peace in Iraq and Afghanistan. Even the US Supreme Court, traditionally subservient to executive excesses during crisis or war and mute during Bush's first term, spoke out in the second term in support of the rights of enemy combatants, despite Bush having pushed the Court to the right with two new appointments (Long, Chapter 4). Internationally, too, Bush was shunned, invading Iraq without United Nations support and in the face of huge demonstrations by citizens around the world. Defense secretary Donald Rumsfeld antagonised many foreign leaders with his remarks about "old Europe", but his statement was emblematic of the divide between America and its traditional allies and of the administration's lack of concern about what others thought of it or wanted (Houghton, Chapter 8). In the realm of liberalising international trade, too, the administration largely failed to promote multilateral agreements. The alternative strategy of pursuing bilateral and regional agreements had the unhappy result – at least as far as the administration was concerned – of provoking increased congressional activity and resistance in the area (Chorev, Chapter 9).

In sum, the Bush administration achieved many significant successes during its first term, despite an ostensible lack of political capital, but the strategy responsible for most of these successes was itself the major cause of the second term's failures, of which there were many. What had appeared a strong, successful but polarising presidency unravelled as the permanent campaign malfunctioned as a governing strategy. Bush's presidency came to an ignoble end with the economy crashing and the country's military engagements unresolved. With Democrats taking control of the legislature and executive in 2009, earlier talk about a Republican electoral realignment and historic legacy looked foolish in retrospect. On his exit from office, the American public rated Bush harshly. It is possible that in the court of history his reputation will be revived – perhaps if his foreign adventures produce democratic and stable regimes or if his government's massive economic intervention provides the foundation for a solid recovery – just as Truman is today held in much higher esteem than when he left office. As we conclude in the final chapter of this volume, our best guess is that this is unlikely, with the first term's successes buried deep below the second term's failures in the nation's collective memory.

# PART I
# INSTITUTIONS AND STRUCTURES

*Chapter 2*

# GEORGE W. BUSH AND THE US CONGRESS

Robert Singh

During the 2000 presidential election campaign, George W. Bush had promised to seek an end to the vicious partisanship of the Clinton years and, if elected, be a "uniter, not a divider". His record as governor of Texas (1995–2001) had indeed seen considerable bipartisan co-operation with the state legislature and Bush had proven a popular chief executive. Gaining the presidency after losing the popular vote to Al Gore, through a controversial US Supreme Court intervention (*Bush* v. *Gore,* 2000), and with a bare majority of Republicans in Congress, Bush was widely expected to deliver on his promise and reach out across the aisle to forge bipartisan consensus. Moreover, in his 13 December 2000 victory speech after Gore finally conceded defeat, Bush spoke from the chamber of the Texas House of Representatives and declared that, "The spirit of cooperation I have seen in this hall is what is needed in Washington, DC."

By the end of his two terms in office, however, it was self-evident that Bush had been "a divider, not a uniter" (Jacobson 2007). Having successfully made the 2006 mid-term elections a referendum on Bush's faltering leadership, congressional Democrats viewed the president with a mixture of contempt, derision and disgust – though they subsequently proved unable to reverse his policies on Iraq despite their majorities in the 110th Congress (2007–8). Congressional Republicans, for the first time in the minority since 1993–4, and running for re-election in 2008, vigorously distanced themselves from the president, whose controversial policies and executive incompetence had effectively made the Republican brand a toxic one: by 2008, Americans viewed Democrats as more competent than Republicans by a margin of five to three, and as more ethical by a margin of two to one. Many economic conservatives in both parties loathed the fiscal irresponsibility, the growth of government entitlement spending programmes such as Medicare, and the apparent reversal by Bush of the historic conservative gains that had culminated in Bill Clinton's 1996 State of the Union declaration that "the era of big government is over". Few could have anticipated in January 2001 that the Bush era would end with a $700 billion economic rescue package, the partial nationalisation of the US banking system by a supposedly conservative administration, a federal budget deficit heading in excess of one trillion dollars, and a national debt of more than ten trillion.

On the morning after the 2004 presidential election – "an accountability moment", as Bush had phrased it with typical inelegance – it looked to some as if the age of an enduring Republican majority had dawned. Bush had not only won re-election with more votes than any previous American president but he had become the first in seventy years to achieve re-election while increasing his party's majorities in both houses of Congress. Just two years later, however, the president received what he called a "thumpin'" in the mid-term elections, with the Democrats winning control of Congress along with six more governorships and 321 additional state legislative seats. The Democrats defeated six incumbent United States senators and picked up thirty House seats. By 2008, the trends were so strongly favouring the Democrats that a nascent Republican realignment a mere four years earlier appeared to some to have instead morphed into an emergent Democratic majority.

This chapter places such volatile political fortunes within the context of Bush's relations with Congress, especially in the light of two competing interpretations of presidential–congressional relations. It argues firstly that, whatever one thinks of the merits or demerits of the particular policies he pursued, Bush was generally a relatively skilled president in terms of his understanding of what he could or could not get out of Capitol Hill. Despite his rightly earned reputation for stubbornness, Bush would generally seek the maximum he could hope for before compromising on the most feasibly available from lawmakers. In the poker idiom he, more often than not, "knew when to hold 'em, knew when to fold 'em". But, secondly, Bush's style of presidential unilateralism – while in some respects effective in policy terms – profoundly alienated lawmakers and cost Bush significant reserves of trust and respect on the Hill, especially by and during his second term. Third, Bush's very mixed legislative record demonstrated that, despite charges that the administration pursued an imperial "power play" (Pfiffner 2008) to subvert and shred the American Constitution, the reality of America's separated system of government remains robust. Crucial to the relative willingness of the president and Congress to co-operate is the partisan balance, the partisan style of the respective parties and the external environment confronting both institutions. In the volatile international and domestic conditions of the post-9/11 years, presidential–congressional relations reflected and reinforced a highly polarised and fractious environment.

## 1. CONGRESS: TO PERSUADE OR NOT TO PERSUADE?

Scholars have long debated the institutional relationship between Congress and the presidency as formally coequal branches of the national government. The growth of the federal government since Roosevelt's New Deal and the emergence of a national security state after World War II empowered significantly the executive branch. George W. Bush assumed office in January 2001 as the latest of a succession of chief executives whose executive branch of government possessed enormous resources, authority and legitimacy to speak both to and for the American nation.

Since Richard Neustadt's legendary definition of presidential power as "the power to persuade", observers of the interaction of the White House and Capitol Hill typically stressed the centrality of bargaining and cajoling over coercion. To succeed as president, the incumbent needed to establish good relations with Congress, devise effective legislative liaison strategies, and manoeuvre tactically to build minimal winning coalitions in the two houses of the national legislature. Even with supportive party majorities in both houses, a good reputation in Washington and public support, presidential success could not reliably be assured in a notoriously slow, reactive and obstructionist legislative body. The US Senate, especially, prized its various institutional mechanisms that made the body highly individualistic and resistant to coercive "top-down" command. The House, while somewhat more amenable to party discipline, nonetheless also constituted a decentralised, fragmented and often obdurate body. Add to this that, since 1968, the norm has been divided party control of the White House and Congress, and it has been easy to understand why enduring presidential success in Congress has typically been more the exception than the rule.

More recently, however, a rather different interpretive picture has emerged. While the Neustadtian perspective remains valid in terms of the president "in the legislative arena" – that is, in seeking to persuade Congress to approve or disapprove new legislation – the new interpretation holds that the president retains extensive resources that are extraordinarily difficult for Congress to check and balance. In terms of influencing the content of public policy, "the president's freedom to act unilaterally is defined by Congress's ability, and the judiciary's willingness, to subsequently overturn him" (Howell 2003: xv). But mobilising collective action is typically very difficult in Congress (not least reaching the supermajority required to achieve a filibuster-proof sixty and presidential veto-proof sixty-seven votes in the Senate). Moreover, the unelected and unaccountable judiciary lacks the democratic legitimacy to check executive actions frequently. As a result, the president can legitimately exploit his unique position within the separated system to take independent action, with or without the consent of either Congress or the courts:

> The fact of the matter is that presidents have always made law without the explicit consent of Congress, sometimes by acting upon general powers delegated to them by different congresses, past and present, and other times by reading new executive authorities into the Constitution itself. (Howell 2003: 13)

In pursuing the politics of direct presidential action, presidents regularly exert "power without persuasion". In sum, through executive agreements, executive orders, presidential declarations and other mechanisms, the expressly co-operative model of presidential–congressional relations of American civics textbooks can be circumvented via bold assertions of presidential unilateralism, especially during times of perceived crisis. In assessing both the propriety and political effectiveness of congressional–presidential relations in the Bush years, these competing interpretations merit careful emphasis.

## 2. THE TURBULENT BUSH YEARS

George W. Bush's relations with Congress from 2001 to 2009 were punctuated by a series of key events that repeatedly and rapidly reshaped Washington politics: the defection of Republican Senator James Jeffords that handed control of the Senate to the Democrats in June 2001; the terrorist attacks of 11 September 2001; the regaining by the Republicans of both houses of Congress in the November 2002 elections; the invasion of Iraq in March 2003 and the subsequent war; Bush's re-election in November 2004; and the Democrats' triumph in the mid-term elections of 2006. Were one to take a snapshot of presidential power at each of these points, the overall picture that would emerge would be of a rapidly oscillating White House, at times able to dominate both ends of Pennsylvania Avenue aggressively, at others in a defensive and frustrated state of near meltdown.

Rather than going through chronologically the various stages of Bush's years in office, however, it is perhaps more useful to consider why such rapid ebbs and flows in presidential–congressional relations occurred. Changes in the partisan balance, and especially in partisan control of one or other house, naturally account for some of this evolution. But much of this is also inseparable from the president's approach to relations with Congress and the long-term costs that accompanied short-term presidential victories. Bush did not pursue a consistent approach on Capitol Hill, at times following a narrowly partisan strategy, at others reaching out to Democrats, and often employing both at the same time on distinct issues. In some regards, this was unsurprising and rational; although he was the first Republican president to see his party in control of both houses of Congress since Dwight D. Eisenhower (1953–61), Bush never enjoyed the kinds of decisive congressional majorities that could assure the enactment of a consistent reform programme through a one-party style of government. But when combined with a highly autocratic, secretive and unconsultative executive style, especially in his first term, along with the controversial aspects of the war on terror, Bush's mix of methods ultimately cost the president dearly on the Hill in his second term.

## 3. "BENDING SO AS NOT TO BREAK"

Both before and after 9/11, it was evident that the president picked and mixed between sharply different approaches to governing relations with Congress at different times and on different issues. Bush was certainly capable of highly aggressive partisanship and brusquely unilateral measures. In 2001, for example, the White House pursued a highly partisan budgetary strategy to push through large tax cuts that essentially rejected the need for substantial Democratic support. Relying on rigid party discipline in the House, especially, this approach managed to win through. Similarly in 2001, with minimal consultation of Congress, the administration withdrew from the 1972 Anti-Ballistic Missile Treaty to advance its missile defence system, stated its emphatic rejection of the Kyoto Treaty, and rejected US participation in the International Criminal Court. These represented just a few of many instances of the "bad Bush" depicted in the voluminous critical assessments of his presidency: rigid, disdainful of bipartisanship at home and alliances abroad, uninterested in complex and nuanced policy debates, and wilfully ignorant of matters beyond what he regarded as his presidency's overarching focus after 9/11, winning the war on terror. This highly partisan Bush was the distinctly "uncompassionate conservative" who rejected compromise on Social Security reform, amid other initiatives, across both his terms in office.

Yet, at the same time in his first year in office, the Bush administration secured a major bipartisan education reform (No Child Left Behind), regularly consulting with Democratic Senator Edward Kennedy and other supportive liberal Democrats, and rejecting the concerns of conservative Republicans about the extension of the federal government into an area traditionally the responsibility of the states. This "good Bush" was (with the key exception of Iraq) also, subsequently, much more in evidence once the Democrats took control of Congress in January 2007 – less rigid and doctrinaire, less partisan, less blinded by a limited range of priorities and policy instruments, and more prepared to tackle emerging problems and make concessions to secure policy outputs.

This seemingly schizophrenic approach owed itself to three factors: the president's strong personal commitment to exercising presidential power; the "facts on the ground" when it came to bargaining with the Hill on specific legislative priorities and positions; and the evolving turn of international events that first elevated powerfully, and then diminished significantly, Bush's capacity to command support in Congress.

Even prior to 9/11, Bush agreed with the long-held conviction of Vice President Dick Cheney that the Congress had steadily usurped legitimate presidential powers since the Nixon years. Cheney strongly ed to the view of the unitary executive advanced by conservative stitutional scholars such as Calabresi and Yoo (2008). Reading ansively into Article II's grant of executive power to the president, is approach legitimated – in the president's view, at least – an extensive executive privilege, privacy and autonomy upon which Congress could not intrude, whether during times of crisis or in more normal periods. This even extended to the president being able to append signing statements to laws passed by Congress and signed into law by the president, which recalibrated the terms of the legislation in terms of the president's perceived constitutional authority and concomitant willingness or otherwise to implement measures in full.

On specific issues, moreover, the utility of partisan versus bipartisan efforts differed. Tax cuts and education reform had both been priorities of the 2000 campaign for Bush, for example, but each faced difficult and distinct legislative paths in 2001. Most congressional Democrats opposed, on principle, substantial tax reductions not targeted at the middle class. By contrast, many Republicans saw no role for the Department of Education at all, let alone its extension into the states to impose school testing and assessment requirements. In Bush's second term, similarly, when he declared that his re-election had afforded him "political capital" – perhaps the first occasion a president had publicly employed a term long the preserve of political scientists – that he intended to spend on entitlement reform, it rapidly became clear that neither the Democrats nor large numbers of Republicans would back him on such a politically sensitive issue, and he eventually abandoned the effort. Given the sharp ideological differences between the two congressional parties, the starkly different world-views of their activist bases, and the consistently narrow majorities on the Hill, neither a consistently one-party nor a consistently bipartisan approach to congressional relations would have proven politically effective.

But what, arguably, transformed an initially rational and prudent "horses-for-courses" approach to relations with the Hill were the attacks of 9/11. Initially, of course, these proved a rare opportunity for national unity, and even Bush's critics conceded that he did an effective job of rallying congressional and public support, with his approval ratings rising to 90 per cent. Partly as a result of this rallying of bipartisan sentiment at a time of national crisis, the legislative productivity of Bush's first two years grew exponentially (see Table 1 below), encompassing not only tax cuts and education reform but the McCain–Feingold campaign finance reform law, a $48 billion increase to the defence budget (larger than the entire defence budget of the United Kingdom), the Sarbanes–Oxley corporate accountability law, the USA Patriot Act's revisions to domestic security law, and the creation of the Department of Homeland Security – part of the largest administrative reform of the entire federal government since President Truman's passage of the National Security Act (1947) and other measures in the immediate onset of the Cold War. In total, seventeen major legislative acts were signed into law during the first two years of the Bush presidency, the second highest number among first-term presidents in the entire post-World War II period (the highest being Lyndon B. Johnson and the Great Society period of 1965–9).

But it was also during this period, in the run-up to the Iraq war, that the electoral and partisan politics of the war on terror simultaneously liberated and confined Bush. In requesting that Congress vote on the resolution authorising the Iraq war in October 2002, with mid-term elections the following month, the administration effectively made national security the defining issue of the day and the prism through which Bush hoped national politics was to be viewed long into the future – one on which Republicans had long enjoyed a partisan advantage. The election results, returning the Senate to Republican control and consolidating the party's majority in the House, both

> vindicated their strategy but also trapped the party within it. In firm control of both branches, Bush and congressional Republicans embarked on an experiment in one-party government. Thanks to superbly honed party discipline, the plan worked for a while, but the price was high. Republicans had to govern from the center of their party, rather than the center of the country. Democrats were absolved from responsibility for the results. (Rauch 2008: 24)

Such a hard-headed approach did not preclude legislative successes; far from it, in fact. Since Bush was amenable to getting what he could from Congress, plenty of instances occurred where, after initial declarations of implacably principled refusal to budge, the administration compromised. When Bush could afford to spurn

Table 1: Selected Laws Enacted by the 107th (2001–2) and 108th Congresses (2003–4)

| *Subject* | *Signed into law by president* |
|---|---|
| Tax cuts | 7 June 2001 |
| Use of force military authorisation | 18 September 2001 |
| Fiscal 2001 supplemental appropriations bill | 18 September 2001 |
| Airline industry bail-out | 22 September 2001 |
| Anti-terrorism powers (Patriot Act) | 26 October 2001 |
| Aviation security legislation | 19 November 2001 |
| Education reform (No Child Left Behind Act) | 8 January 2002 |
| Economic stimulus package | 9 March 2002 |
| Campaign finance reform | 27 March 2002 |
| Farm bill | 13 May 2002 |
| Border security legislation | 14 May 2002 |
| Bioterrorism legislation | 12 June 2002 |
| Yucca Mountain nuclear-waste repository law | 23 July 2002 |
| Corporate accountability bill | 30 July 2002 |
| Presidential trade-negotiating authority | 6 August 2002 |
| Use of military force authorisation (Iraq) | 16 October 2002 |
| Election process reform | 29 October 2002 |
| Temporary extension of 1996 welfare law | 23 November 2002 |
| Homeland Security Department creation | 25 November 2002 |
| Terrorism insurance legislation | 26 November 2002 |
| Fiscal 2003 omnibus spending bill | 20 February 2003 |
| Fiscal 2003 supplemental appropriations bill for wars in Iraq and Afghanistan | 16 April 2003 |
| "Amber Alert" child abduction legislation | 30 April 2003 |
| International AIDS relief bill | 27 May 2003 |
| Tax cuts | 28 May 2003 |
| Fiscal 2003 supplemental appropriations bill for disaster relief | 8 August 2003 |
| Chile and Singapore trade pacts | 3 September 2003 |
| Medicare Modernization Act | 8 December 2003 |

Source: *National Journal*, 20 September 2003, pp. 2868–9

co-operation and compromise, he did. But whether by design or not, Bush was often forced to embrace compromise and flexibility, a pragmatism that recalled his "compassionate" rather than "dogmatic" conservatism of the 2000 campaign.

Moreover, Bush's use of the veto was notably rare. Bush vetoed eleven bills, with four vetoes overridden by Congress. The 107th and 108th Congresses did not see a single presidential veto and the 109th only one – the last president to use the veto in only single figures was Warren Harding (1921–3). Such rare formal rejection of legislation passed by Congress offers additional evidence of Bush's willingness to bargain and compromise in order to get measures enacted.

While this approach ("bending so as not to break", as Howell and Kriner [2007] term it) yielded positive legislative results, the "my-way-or-the-highway" partisanship that accompanied it – exacerbated by the bitterness and narrowness of Bush's election victory in 2004 – ultimately destroyed the president's ability to push through two of his major second-term priorities: entitlement reform and immigration reform. On two issues of profound national concern, both entailing substantial political risk and provoking social division, the incentive for congressional Democrats to gamble by helping to change the broken systems, when Bush was likely to take all the credit for success, was absent. Such a context, poisoned especially by the woeful response to Hurricane Katrina and the deeply divisive fallout from the mismanaged occupation of Iraq, inevitably prompted an increase in partisanship on both sides. When *Congressional Quarterly* (CQ) assessed President Bush's presidential success rating in 2001, it was 87 per cent. But, in the period from January to August 2007, with the Democrats back in the majority, it had fallen to a half-century low: Bush prevailed on only 14 per cent of the seventy-six roll-call votes on which he took a clear position (Jansen 2007). The previous low for any president was in 1995, when Bill Clinton won just 26 per cent of the time during the first year after Republicans took control of the House. A study of House and Senate floor votes, compiled by *CQ* over the August 2007 congressional recess, also showed that House Democrats backed Bush's legislative positions only 6 per cent of the time, making for the strongest opposition from either party against a president in the fifty-four years that *CQ* has kept score. Unsurprisingly, the majority Democrats also became more unified. The average House Democratic unity score (in which a majority of one party's lawmakers opposes a majority of the other party's) of 91 per cent was the highest Democratic unity score in fifty-one years and matched the high-water mark that Republicans scored three times: in 1995, 2001 and 2003. The average Senate Democratic unity score was similarly high at 88 per cent, almost reaching the party's peak score of 89 per cent posted twice: in 1999 and 2001. By comparison, House Democrats supported Nixon 46 per cent of the time in 1974, the year he resigned. Nixon prevailed on votes 68 per cent of the time that year, despite the intense political divisions over Watergate. House Republican support for President Lyndon B. Johnson also stood at 51 per cent in 1968, during the height of the Vietnam War, and Johnson succeeded 84 per cent of the time on votes that year (Jansen 2007).

Although any president can count on a certain amount of discontent from the opposing party, especially one that controls Congress, Bush's remarkably feeble success ratings and his very low support scores among House Democrats were a direct function of disagreements over the Iraq War, spending priorities, executive secrecy and evasion, and the poisoned relations that had culminated since the unity moment in the immediate aftermath of 9/11.

## 4. BANKING ON CONGRESS: A MICROCOSM OF A MACRO-POLITICAL FAILURE

The combination of a polarising and ideological presidency with tactical pragmatism and realpolitik was vividly manifest in the financial crisis of autumn 2008. The banking crisis underlined Bush's two biggest personal weaknesses in dealing with Congress throughout his presidency: a failure to articulate a clear and appealing message, and an indecisiveness that belied his self-styled status as "the decider". Bush failed to explain in simple language that a crisis on Wall Street also means a crisis on Main Street. Ever the delegator, the "MBA president" handed responsibility for the bail-out to a technocrat, his treasury secretary, Hank Paulson, but then failed to provide him with the necessary political support. The president started lobbying legislators only days before the key vote and never went personally to Capitol Hill to appeal to Congress. On 29 September 2008 Bush saw his rescue package torn apart by two groups of people who had been enraged by his political style – progressive Democrats and conservative free-market Republicans. Catastrophe was ultimately averted when the rescue package passed the House of Representatives on 3 October, having been approved by the Senate on 1 October. But this owed less to the administration than to a run on the markets that powerfully concentrated the minds of legislators, most of whom were shortly to face an outraged electorate at the polls.

In one sense, Bush also paid the price for the defining cause of his presidency, the invasion of Iraq – the single most important factor that destroyed the brief bipartisan spirit created by 9/11. The most forceful complaint on the Hill against the Emergency Economic Stabilization Act of 2008 was that it bore an uncanny and unfortunate family resemblance to the Iraq War Resolution of 2002: the same bid for untrammelled authority (Secretary Paulson's initial request for $700 billion was a mere three pages in length; over the following week Congress increased it to 450 pages); similar alarmist and fearful rhetoric about "our entire economy" being in imminent danger; and the same insistence that Congress should limit deliberation in the face of the need to act immediately. Nor was such scepticism and resentment confined to Democratic lawmakers: 133 Republicans initially had decided to vote against a Republican administration.

But Bush the practitioner of pragmatism emerged again once the president became fully engaged with the financial crisis in late September. When it became clear that investors were doubting his commitment to a rescue package, the president delivered a sober, televised, prime-time address to explain how the crisis had originated. Subsequently, he took the lead in introducing new initiatives and lobbying for congressional support. When his own party's lawmakers threatened to reject the rescue package as an affront to conservative free-market principles, Bush threw in his lot with the Democrats and accepted many of their suggestions while cajoling House Republicans to drop their opposition. When foreign governments balked at joining the US rescue, he pressed for international co-ordination and reached greater unity with European leaders than had been apparent for several years. Finally, when investors doubted the mortgage-security-focused strategy underpinning the $700 billion rescue plan, Bush abandoned it and instead adopted the bank-centred approach advanced by European heads of government, especially Britain's Gordon Brown. Like Roosevelt previously, albeit on a much smaller scale, Bush proved politically able and willing to try different approaches and to start again from scratch when a new proposal did not work effectively.

Unlike Roosevelt, however, the recovery of pragmatism came far too late in the day to assist his party's teetering political fortunes. Bush had devoted much of his energy as president to forging a lasting Republican majority but his second term saw not only his ideological opponents, the Democrats, but also partisan conservatives oppose the president on measures from immigration reform to the budget to financial management. Far from creating a majority Republican Party, Bush left the Republicans in the most parlous state since 1964, characterised by profound internal divisions over both foreign and domestic policies, confused about their identity as a party and confronting their most substantial electoral defeat since 1974.

## 5. THE COSTS AND BENEFITS OF PRESIDENTIAL UNILATERALISM

To his sternest critics, Bush's polarising and disdainful treatment of Congress and his extraordinary claims to executive authority together "undermined two of the fundamental principles upon which the United States was established: the rule of law and the Constitution" (Pfiffner 2008: 245). On matters such as the appointment of federal judges and the ratification of US treaties, the president is required to obtain the advice and consent of the Senate. Instead, Bush's general approach to Congress was, to his critics, more one of "ignorance and contempt".

But, as argued above, relations between Congress and the White House were far from consistent. Moreover, even on the most contentious of issues, the separated system of government remained a reality. Take, for example, the Iraq war. Congress was indicted by some observers for a virtual collapse of oversight of the Bush administration's conduct of the war and, indeed, a failure to monitor the administration's foreign and national security policies more broadly (Ornstein and Mann 2006). But the decisive factor in determining whether lawmakers will oppose or support presidential calls for war, and then closely oversee its execution, is the partisan composition of Congress (Howell and Pevehouse 2007a). As Howell and Pevehouse (2007b: 96) contend, "Partisan unity, not institutional laziness, explains why the Bush administration's Iraq policy received such a favourable hearing in Congress from 2000 to 2006." When the president's party dominates the legislative branch during war, the White House can anticipate a quiescent Congress. When the opposition party holds a large number of seats or controls one or both houses, legislators routinely challenge the executive and step up oversight of foreign conflicts, as occurred in 2007–8. The Democrats lacked the sufficient two-thirds majorities in both chambers to overcome a presidential veto of their efforts to end the Iraq war. But, in approving or disapproving funding requests, dictating how appropriations be spent, establishing reporting requirements, and launching hearings and investigations into the mishaps, scandals and tactical errors that plagued the Iraq war, the 110th Congress illustrated that "When they choose to do so, members of Congress can exert a great deal of influence over the conduct of war" (Howell and Pevehouse 2007b: 97).

To the extent that the Bush administration was able to pursue its vision of expansive executive branch powers, then, much of the explanation lies in the active support or passive acquiescence of a Congress under Republican majorities for most of the Bush years. Under changed conditions – a Democratic administration and Congress – one might reasonably expect not a wholesale shift in the institutional balance of powers over legislation, investigations and oversight but, rather, policy shifts that a new partisan partnership favours. As such, there is little here that is entirely novel in the history of congressional–presidential relations.

Congress remains, however, a coequal partner in the business of government. As Bush discovered, trust, respect and perceptions matter deeply in Washington. The somewhat hubristic treatment that he and senior members of his administration accorded not only congressional Democrats, but also some Republicans, emptied the reservoir of support that the president could anticipate when conditions became less favourable. By 2007–8, Congress reasserted its prerogative strongly, and the president's authority and power were reduced to a shred of what they had been in 2001–2. Presidential unilateralism and power without persuasion are enticing to occupants of the Oval Office in domestic and foreign policy. But in an interdependent environment at home and abroad, persuasion usually bests coercion.

## CONCLUSION

To its many critics, and many lawmakers, the Bush administration treated Congress with something approaching contempt. President Bush, the first MBA (Master of Business Administration) president, liked to think of himself as a CEO (Chief Executive Officer) at the head of a government machine rather than as another politician in a town full of politicians. But while bold, committed and highly ideological, Bush was also highly strategic, sometimes making concessions to achieve the bulk of what he wanted, at other times pre-empting congressional action that threatened cherished goals. Congress rarely, especially under Republican control, acted to rein in the president when he sought to act unilaterally and controversially. This, however, was at least as much a function of the increasingly conservative cast of the congressional Republicans and their majority status for most of the Bush years as it was the strategic and tactical nous of the White House.

But, despite the fears of critics, the American system of separated government remains robust and competitive at the end of the Bush years. The Democratic triumph in the 2006 mid-term elections ushered in the least pliant Congress of the Bush presidency and saw the disciplined loyalty of Republican congressional leaders such as Dennis Hastert, Trent Lott and Tom DeLay replaced by the equally disciplined hostility of Democrats Nancy Pelosi and Harry Reid. While the lack of two-thirds majorities in either chamber precluded the Democrats from establishing complete congressional dominance, the president found his ability to enact new legislation powerfully curtailed.

As George Edwards (2009) argues, presidential persuasion is in fact a rare commodity. Presidents typically need both to recognise their strategic environment accurately and, where possible, exploit auspicious opportunities to advance policy change. The September 2001 terrorist attacks afforded George W. Bush a rare opportunity to do precisely this, but both the substance and the style of his strategic vision entailed at least as many costs as it did benefits for his overall presidential legacy. The significant capital that Bush accrued in the year following 9/11 was subsequently squandered with equal rapidity. Perhaps the most powerful irony in this regard was not so much that the erstwhile uniter became one of the most divisive presidents in American history but more that the presidential office that he bequeathed his successor was, in important respects, arguably weaker than the one he inherited. In its own fashion, the Bush presidency will provide a vivid set of lessons about strategic leadership and the management of congressional relations for many years to come.

## BIBLIOGRAPHY

Calabresi, Stephen G. and Christopher S. Yoo (2008), *The Unitary Executive: Presidential Power From Washington to Bush*, New Haven: Yale University Press

Edwards, George C. (2009), *The Strategic President: Persuasion and Opportunity in Presidential Leadership*, Princeton: Princeton University Press

Howell, William G. (2003), *Power Without Persuasion: The Politics of Direct Presidential Action*, Princeton: Princeton University Press

Howell, William G. and Douglas L. Kriner (2007), "Bending so as Not to Break: What the Bush Presidency Reveals About the Politics of Unilateral Action", Chapter 4 in George C. Edwards III and Desmond King, eds, *The Polarized Presidency of George W. Bush*, Oxford: Oxford University Press

Howell, William G. and Jon C. Pevehouse (2007a), *While Dangers Gather: Congressional Checks on Presidential War Powers*, Princeton: Princeton University Press

Howell, William G. and Jon C. Pevehouse (2007b), "When Congress Stops Wars: Partisan Politics and Presidential Power", *Foreign Affairs* 86 (5), pp. 95–107

Jacobson, Gary C. (2007), *A Divider, Not a Uniter: George W. Bush and the American People, the 2006 Elections and Beyond*, New York: Longman

Jansen, Bart (2007), "Bush Success Rating at Historic Low", *CQ Today*, 31 August

Ornstein, Norman J. and Thomas E. Mann (2006), "When Congress Checks Out", *Foreign Affairs* 85 (6), pp. 67–82

Pfiffner, James P. (2008), *Power Play: The Bush Presidency and the Constitution*, Washington, DC: Brookings Institution Press

Rauch, Jonathan (2008), "Small Ball After All?", *National Journal*, 20 September, pp. 22–8

*Chapter 3*

# GEORGE W. BUSH AS CHIEF EXECUTIVE

James P. Pfiffner

Those who observed President Bush in office were struck by his self assurance, his confidence in his "gut" judgement, his lack of self-doubt, his impatience with lengthy policy debate, and his willingness to delegate large swaths of public policy to Vice President Dick Cheney. These characteristics can lead to certainty in decision-making, but they may also prematurely constrain the range of options considered in addressing far-reaching decisions of state. While President Bush was able to make important policy decisions with confidence and dispatch, his approach to the use of executive power had some drawbacks. Important decisions, particularly in his first term, were often made without the depth of policy analysis or consultation within the administration that previous presidents displayed. Often when disagreement or reservations were expressed by experts and professionals within the executive branch, they were ignored or dismissed. In addition, President Bush was committed to an expansive approach to the constitutional prerogatives of the presidency, and he asserted his right to ignore the usual checks and balances built into the separation of powers system.

This chapter will examine several cases of policy decisions that illustrate these characteristics. To illustrate President Bush's unwillingness to subject his policy preferences to expert scrutiny, it will examine his order that created military commissions to prosecute suspected terrorists in November 2001 and his decision to disband the Iraqi army in May 2003. His penchant to ignore or to dismiss the judgement of professionals in the executive branch will be illustrated by his decision to suspend the Geneva Conventions in the war on terror and his insistence that Saddam was connected to al-Qaeda and 9/11, despite

CIA evidence to the contrary. Finally, his broad assertions of presidential power will be illustrated with his order to the National Security Agency to conduct surveillance on Americans, without the warrants required by law, and his unprecedented use of signing statements. Most of these policy decisions were made and carried out through Vice President Cheney's mastery of the levers of power within the executive branch of the United States government (Gellman 2008).

## 1. LACK OF CONSULTATION

This section will first consider President Bush's Military Order of 13 November 2001 to establish military commissions to try terrorist suspects in the war on terror, a decision that was tightly held to a few lawyers in the White House until the order had been signed. It will then take up the decision to disband the Iraqi army in May of 2003, which drastically reduced the ability of American forces to provide security in Iraq and made the anti-coalition insurgency much more effective.

### *a. The Military Commissions Order*

The decision-making process that led to the issue of President Bush's military commissions order in November 2001 illustrates the unwillingness of the administration to consult even its own political appointees about the wisdom of proposed policies. The administration feared that there might be some objection and that the president and vice president might be forced to alter their original policy plans. Ironically, such consultation might have avoided the legal and political trouble this decision caused them.

The small group of lawyers preparing the order felt that normal trials, whether civilian or under the Uniform Code of Military Justice, would afford too many legal protections to terrorists, and thus were "not practicable", so the order required that military commissions be established entirely within the executive branch to try suspected terrorists (Bush 2001). In the order, President Bush declared that any non-citizen "whom I determine" was or abetted a terrorist could be "detained at an appropriate place" by the secretary of defense and tried by military tribunals created by the secretary (Fisher 2005: 168). Evidence could be admitted that would "have probative value to a reasonable person", possibly including that obtained by torture. The order also declared that no court would have jurisdiction to hear an appeal to a military commission's decision or consider a writ of habeas corpus.

An inter-agency working group had been examining the legal implications of how to handle detainees who might have been members of the Taliban or al-Qaeda. It was led by Pierre Prosper, ambassador at large for war crimes. National Security Advisor Condoleezza Rice and Secretary of State Colin Powell knew that the Prosper committee was working on the issue and believed that they would have some input in drafting the order. In late October 2001, however, Vice President Cheney determined the process was taking too long and short-circuited it by ignoring and secretly bypassing the committee (Gellman and Becker 2007).

The order was drafted by David Addington, the vice president's legal counsel, and purposefully kept secret from the rest of the administration. Addington forcefully expressed his attitude towards consultation: "Fuck the interagency process", he opined (Mayer 2008: 80). One of the few lawyers who did see the draft said that it "was very closely held because it was coming right from the top" (Gellman and Becker 2007). One might expect that such an important and far-reaching order would involve consultation with administration officials who had expertise or who would be involved with implementing the order. But Cheney gave strict instructions that others in the White House and cabinet be bypassed, specifically Rice, Powell and their lawyers.

Military lawyers were also generally excluded from commenting on the draft of the military order. Rear Admiral Donald J. Guter, the Navy Judge Advocate General, said "I can't tell you how compartmented [*sic*] things were. This was a closed administration" (Golden 2004). On 9 November, four days before the president signed the order, Department of Defense General Counsel Jim Haynes allowed a small group of lawyers, headed by Lawrence J. Morris, to look at a draft of the order, but they were not allowed to have a copy or take notes. At the last minute, Army Judge Advocate General Major General Thomas Romig called a group of military lawyers together over the weekend to try to make some changes, but their efforts were unavailing (Ragavan 2006: 37; Golden 2004).

On 13 November Cheney had Addington take the draft to the

White House staff secretary to put it in final form in strict secrecy. Once the order was put into a formal document, Cheney took it to Bush in the Oval Office and the president signed it immediately. White House aides present said they did not know that the vice president had been involved in the drafting of the memo. Thus Cheney had engineered the president's approval and signature without any policy process or sign-off by relevant White House and cabinet officials, most importantly National Security Advisor Rice and Secretary of State Powell. On the evening of 13 November, when CNN broadcast that the military order had been signed by the president, Colin Powell exclaimed "What the hell just happened?" and Rice sent an aide to find out about the order (Gellman and Becker 2007).

The order was important because it created a new category of "enemy combatant" to avoid the "prisoner of war" designation that would have invoked the Geneva Conventions. People could be labelled enemy combatants at the president's discretion. In accordance with the president's subsequent decision to suspend the Geneva Conventions made the following month, discussed in detail below, enemy combatants would not be entitled to the protections of the Geneva rules, either for prisoners of war or for others held at the mercy of opposing forces. This determination led to the abuse and torture of detainees. If the draft order had been circulated more widely, the administration might have avoided the Supreme Court's 2006 ruling in *Hamdan* v. *Rumsfeld* that struck down the military commissions plan because it was not set up in accordance with the Geneva Conventions or United States law, including the Uniform Code of Military Justice.

### *b. Disbanding the Iraqi Army*

Once American forces had captured Baghdad, several key decisions were made that gravely jeopardised wider success in Iraq. First, Paul Bremer alone was made the supreme United States authority in Iraq. Second, the decision was taken to bar from government work those who ranked in the top four levels of Saddam's Baath Party and the top three levels of each government ministry. Third, it was decided to disband the Iraqi army and replace it with a new army built from scratch. These fateful decisions were made against the advice of military and CIA professionals and without consulting important members of the president's staff and cabinet.

The decision to give Bremer sole authority in Iraq, rather than, as had been planned, his sharing it with Zal Khalilzad, an expert on Iraq, was made by President Bush during an informal lunch with Bremer and without consulting his secretary of state or national security adviser (Gordon and Trainor 2006: 475). According to Powell, "The plan was for Zal to go back. He was the one guy who knew this place better than anyone. I thought this was part of the deal with Bremer. But with no discussion, no debate, things changed. I was stunned." Powell observed that President Bush's decision was "typical". There were "no full deliberations. And you suddenly discover, gee, maybe that wasn't so great, we should have thought about it a little longer" (Cohen 2007).

The decision by Bush to put Bremer fully in charge led to the first of the other two blunders. In order to rid the country of any vestiges of Saddam's brutal regime, Bremer issued his de-Baathification Coalition Provisional Authority Order Number 1 on 16 May 2003. The order involved up to 85,000 civilian, managerial-level technocrats who managed the economic and energy infrastructure of the country. Despite Under Secretary of Defense Douglas Feith's assertion that the decision had been cleared in an inter-agency process, the military had a distinctly different understanding of what the policy had been and thought that the CPA order cut too deeply into the administrative infrastructure of the country. CIA Director George Tenet noted his agency "knew nothing about it until de-Baathification was a fait accompli . . . Clearly, this was a critical policy decision, yet there was no NSC [National Security Council] Principals meeting to debate the move" (Tenet 2007: 426). The lack of an NSC meeting to deliberate fully before President Bush's decision was characteristic of his presidency.

The third key decision was to disband the Iraqi army, which threw hundreds of thousands out of work and immediately created a large pool of unemployed and armed men who felt humiliated by, and hostile to, the American occupiers. According to one US officer in Baghdad, "When they disbanded the military, and announced we were occupiers – that was it. Every moderate, every person that had leaned toward us, was furious" (Ricks 2006: 164). The pre-war plans of the State Department, the Army War College and the Center for

International and Strategic Studies had all recommended against disbanding the army (Fallows 2004: 74).

In a NSC meeting on 12 March 2003 there had been a consensus that the American forces would use the Iraqi army to help provide internal and external security in post-war Iraq. But one week after the de-Baathification order, Bremer issued CPA Order Number 2 on 23 May 2003 dissolving the Iraqi security forces. There had been an NSC meeting in which Bremer, via teleconference, had casually mentioned his intentions, but other participants did not conclude that President Bush had made a decision about disbanding the army.

Importantly, Colin Powell was out of town when the decision was made, and he was not informed about it, much less consulted. Even President Bush did not remember deciding. When asked in 2006 by his biographer, Roger Draper, about the decision, Bush replied, "Well, the policy was to keep the army intact. Didn't happen" (Draper 2007: 211, 433). "Yeah, I can't remember, I'm sure I said, 'This is the policy, what happened?'" (Andrews 2007). What is known is that the decision was made against the judgement of military planners and without consultation with Secretary of State Powell, CIA Director Tenet or Chair of the Joint Chiefs of Staff General Richard Myers.

The security forces included 385,000 in the armed forces, 285,000 police in the Interior Ministry and 50,000 in presidential security units (Ricks 2006: 162, 192). Of course, those in police and military units that were Saddam's top enforcers, such as the Special Republican Guard, had to be barred from working in the government. But many officers in the army were professional soldiers, and the rank-and-file enlisted soldiers could have constituted a source of stability and order.

Both de-Baathification and disbanding the security forces fuelled the insurgency by alienating hundreds of thousands of Iraqis who could not support themselves or their families, and by undermining the infrastructure required for social and economic activity. They also ensured that there was insufficient security to carry on normal life and created more insurgents who were angry at the United States, many of whom had weapons and were trained to use them. It is probable that a more thorough consultation process could have given President Bush a much more realistic understanding of what the likely consequences would be.

## 2. IGNORING PROFESSIONAL ADVICE

The problem of failing to consult more broadly within the administration was often compounded by President Bush's tendency to ignore or dismiss the advice of expert political appointees and career professionals on important policy matters. This section will illustrate this tendency by examining Bush's decision to suspend the Geneva Conventions in the war on terror and his rejection of the CIA's conclusion that there was no meaningful link between Saddam Hussein and al-Qaeda.

### *a. Abandoning the Geneva Conventions*

In autumn 2001 the Bush administration felt tremendous pressure not only to pursue those who had committed the 9/11 atrocities but also to prevent future attacks, which it assumed were in the planning stages. To obtain crucial intelligence, the United States would have to depend on the interrogation of prisoners to discover plans for future attacks. Thus, some thought that the traditional interrogation techniques developed by the US military and limited by the strictures of the Geneva Conventions would not be sufficient. In late 2001 and early 2002 the administration went about exempting American interrogators from the Geneva rules. In addition, the administration wanted to ensure that its interrogators did not get charged with war crimes; the United States war crimes statute referred to the Geneva rules, and if Geneva did not apply, the statute was unlikely to be invoked regarding the harsh treatment of detainees.

The Judge Advocate Generals of the services (JAGs or TJAGs), however, were not consulted about the decisions (Sands 2008: 32). That is, those who, because of their training and years of experience, were among the most informed and qualified lawyers on the laws of war, were excluded from consultations on this important decision. As David Addington reportedly said, "Don't bring the TJAGs into the process, they aren't reliable" (Sands 2008: 32). President Bush made his decision on 8 January 2002 and Secretary Powell was informed on 18 January while in Asia (Mayer 2008: 123; DeYoung 2007: 368).

When Powell returned to the United States, he objected to the policy of abandoning the Geneva Conventions. In a 26 January memo he argued that "It will reverse over a century of policy . . . and undermine the protections of the law of war for our troops, both in this specific conflict and in general; It has a high cost in terms of negative international reaction . . .; It will undermine public support among critical allies" (Powell 2002). He also noted that applying the Conventions, "maintains POW status for US forces . . . and generally supports the US objective of ensuring its forces are accorded protection under the Convention".

Despite Powell's memo, but in accordance with the Justice Department's and his counsel's recommendations, President Bush signed a memorandum on 7 February 2002, stating: "Pursuant to my authority as Commander in Chief . . . I . . . determine that none of the provisions of Geneva apply to our conflict with al Qaeda in Afghanistan or elsewhere throughout the world because, among other reasons, al Qaeda is not a High Contracting Party to Geneva." The memo argued that the Geneva Conventions apply only to states and "assumes the existence of 'regular' armed forces fighting on behalf of states", and that "terrorism ushers in a new paradigm" that "requires new thinking in the law of war". The memo also stated that "As a matter of policy, the United States Armed Forces shall continue to treat detainees humanely and, *to the extent appropriate and consistent with military necessity*, in a manner consistent with the principles of Geneva" (Bush 2002, emphasis added).

Suspending the Geneva rules drastically changed United States policy on the treatment of prisoners and reversed firm Defense Department guidelines on prisoner treatment during wartime. It allowed the use of the aggressive techniques of interrogation used by the CIA and military intelligence at Guantánamo that were later, in autumn 2003, transferred to the prison at Abu Ghraib. The president had been successful in exempting interrogators from having to conform to the Geneva rules (although the Court would later overturn the president in *Hamdan*) and consequences were profound: the harsh interrogations of detainees by American personnel aided the recruitment of terrorists and drew the opprobrium of America's allies and adversaries.

### *b. Insisting on a Link between Saddam and Al-Qaeda*

Immediately after the 9/11 attack, much of the American public believed that Saddam Hussein was responsible or connected in some way, and statements by the president and other administration officials reinforced this impression over the next several years. Within twenty-four hours of the attack, President Bush told White House terrorism adviser Richard Clarke several times to look into "any shred" of evidence of a link, despite Clarke's report that the intelligence community had concluded that Saddam was not behind the attacks (Clarke 2004: 30–3). In September 2002 Secretary of Defense Donald Rumsfeld said evidence for the link was "bulletproof", "factual" and "exactly accurate" (Schmitt 2002). In his 7 October 2002 address, President Bush asserted, "we've learned that Iraq has trained al-Qaeda members in bomb-making and poisons and deadly gasses". The main items of evidence adduced to prove the relationship were an asserted meeting of hijacker Mohamed Atta with an Iraqi intelligence official in Prague on 9 April 2001 and the confession under aggressive interrogation of Ibn al-Shaykh al-Libi, who had been a senior member of al-Qaeda. The CIA and FBI, however, found no evidence of the alleged Prague meeting, and in February 2002 the Defense Intellignce Agency judged that al-Libi's statements were suspect because he could not provide credible details about the types of weapons involved, the Iraqis he dealt with, or the locations of the meetings, and was, in addition, subjected to torture to obtain his confession (Isikoff 2004; Jehl 2004b; Priest 2004; Levin 2005). Al-Libi later recanted his claims in February 2004 after being returned to United States custody at Guantánamo Bay. In the President's Daily Brief of 21 September 2001 the CIA reported that there was no evidence demonstrating a link between Saddam and al-Qaeda (Waas 2005), but Secretary Rumsfeld and Vice President Cheney continued to claim a connection, and on 25 September 2002 President Bush said, "You can't distinguish between al Qaeda and Saddam when you talk about the war on terror" (Waas 2005).

Paul Pillar, who was in charge of co-ordinating the US intelligence community's assessment of Iraq from 2000 to 2005, concluded that

> the greatest discrepancy between the administration's public statements and the intelligence community's judgments concerned . . . the relationship between Saddam and al Qaeda. The enormous attention devoted to this subject did not reflect any judgment by intelligence officials that there was or was likely to be anything like the "alliance" the administration said existed. (Pillar 2006)

Thus the administration's decision to go to war in Iraq was based in part on its conclusion that Saddam was allied with al-Qaeda – a conclusion explicitly challenged by the intelligence community, especially the CIA and the Office of Intelligence and Research within the State Department.

## 3. BROAD ASSERTIONS OF CONSTITUTIONAL AUTHORITY

The modern tradition of constraining the power of political executives has deep roots in Anglo-American governmental traditions. The Magna Carta of 1215, Habeas Corpus Act of 1679, English Bill of Rights of 1689, Common Law, and other documents and traditions of the un-codified British constitution all provided precedents upon which the framers of the United States Constitution drew. The writing of the United States Constitution also benefited from the centuries of struggle between the British monarch and parliament over the control of public policy. The US Constitution created a separation of powers system in which the legislature is clearly superior to the executive in the formulation of public policy. Article II of the Constitution also provides that the president "shall take care that the laws be faithfully executed". This section will examine President Bush's assertion that he could ignore the law and order secret surveillance in the United States, and his broader assertion that he could selectively ignore parts of laws that he claimed impinged on his prerogatives as chief executive.

### *a. NSA and the Terrorist Surveillance Program*

Shortly after 9/11 President Bush ordered the National Security Agency (NSA) to listen in on conversations between al-Qaeda suspects in foreign countries and people within the United States. Public law permits the NSA to monitor calls and other transmissions in foreign countries, but the Foreign Intelligence Surveillance Act of 1977 (FISA) required that all domestic wiretapping or surveillance be undertaken pursuant to a warrant, and set up a special court for that purpose. President Bush asserted that he had the inherent authority as commander-in-chief to disregard the law and order surveillance in the domestic United States without obtaining a warrant issued by FISA judges.

Bush's actions were problematic because the Fourth Amendment protects citizens against unreasonable searches and seizures without a warrant, and FISA set up a special court for the consideration of warrants for electronic surveillance, if probable cause is shown that the suspect is likely to be an agent of a foreign power. The Act covers any wire, radio, or other communication "sent by or intended to be received by a particular, known United States Person who is in the United States". And in three cases a warrant is not even required: (1) if the Attorney General determines that the communication is among foreign powers or their agents and "there is no substantial likelihood that the surveillance will acquire the contents of any communication of which a United States person is a party"; (2) if the Attorney General determines that there is insufficient time to obtain a warrant, but in such a case a FISA judge shall be notified within seventy-two hours (changed from twenty-four hours on 28 December 2001); and (3) surveillance can be conducted without a warrant for fifteen days after Congress declares war. It is also worth noting that FISA provides a strong presumption in favour of the president; a FISA court judge "must" issue a warrant under a set of relatively liberal circumstances.

It is not as if President Bush did not have the means to undertake the NSA spying within the law. He could have sought FISA warrants for that very purpose. If speed was of importance, the NSA could have carried out the surveillance and come back to the FISA court within seventy-two hours for retrospective authorisation, as provided for by the law. Or if the law, as written, was too narrow to allow the kind of surveillance deemed necessary, such as data mining, the president could have asked Congress to change the law – as he eventually did in 2007. President Bush did none of these things, however, even though between 1978 and 2005 the FISA court had approved more than 18,000 requests for warrants and disallowed only five, suggesting that requests for warrants by the administration would almost certainly have been granted. Instead, he secretly ordered the NSA to conduct the surveillance without warrants and then, when his actions were disclosed, asserted that the Constitution's Article II commander-in-chief clause gave him the authority to ignore the law. President Bush's belief that he had the constitutional authority to undertake such warrantless surveillance amounts to a claim that the executive has the authority to ignore the law if he or she determines that it is in the interest of national security to do so.

The above episode illustrates the importance the Bush administration placed on secrecy and its unwillingness to comply with the law and subject itself to the checks and balances built into the Constitution. The irony is that the surveillance would have been unremarkable if only the administration had complied with the law and sought the required warrants, which almost certainly would have been granted by a pliant FISA court.

### *b. Signing Statements*

A signing statement is a written statement by the president about a bill that he has just signed into law. Often these statements are hortatory and either praise or criticise the purpose of the just-enacted law. The Bush administration, however, frequently used signing statements to declare that the president was not bound by the bill that he had just signed. Although many other presidents had issued signing statements, Bush used them to an unprecedented extent, issuing more than a thousand challenges to provisions in 150 laws in his first six years in office (Savage 2007). He used signing statements to assert the unilateral and unreviewable right of the executive to choose which provisions of laws to enforce and which to ignore. For instance, he used them to indicate that he did not feel bound by all of the provisions of laws regarding: reporting to Congress pursuant to the Patriot Act; the torture of prisoners; whistle-blower protections for the Department of Energy; the number of American troops in Colombia; the use of illegally gathered intelligence; and the publication of educational data gathered by the Department of Education (Savage 2007: 228–49).

The implications of these sweeping claims to presidential authority are profound and undermine the very meaning of the rule of law. Despite the Constitution's grant of lawmaking power to Congress, the Bush administration maintained that executive authority and the commander-in-chief clause could overcome virtually any law that constrained the executive. President Bush thus claimed unilateral control of the laws. If the executive holds that it is not subject to the law as it is written but can pick and choose which provisions to enforce, it is essentially claiming the unitary power to say what the law is and the "take care" clause of Article II is effectively nullified.

Even though some limited circumstances might justify the president not obeying a law – such as President Lincoln's (1861–5) decision to suspend habeas corpus during the Civil War to maintain the Union and protect the Constitution – expanding those limited circumstances to more than 1,000 threats not to execute the law constituted an arrogation of power by President Bush. The Constitution does not give the president the option to decide *not* to execute the law faithfully. If there is a dispute about the interpretation of a law, the interaction of the three branches in the constitutional process is the appropriate way to settle the issue. The politics of passage, the choice to veto or not, and the right to challenge laws in court all are legitimate ways to deal with differences in interpretation. But the assertion by the executive that it alone has the authority to interpret the law and that it will enforce the law at its own discretion threatens the delicate constitutional balance established by the founding fathers more than two centuries ago.

## CONCLUSION

The patterns that emerge from an examination of the actions of President Bush are secrecy, even within his own administration; the exclusion from deliberation of qualified executive branch experts and disregard for their judgements; and the assertion of extraordinary constitutional authority of the president. Colin Powell, particularly, was marginalised by the White House staff and the vice president. Ironically, Powell arguably had more relevant experience than any of the other NSC principals: two tours of combat experience in Vietnam, chairman of the joint chiefs of staff under Presidents G. H. W. Bush and Clinton, national security adviser to President Reagan, and secretary of state to President Bush.

The above problems were exacerbated by the failure of the president to bring together his major staffers and departmental secretaries and deliberate about the wisdom of many decisions. The decision itself to go to war in Iraq was never considered in a formal meeting of the NSC principals, for example.

Arguably the decisions examined in this chapter were unwise. The military commissions order designed a flawed process that was invalidated by the Supreme Court. The NSA's surveillance, which could have been undertaken easily within the law, became a scandal and constitutional confrontation when it was revealed that the president had ignored the law. The abandonment of the Geneva Conventions led to the abuse and torture of detainees in the war on terror. The insistence by the administration that there was a link between Saddam and al-Qaeda helped convince Americans that the war was justified, but was exposed as an exaggeration or fabrication. And President Bush's use of signing statements made extremely broad claims to unilateral presidential authority.

Broader consultation would not necessarily have led to different outcomes, but listening to dissent from his own political appointees and the considered judgement of career professionals might have exposed President Bush to alternative judgements about the consequences of his decisions. Even if one posits that Bush did not and would not abuse his executive power, his claim to be able to ignore the law set a dangerous precedent that future presidents might use to justify their own claims to power.

## BIBLIOGRAPHY


Andrews, Edmund (2007), "Envoy's Letter Counters Bush on Dismantling of Iraq Army", *New York Times*, 4 September

Bloom, Robert M. and William J. Dunn (2006), "The Constitutional Infirmity of Warrantless NSA Surveillance", Boston College Law School, Legal Studies Research Paper Series, 6 August, pp. 20–2

Bush, George (2001), "Detention, Treatment, and Trial of Certain Non-Citizens in the War Against Terrorism", 13 November, http://www.whitehouse.gov/

Bush, George W. (2002b), Memorandum for the Vice President, et al., Subject: Humane Treatment of al Qaeda and Taliban Detainees, 7 February, in Karen J. Greenberg and Joshua L. Dratel, eds, (2005), *The Torture Papers*, Cambridge: Cambridge University Press

Clarke, Richard A. (2004), *Against All Enemies*, New York: Free Press

Cohen, Roger (2007), "The MacArthur Lunch", *New York Times*, 27 August

DeYoung, Karen, (2006), *Soldier*, New York: Knopf

Draper, Robert (2007), *Dead Certain: The Presidency of George W. Bush*, New York: Free Press

Fallows, James (2004), "Blind Into Baghdad", *Atlantic Monthly*, January/February, pp. 52–74

Fisher, Louis (2005), *Military Tribunals and the War on Terror*, Lawrence, KS: University Press of Kansas

Gellman, Barton (2008), *Angler: The Cheney Vice Presidency*, New York: Penguin Press

Gellman, Barton and Jo Becker (2007), "'A Different Understanding With the President'", *Washington Post*, 24 June

Golden, Tim (2004), "After Terror, a Secret Rewriting of Military Law", *New York Times*, 24 October

Gordon, Michael and Bernard Trainor (2006), *Cobra II*, New York: Pantheon

Isikoff, Michael (2004), "Forget the 'Poisons and Deadly Gasses'", *Newsweek*, 5 July

Jehl, Douglas (2004), "A New C.I.A. Report Casts Doubt on a Key Terrorist's Tie to Iraq", *New York Times*, 6 November

Mayer, Jane (2008), *The Dark Side*, New York: Doubleday

Pillar, Paul (2006), "Intelligence, Policy, and the War in Iraq", *Foreign Affairs*, March/April, pp. 15–27

Powell, Colin (2002), "Memorandum to: Counsel to the President and Assistant to the President for National Security Affairs, 26 January, SUBJECT: Draft Decision Memorandum for the President on the Applicability of the Geneva Convention to the Conflict in Afghanistan", in Karen J. Greenberg and Joshua L. Dratel, eds, (2005), *The Torture Papers*, Cambridge: Cambridge University Press

Priest, Dana (2004), "Al Qaeda–Iraq Link Recanted", *Washington Post*, 1 August

Ragavan, Chitra (2006), "Cheney's Guy", *U.S. News and World Report*, 29 May

Ricks, Thomas (2006), *Fiasco*, New York: Penguin Press

Sands, Phillippe (2008), *Torture Team*, New York: Palgrave Macmillan

Savage, Charlie (2006), *Takeover*, Boston: Little, Brown

Schmitt, Eric (2002), "Rumsfeld Says U.S. Has 'Bulletproof' Evidence of Iraq's links to Al Qaeda", *New York Times*, 28 September

Tenet, George (2007), *At the Center of the Storm: My Years at the CIA*, New York: HarperCollins

Waas, Murray (2005), "Key Bush Intelligence Briefing Kept from Hill Panel", *The National Journal*, 22 November

*Chapter 4*

# GEORGE W. BUSH AND THE US SUPREME COURT

Emma Long

Few of a president's powers offer such opportunity and danger as an appointment to the Supreme Court. A good choice offers a president the chance to influence public policy long after he leaves office; a poor choice can undermine his legacy. Conservatives expected George Bush to nominate candidates sympathetic to their policy preferences, liberals feared the same, and both sides were ready for a battle after eleven years without change on the Court. But when his opportunity finally came early in his second term, Bush faced additional difficulties in achieving a successful appointment, stemming from growing public and political opposition to the administration's foreign policy and a series of political scandals involving leading Republicans. A failed nomination threatened to weaken further Bush's authority and political credibility. Thus the stakes were high for Bush and his administration as, in the summer of 2005, they sought a replacement for one of the Court's most important members.

## 1. THE ROBERTS NOMINATION

The announcement of Justice Sandra Day O'Connor's resignation on 1 July 2005 took many Supreme Court watchers by surprise. As the end of the 2004 term approached, most speculation focused on Chief Justice Rehnquist who, battling thyroid cancer, had been absent for much of the term. As the first vacancy to appear since Justice Harry Blackmun's departure in 1994, O'Connor's retirement was significant; the long period of unchanging membership on the Court was unusual for an institution that on average saw one vacancy every two years. That it was O'Connor's seat Bush would have the opportunity to fill made the appointment more than usually significant. For over a decade O'Connor had been at the Court's centre, holding the balance between the liberals and conservatives on issues such as abortion, affirmative action and separation of church and state. Bush stated that he was looking for a nominee with "a high standard of legal ability, judgment and integrity, who will faithfully interpret the Constitution and laws of our country", but conservatives sensed the opportunity finally to tilt the balance decisively in their favour (Bush 2005).

Replacing O'Connor offered Bush the chance to reshape the Court in a way individual appointments had rarely done, but the nomination was fraught with difficulties. Conservatives expected Bush to fulfil his campaign pledge and nominate someone sympathetic to their interests, like Justices Antonin Scalia or Clarence Thomas. Liberals, equally aware of the potential for change presented by O'Connor's retirement, were prepared to fight hard against any nominee considered too conservative. As early as 14 July, the liberal advocacy group MoveOn.org was running television advertisements in Maine, Nebraska, South Carolina and Virginia urging senators not to vote for an extremist candidate (Stolberg 2005a). Already facing criticism over the wars in Iraq and Afghanistan and the federal government's response to Hurricane Katrina, Bush could not afford a protracted fight with either side of the political spectrum. A bitter partisan nomination battle only risked further damage to the administration.

In Judge John Glover Roberts Jr of the United States District Court of Appeals for the District of Columbia Circuit, Bush made a shrewd choice. Undoubtedly qualified for the position, Roberts's choice of clerkships (for Judge Henry J. Friendly of the federal appeals court of New York and for Chief Justice Rehnquist), legal experience in the Reagan and the first Bush administrations and personal financial donations also revealed his Republican credentials. Testimony from friends and colleagues about his devout Roman Catholic faith and support from leading Christian conservative lawyers suggested Roberts was a nominee social conservatives could support (Purdum et al. 2005; Kirkpatrick 2005a). At the same time, opinions from Roberts's two years on the Court of Appeals revealed little beyond his support for a limited view of federal power, a strong executive, a cautious judiciary governed by judicial restraint, and individual responsibility (Liptak 2005; Greenhouse 2005; Purdum et al. 2005). On issues such as abortion, church and state, freedom of speech, the death penalty and criminal procedure, Roberts presented a limited or non-existent record. Neither conservatives, who were generally inclined to support Roberts's nomination, nor liberals, who were more suspicious, could find anything objectionable in Roberts's record.

By September 2005, as the Senate judiciary committee hearings loomed, Roberts's successful appointment to the Court seemed likely. Despite opposition from liberal interest groups and continued scepticism from some Democratic senators who complained Roberts was less than forthcoming in personal meetings, nothing suggested Roberts was unsuitable for the job or that his nomination would be rejected. Then, on 3 September 2005, Chief Justice Rehnquist died. Two days later Bush announced that Roberts was now his nominee to replace Rehnquist rather than O'Connor. The switch had a number of benefits for Bush. O'Connor had agreed to remain on the Court until her successor was appointed, giving Bush time to find a suitable replacement, while Rehnquist's death left an immediate vacancy to be filled. Roberts's successful nomination would ensure a full Court for the start of the new term in October. More importantly, replacing the conservative Rehnquist with the similarly inclined Roberts meant avoiding politically dangerous ideological battles as the nomination no longer threatened the existing balance of the Court. O'Connor's position as a swing vote made her seat the more politically crucial. With that seat still needing to be filled, liberals were unwilling to risk political capital fighting Roberts's nomination, which would not affect the status quo. Kate Michelman, former president of NARAL Pro-Choice America, argued that Roberts's hearing should be used not to prevent his appointment but to "show people what it means to have his views on the court and lay the groundwork for the next nomination fight" (Becker 2005). A similar pattern was seen in the Senate. Although pledging to scrutinise Roberts carefully, Democrats in particular acknowledged that O'Connor's seat was the most crucial (Baker and Becker 2005; Kirkpatrick 2005b). The philosophical similarities between Roberts and Rehnquist thus reduced opposition to his appointment and made an already likely event appear almost inevitable.

Little unexpected or remarkable occurred during the Senate judiciary committee hearings between 13 September and 16 September 2005 except, perhaps, the performance of the candidate himself. Committee members found themselves exasperated at Roberts's refusal to answer questions about issues he asserted could come before the Court, but impressed at his ability to sidestep them. The impression was of a judge concerned for the significance of precedent but not unquestioningly bound by it, not an ideologue but a pragmatist who would judge each case on its merits but who did not see the Supreme Court as the cure for society's ills. Although Roberts's testimony gave away nothing as to the kinds of decisions he might make as chief justice, it showed him more than capable of the job. The judiciary committee agreed, recommending his appointment thirteen to five, with three Democrats voting with the committee's ten Republicans. On 29 September 2005, the Senate approved his nomination by a seventy-eight to twenty-two vote, and only a few hours later Roberts was sworn in as the seventeenth chief justice of the Supreme Court.

The Roberts nomination was a case study in effective organisation and planning by the Bush administration and showed its ability to respond quickly to events. Roberts was a strong choice, reflecting the political circumstances on the Court and in the country. The administration worked hard to highlight Roberts's qualifications for a place on the Court and made some effort towards bipartisan consultation. His personality and temperament, along with Rehnquist's death, undoubtedly made the appointment easier. Roberts's appointment as chief justice, however, both in manner and conclusion, was a clear success of Bush's second term.

## 2. THE CASE OF HARRIET MIERS

If the nomination of Roberts was a case study of a successful appointment to the Supreme Court, Bush's nomination of Harriet Miers was a study in how to get it wrong. Four days after Roberts took the oath of office, Bush announced Miers as his nominee for O'Connor's seat. A Roman Catholic who had converted to become an evangelical Christian, Miers spent many years in Texas politics before joining the White House counsel's office and had played a leading role in Roberts's nomination. Her background and experience suggested a moderate conservative, sympathetic to the social conservative agenda. Yet, on 26 October 2005, three weeks after her nomination, Miers withdrew her candidacy.

Miers herself was part of the problem. "There are a lot more people – men, women and minorities – that are more qualified in my opinion by their experience than she is. Right now, I'm not satisfied with what I know", commented Republican Senator Trent Lott only two days after her nomination, reflecting concerns that Miers lacked the experience and the ability to fill O'Connor's seat (Kirkpatrick 2005c). As a private lawyer working mostly on business deals and contract disputes, Miers's experience did not extend to the key social and constitutional issues of interest to those concerned with Court nominees. Senator Arlen Specter, chairman of the Senate judiciary committee, added to the perception by commenting that Miers had "a fair sized job to do" to become fluent in constitutional law in which she needed a "crash course" (Stolberg 2005b). Although apparently intended simply as recognition of Miers's past work in areas unrelated to constitutional law, Specter's comments reinforced a growing sense among leading Republicans that Miers was underqualified.

Miers's failure was equally the result of disillusion with her among the Christian right and, increasingly, with Bush's conservative record. Her lack of a record on key social issues, particularly abortion, riled conservatives far more than it did liberals. Unlike Roberts, who also had a limited public record, Miers's background did not convince conservatives of her affinity with their policy preferences. Whereas Roberts's roles in the Attorney General's and Solicitor General's offices during the Reagan and Bush administrations suggested clear similarities between his personal philosophy and the aims of social conservatives, Miers's experience as White House counsel did not. Bush had pledged to nominate only judicial conservatives to the Court but Miers's silence on abortion in particular suggested to conservatives either no fixed position or an unwillingness to state one publicly. Either way, Miers was no Scalia or Thomas. Already concerned about Bush's limited support for their agenda, social conservatives saw no reason to give Miers the benefit of the doubt. "I want to be assured that she is not going to be another [David] Souter", commented Republican Senator George Allen, referring to President George H. W. Bush's nominee to the Supreme Court in 1990 who had a limited public and political record on taking his seat and had failed to vote to overturn *Roe*, disappointing conservatives (Kirkpatrick 2005c). But to many, Miers appeared to be in the same vein. Conservatives were suspicious of Bush's commitment to their cause and Miers did nothing to assuage their concern.

The administration's approach to the nomination did not help

Miers's cause, either. Although Roberts had been a relative unknown when his nomination was announced, it became clear that the administration had been discussing him and his credentials with leading conservatives for some time before a vacancy appeared on the Court. It was equally clear that this had not occurred with Miers. Conservatives, unaware of her background, were forced to conduct a painfully public examination and discussion of her credentials. The Bush administration's choice appeared rushed and ill-considered, an impression, given O'Connor's position at the Court's centre, more than normally ill-advised. The mishandling of Miers's nomination seemed further evidence of an administration already weakened by criticism over Hurricane Katrina, Iraq and Afghanistan, a leak investigation involving Bush's close political adviser Karl Rove, and the indictment of Representative Tom DeLay, former House majority leader and leading Republican strategist, on charges of conspiracy to violate election laws.

The Miers debacle exemplifies the "two terms" thesis of Bush's presidency. Democrats had little involvement in the failure of Miers even to reach hearings before the Senate judiciary committee: the nomination was undermined by divisions between the Christian right and mainstream Republicans and mistakes by an already weakened White House. Whereas Roberts's clear qualifications overcame existing divisions, Miers's more opaque background allowed divisions to surface and ultimately defeat her candidacy. The problem facing the administration was to find a candidate who could placate the increasingly frustrated Christian right without alienating moderate Republicans or forcing frustrated Democrats into considering a filibuster.

## 3. THE ALITO NOMINATION

Bush's nomination of Samuel A. Alito Jr appeared deliberately designed to placate conservative Republicans after Miers withdrew her nomination. By nominating an Italian American, Bush could not be accused of failing to consider issues of diversity, and there could be no doubt about Alito's legal or political credentials. Alito spent seven years in the Justice Department under Reagan before George H. W. Bush appointed him to the Third Circuit Court of Appeals in 1990. After fifteen years as an appellate judge, he had a substantial written record to demonstrate both his experience and his jurisprudence. It was this record that most concerned Democrats and liberal advocacy groups and dominated discussions within and outside Congress in the weeks after his nomination.

Of most concern was a letter written by Alito in 1985 in application for the position of Deputy Assistant Attorney General in the Reagan White House. The letter suggested that Alito shared conservatives' opposition to Warren Court decisions involving criminal procedure, separation of church and state, legislative reapportionment, affirmative action and *Roe* (Becker and Russakoff 2006). Critics' suspicions were strengthened by a 1995 brief Alito co-wrote for the Reagan administration challenging the constitutionality of affirmative action, a 1996 opinion arguing Congress had exceeded its power by passing a law banning machine guns, and a 1991 dissent arguing that a 1989 Pennsylvania law requiring married women seeking abortions to notify their husbands did not place an undue burden on those women. The latter was of particular concern to critics because, when heard by the Supreme Court as *Planned Parenthood of Southeastern Pennsylvania* v. *Casey* in 1992, it rejected Alito's approach in a five to four decision with O'Connor in the majority. Critics accused Bush of making a needlessly provocative nomination. "Instead of uniting the country through his choice, the president has chosen to reward one faction of his party, at the risk of dividing the country", argued Senator Patrick Leahy, the senior Democrat on the judiciary committee who earlier had voted in favour of John Roberts (Bumiller and Hulse 2005). Unlike Roberts, for liberals there seemed little doubt that Alito was exactly the kind of nominee they had feared from the Bush White House.

Supporters of Alito argued that such individual cases, taken out of context, gave a misleading impression of Alito and his jurisprudence. The picture they painted was of a decent, methodical and open-minded man whose judicial philosophy was undoubtedly conservative, but not dogmatically so. Analysis of his opinions from the third circuit suggested he generally favoured government and corporations, deferred to "good faith judgments" of other participants in the justice system, including police officers, prosecutors and juries, and showed deference to the views of the people and the agencies closest to the facts (Liptak and Glater 2005). In cases involving the death penalty, employment discrimination and immigrants' rights, Alito frequently read statutes narrowly to limit the ability of individuals involved to obtain relief from the courts (Bumiller and Hulse 2005). Nothing in these positions, supporters argued, placed Alito outside the jurisprudence of the Rehnquist Court.

Alito's confirmation hearings before the Senate judiciary committee between 9 and 12 January 2006 reflected both his conservative record and the significance of Justice O'Connor, whose seat he might take. In many ways they were the hearings Roberts would have faced had Bush not elevated him to chief justice. Democrats in particular challenged Alito repeatedly, and at times aggressively, on key issues. "In case after case, you give the impression of applying careful legal reasoning but too many times you happen to reach the most conservative result", stated Senator Charles Schumer, one of Alito's fiercest critics during the hearings (Stevenson and Lewis 2006). The more partisan tenor of the hearings reflected the importance of O'Connor's seat but also the changed political circumstances since Roberts's hearings a few months earlier. Criticism over the administration's policies in Afghanistan and Iraq, plus ongoing investigations into Karl Rove and Tom DeLay had weakened the administration, as seen in the Miers debacle. This was exacerbated by Miers's defeat and by the discovery of Bush's domestic surveillance programme, which was widely criticised by many Democrats as an unconstitutional expansion of executive power. Ultimately, however, the political battles and aggressive questioning had little impact. Alito argued in his opening statement that judges should have no agenda and no preferred outcome in a case and should always be open to the possibility of changing their minds. Nothing in his answers to the committee provided evidence that he would not follow this principle and, at times, his frank answers gave the impression of a judge far less ideological than Democrats suggested (Liptak and Nagourney 2006). Democrats remained unconvinced but the committee approved Alito's nomination ten to eight, entirely along party lines. The trend continued in the Senate, which ultimately approved his nomination on 31 January 2006 by a fifty-eight to forty-two vote, the narrowest margin since that of Clarence Thomas in 1991.

Alito's successful appointment to the Court was a greater achievement for Bush than that of Roberts. Facing a more partisan political climate and following a highly public defeat with Miers, Bush nevertheless achieved the appointment of a well-qualified but undoubtedly conservative justice to replace O'Connor. Among the problems and difficulties of Bush's second term, Alito's nomination was an undoubted highlight.

## 4. THE CASES

Arguably the most significant cases heard by the Court during Bush's presidency were those tied to issues of national security and the war on terror. Despite claims made by civil liberties groups of the erosion of personal freedoms and constitutional rights, the Patriot Act was passed by Congress with massive bipartisan support in the aftermath of the 9/11 attacks. Arguments about the need for national security trumped most opposition, with supporters arguing that freedom of speech is useless to people killed in a terrorist attack. Likewise, as Guantánamo Bay was turned into a prison camp for "enemy combatants" to be held indefinitely without trial, those who sought to argue for the legal and civil rights of detainees were met with claims of national security. Despite complex debates over the rights of non-US citizens and those of US citizens committing crimes abroad, as well as the term enemy combatant, popular discourse suggested that because detainees threatened the security of the United States, they had no right to be treated in the same way as decent, law-abiding citizens. Civil liberties groups, who looked to the Supreme Court to defend the constitutional rights of citizens and detainees alike, were disappointed. For most of Bush's first term the Court remained silent on issues stemming from the war on terror.

Starting in 2004, however, the Court began to challenge Bush over Guantánamo Bay. In *Rasul* v. *Bush* (2004) the Court held that the military base came within the jurisdiction of the federal courts. Two years later, with Roberts and Alito on the Court, the government was denied the ability to try detainees by military commission in *Hamdan* v. *Rumsfeld* (2006). Both moved the status of those at Guantánamo Bay towards that of civilian prisoners rather than that of enemy combatants despite strenuous objections from Bush. This process continued in 2008 when a bare majority held in *Boumediene* v. *Bush* that prisoners at Guantánamo Bay have a constitutional right to challenge in a federal court their continued detention. The decision overturned parts of the 2006 Military Commissions Act that had removed the jurisdiction of federal courts to hear habeas corpus petitions from the detainees. By the time Bush left office, the Court had undone much of his plan for those held at Guantánamo Bay.

One interpretation of the Court's inaction in Bush's first term suggests that the justices were overly deferential to a popular president and scared of public opinion, which demanded action to defend the country and which might view Court action in defence of civil liberties as a threat to national security – it did nothing because it could do nothing else. The Court was rendered impotent to protect civil liberties by a strong president and overwhelming public opinion, but as Bush's support declined after 2004 and public opinion about the war on terror changed, it became bolder and began to challenge the administration. The argument has some merit but assumes a close link between Court action and public opinion that has yet to be demonstrated convincingly, despite the old adage that the Court follows the election returns.

A second interpretation argues that the Court deliberately chose to do nothing in Bush's first term. The Court's opinions reveal an institutional history of deference to presidential decision-making in foreign affairs and national security that might well explain its silence. In *US* v. *Curtiss-Wright Export Corporation* in 1936 the Court stated that the president has primary power in dealings with foreign nations, and in 1981 in *Rostker* v. *Goldberg* held that judicial deference is at a peak when considering combined executive–legislative power over national security. As civil liberties issues became more prominent in Bush's second term, in part due to the prisoner abuse at Abu Ghraib, the balance of power shifted away from the executive and towards the Court. (Again, there is Court precedent for this. In *Ex Parte Milligan* in 1866 the Court held that military tribunals cannot replace civilian courts where those courts remain open, and *US* v. *US District Court* in 1972 argued that First Amendment rights outweighed a vaguely defined concept of national security). In addition, holding the power of neither the purse nor the sword, the Court's authority rests on an ability to ensure co-operation with, and acceptance of, its rulings. Fear that an unpopular ruling might simply be ignored, damaging the Court's authority, led the Court, in this view, to its initial silence as an act of self-preservation. As Bush's popularity fell, the Court's relative strength increased and it began to take action. Irrespective of the causes, the results of the Court's actions were the same. On issues relating to national security, the two terms thesis of Bush's presidency seems entirely apt: no interference in the first term, clear and decisive opposition in the second.

In other areas of interest to Bush and his supporters, however, success came in the second term, partly as a result of the presence of Roberts and Alito. Abortion had been a key issue dividing conservatives (mostly anti-abortion) and liberals (mostly pro-choice) since 1973 when the Court in *Roe* v. *Wade* restricted the right of states to interfere with a woman's choice to terminate a pregnancy. Under Rehnquist, the Court narrowed the application of *Roe* but did not overturn it. Conservatives hoped Roberts and Alito would provide the votes to do so. The Court's April 2007 rulings in *Gonzales* v. *Carhart et al.* and *Gonzales* v. *Planned Parenthood Federation of America* were eagerly awaited by both sides looking for signs of the new Court's position on abortion. The cases, challenging the 2003 Partial Birth Abortion Ban Act which outlawed a procedure used in late-term abortions, also effectively challenged the Court's ruling in *Stenberg* v. *Carhart* (2000) in which a similar Nebraska law was struck down for failing to provide an exception for preserving the health of the mother. In *Gonzales*, the Court, with Roberts and Alito in the majority, upheld the constitutionality of the 2003 Act and seemingly overruled *Stenberg*, although it failed to do so explicitly. The cases represented the first time that the Court agreed a specific abortion procedure could be banned. For pro-choice advocates, *Gonzales* confirmed their worst fears about the direction of the Roberts Court. For anti-abortion campaigners, Bush and his supporters, the decision was a step in the right direction towards overturning *Roe*. But as of early 2009, the Court has shown no inclination to revisit the legality of abortion and it thus remains unclear as to the full significance of these cases. While undoubtedly a more conservative position on abortion, Kennedy's opinion for the majority also took pains to point to the limited application of the law in question. Whether this is the beginning of a major challenge to *Roe* from within the Court or a case dealing with one particular procedure is, as yet, unclear and awaits future decisions.

A second issue dividing liberals and conservatives is affirmative action. The United States has struggled for more than a century to deal with the legacy of slavery and for decades with the legacy of segregation. So-called affirmative-action policies were designed to make it easier for minorities to overcome disadvantages born of this history of discrimination, but some conservatives, including Scalia and

Thomas, argue that the policies are patronising and no more than reverse discrimination. The Court has been integral to the debates, especially since 1954 when in *Brown* v. *Board of Education* it outlawed segregation in the nation's schools. But the Court has also struggled to find a balance between the demands of equal protection for all embedded in the Constitution, which presumes that different treatment based on race, religion or gender is inherently suspect, and recognition of the very real consequences of the nation's history of race relations. Generally the Court has upheld affirmative-action programmes that are directly related to past discrimination or which are carefully designed to have particular and limited effects while striking down those considered too broad or general. School and university admissions policies have provoked particular concern because of past segregation and the importance of education for later life. In *Grutter* v. *Bollinger* in 2003 the Court held that universities could consider race as one of a number of factors when seeking a diverse student body, reinforcing a 1978 ruling in *Regents of the University of California* v. *Bakke*. But in June 2007 it appeared to reverse *Grutter* in a bitterly divided opinion in *Parents Involved in Community Schools* v. *Seattle School District No. 1* and *Meredith* v. *Jefferson County Board of Education*, which held that school districts cannot take explicit account of race when seeking to achieve or maintain integration. As many liberals had feared, the four conservatives, in an opinion by Chief Justice Roberts, argued that such programmes violate the Constitution's guarantee of equal protection. The fifth vote to strike down the programmes in question, however, came from Justice Kennedy whose concurring opinion moderated the plurality's "all-too-unyielding" position. Under certain conditions, Kennedy asserted, race may be taken into account, but only if the programme was narrowly tailored to meet those conditions: here they were not. As a result of Kennedy's opinion the practical consequences of the ruling remain unclear but the principles espoused by Roberts echoed those of Bush's supporters and suggested a victory for conservatives in another major area of public policy.

In a third policy area, Bush also found support from the Roberts Court: gun ownership. The debate over the Second Amendment's right to bear arms has traditionally divided those who believe it protects an unfettered individual right to gun ownership and those who assert the right is limited and gun control laws are not inherently unconstitutional. The Court, however, had not addressed the Second Amendment since *US* v. *Miller* in 1939 until it handed down *District of Columbia* v. *Heller* (2008), involving a Second Amendment challenge to a District of Columbia law banning handgun possession. In one of the term's few five to four decisions, it struck down the ban and found, for the first time, that the Second Amendment includes an individual right to possess guns that is not tied to participation in a militia. The opinions revealed tensions among the justices: Scalia in typically caustic language referred to Stevens's reasoning as "frivolous" and "absurd" while Stevens responded with claims of "strained and unpersuasive reasoning" by the majority. The clear support for individual rights to gun ownership provided a boost to groups like the National Rifle Association that had long advocated such a view. The decision left open the question of regulation of such ownership on the grounds of public safety, however. The ruling was, like others, narrow and left scope for further litigation.

## CONCLUSION

The applicability of the two terms thesis to Bush's relations with the Supreme Court depends, in part, on how the relevant issues are weighted. On issues relating to Guantánamo Bay, the Court's initial silence and later action undoubtedly reflect the successful first term, weaker second term framework. Likewise, the defeat of Miers's nomination to the Court by Bush's own supporters showed weaknesses in the Republican Party. Rejection of a Court nominee is a significant challenge to presidential authority and for the president's own party to be responsible only exacerbates the sense of weakness. Yet these reflect only part of Bush's relationship with the Court over eight years and, viewed from a broader perspective, the two terms theory seems less appropriate. First, in Bush's first term, the administration sought little direct involvement with the Court. That the generally conservative Rehnquist Court more frequently handed down opinions favoured by Bush and his supporters than opinions challenging their views made involvement beyond filing briefs in cases of particular concern largely unnecessary. Although it is possible to see this as a success of the first term (and it certainly didn't represent failure) it is, at best, a passive success. Second, with the exception of the Miers nomination, in his second term Bush was actively successful with the Court. Given the opportunity to make two new appointments, Bush nominated two reliably conservative justices, saw both confirmed after relatively straightforward hearings and then saw the emergence of a stronger conservative bloc on the Court. From the perspective of the Bush legacy, Bush's impact on the nation's highest court should be considered one of his most important and enduring contributions to American life: and it occurred in his second term.

Yet for all conservatives' hopes and liberals' fears, the full impact of Roberts and Alito remains to be seen. Despite an unusually high number of five–four decisions in the term ending July 2007, which suggested the Roberts Court was ready to move significantly to the right, the term ending July 2008 suggested such claims were premature. Decisions by the Court upholding the ban on partial birth abortions, striking down voluntary school integration plans, and finding an individual right to gun ownership in the Second Amendment suggested the greater influence of the conservatives with O'Connor's retirement. But the rulings granting Guantánamo Bay detainees access to federal courts, rejecting the death penalty for those who rape children, and a number of cases finding in favour of employees in workplace discrimination cases, suggested the liberal justices on the Court are capable of forming a coalition with Kennedy to challenge the conservative bloc. In addition, the narrowness of the rulings in many of the key cases of the two terms of the Roberts Court makes them unreliable predictors of future directions. The Court is undoubtedly more conservative with Roberts and Alito in place. What is less clear is whether that will translate into an eventual overturning of the pillars of the Warren Court's legacy that so enrage conservatives. Ultimately Bush's legacy on the Court may be determined by his successor. Justice Kennedy, now at the Court's centre with O'Connor's retirement, is seventy-three years old, Justice Stevens is eighty-eight, and Justice Ginsburg recently announced she is being treated for pancreatic cancer. Should President Barack Obama have the opportunity to replace one or more of these or other justices in the next four years, and Kennedy in particular, the composition of the Court will change again. The successful nominations of Roberts and Alito were undoubted successes of the Bush administration but their long-term significance remains to be seen.

## BIBLIOGRAPHY


Baker, P. and J. Becker (2005), "Bush Pledges Wide Search for Court Seat", *Washington Post,* 7 September

Barnes, R. (2007), "High Court Upholds Curb on Abortion", *Washington Post,* 19 April

Becker, J. (2005), "Democrats Pledge More Intense Scrutiny of Roberts", *Washington Post,* 6 September

Becker, J. and D. Russakoff (2006), "Proving His Mettle in the Reagan Justice Department", *Washington Post,* 9 January

Bumiller, E. and C. Hulse (2005), "President Picks Judge on Appeals Court for O'Connor Seat", *New York Times,* 1 November

Bush, George W. (2005), "Remarks of President Bush", *New York Times,* 1 July

Greenhouse, L. (2005), "Bush's Supreme Court Choice is a Judge Anchored in Modern Law", *New York Times,* 20 July

Kirkpatrick, D. (2005a), "A Year of Work to Sell Roberts to Conservatives", *New York Times,* 22 July

Kirkpatrick, D. (2005b), "Senate Democrats Are Shifting Focus From Roberts to Other Seat", *New York Times,* 9 September

Kirkpatrick, D. (2006), "New Questions on the Right on Court Pick", *New York Times,* 6 October

Liptak, A. (2005), "In His Opinions, Nominee Favors Judicial Caution", *New York Times,* 22 July

Liptak, A. and J. Glater (2005), "Alito's Dissents Show Deference to Lower Courts", *New York Times,* 3 November

Liptak, A. and A. Nagourney (2006), "Judge Alito Proves a Powerful Match for Senate Questions", *New York Times,* 11 January

Purdum, T., J. Wilgoren and P. Belluck (2005), "Court Nominee's Life is Rooted in Faith and Respect for Law", *New York Times,* 21 July

Stevenson, R. and N. Lewis (2006), "Alito Says Judges Shouldn't Bring Agenda to Cases", *New York Times,* 10 January

Stolberg, S. (2005a), "Senators Who Averted Showdown Face New Test in Court Fight", *New York Times,* 14 July

Stolberg, S. (2005b), "Bush Works to Reassure G.O.P. Over Nominee for Supreme Court", *New York Times,* 9 October

*Chapter 5*

# FEDERALISM IN THE BUSH ERA

M. J. C. Vile

Federalism is a technique for giving the necessary unity to member states to meet common problems, while making possible divergent policies on those issues where there is no national consensus. Of course, over time, changing circumstances require new solutions to policy problems, and a new consensus about the distribution of government functions between federal and state governments emerges. The formal division of powers set out in the Constitution has remained essentially unchanged since 1789, but judicial interpretation of these powers and the development of conventions relating to the exercise of presidential power have transformed the relationship between the federal government and the states. The history of American federalism is one of seemingly inexorable centralisation, punctuated by largely ineffectual attempts to reverse or slow the process. Furthermore, as the processes of urbanisation and industrialisation have reduced the economic and social differences between regions, the states have become less concerned with the representation of geographical interests and more with the channelling of varying political interests in the process of decision-taking. America is a pluralistic society, one in which many interest groups contend over political issues, and although the geographic character of federalism has not been entirely lost, it has increasingly become an institutional mechanism through which the pluralistic battle of differing interest groups is played out (Vile 2007: 20, 28–37). This process was accelerated during the presidency of George W. Bush, for he seemed to have little concern for the values of federalism or for states' rights. Federalism was subordinated to his policy goals, and, where these goals required the centralisation of government power, it was vigorously pursued.

## 1. CENTRALISATION AND DEVOLUTION

The basic constitutional principle of American federalism is that the federal government is a government of enumerated powers. In other words, the federal government's powers are limited to those listed in the Constitution, which are very few. On the other hand, in the words of the Tenth Amendment, "The powers not delegated to the United States by the Constitution . . . are reserved to the states." Thus the legal basis for any Act of the federal government has to be found in a few, rather vaguely worded clauses. The most important for domestic policy have been the power "to regulate commerce with foreign nations and among the several states" and the "power to lay and collect taxes . . . and provide for the common defense and general welfare of the United States". The former has provided the means for the vast expansion of federal regulatory power over American economic life, and the latter has been the basis for the provision of federal social programmes, most of which have taken the form of providing money for the states to undertake programmes in areas over which the federal government had no explicit power, with conditions laid down by Congress as to the way the money should be spent. The vast centralisation of power that has taken place over the past 220 years has been through the progressive elaboration of these techniques.

The process of the centralisation of power and function in the hands of the federal government began early with the decisions of the Supreme Court under Chief Justice Marshall (1801–35). Later, the passage of the Sixteenth Amendment in 1913 authorised the levying of a federal income tax and enhanced the financial strength of the federal government, making it possible to generate the income to provide large federal grants to state governments. The really extensive increase in federal power, however, began with the New Deal of President Franklin Roosevelt. In 1935 Congress passed the Social Security Act. It established the first wholly federally administered welfare programme, providing pensions for the elderly, but it also set up welfare programmes for the disadvantaged, financed jointly by the federal and state governments and administered by the states under conditions set by the federal government. This programme, typical of the "co-operative federalism" initiated by Roosevelt, provided federal grants-in-aid for the states and set conditions that the states had to meet to receive this federal money. Conditional grants-in-aid, which encouraged the states to adopt policies desired by the federal government, became a favourite strategy and were used for a wide variety of programmes in agriculture, civil aviation, education, roads, housing, disaster relief and public health.

In the 1960s centralisation continued with the Great Society programmes of President Lyndon Johnson, including the Medicare and Medicaid programmes. Medicare is a federally administered government health insurance programme for people aged sixty-five or older and for some disabled people under sixty-five. Medicaid is a health-care programme for some individuals and families with low incomes and resources. It is jointly funded by the states and the federal government but managed by the states. Medicaid provides automatic entitlement to medical care for claimants who meet the eligibility requirements for welfare programmes and is financed by conditional grants-in-aid with approximately half the cost coming from state funds. Lyndon Johnson's administration also saw a significant increase in federal regulations (mandates) requiring state action.

But the most important force for centralisation in these years came through the decisions of the Supreme Court. The first ten amendments to the Constitution, the Bill of Rights, adopted in 1791 provided protection to American citizens from the abuse of power by the federal government, but not against actions of the states. Thus, all those state laws which discriminated against blacks in the nineteenth and early twentieth centuries were immune from challenge. In the twentieth century the Supreme Court gradually extended the constitutional protection of the provisions of the Bill of Rights against state government actions, through its reinterpretation of the Fourteenth Amendment. These decisions heralded the end of racial segregation, and provided protection for the civil and political rights of African Americans, as well as for the extension of freedom of speech and the press. In the economic sphere, the Court gradually extended federal power after 1936 until, in *Garcia* v. *San Antonio* in 1985, it seemed to abandon the defence of states' rights altogether, leaving the determination of the boundaries between federal and state power wholly in the hands of Congress.

This transfer of power and function from the states to the federal government raised fears that so-called big government had eroded the entrenched constitutional position of the states and reduced individual liberty. It also impinged upon a variety of groups that would prefer to be regulated, if at all, by the states rather than by a powerful federal bureaucracy. Successive Republican presidents declared their intention to restore power to the states and to curb the expansion of the federal government. In 1953 President Eisenhower called for "a sounder relationship between Federal, State, and local governments", but a much stronger reaction against centralisation came with attempts by Presidents Nixon and Reagan to return power to the states. Nixon's New Federalism centred on giving block grants to the states giving them greater discretion in the administration of federal aid programmes; and President Reagan issued executive order 12612 in 1987, declaring that intrusive federal oversight of state administration is neither necessary nor desirable and instructing federal agencies to grant the states the maximum administrative discretion possible. Agencies were further instructed that any statutory federal regulations which would pre-empt state law must be "restricted to the minimum level necessary to achieve the objectives of the statute". In 1990 President George H. W. Bush confirmed Reagan's executive order and instructed the heads of federal departments to comply with it.

## 2. BIG GOVERNMENT CONSERVATISM

From the 1930s, liberals and Democrats, with the exception of some mostly from southern states, were generally in favour of expanding federal power in order to pursue national economic and social policies, albeit involving state co-operation where possible. Republicans and conservatives, on the other hand, were more protective of states' rights, in part as a strategy for using the power of the states to resist federal policies of which the conservatives disapproved. President George W. Bush, however, did not fit into this mould. He was a conservative, but he was not a traditional conservative concerned primarily with limited government.

The Bush administration was deeply influenced by the neo-conservative philosophy. Neo-conservatives are not necessarily opposed to big government, provided that the exercise of federal power is necessary to achieve their aims. In fact, Republicans had for some time been moving away from being straightforward defenders of states' rights, realising that public concern for such things as educational standards was a more persuasive electoral position (Posner 2007: 393). Furthermore, in approaching the relationship of the federal government to the states, most presidents have made an effort to maintain a bipartisan stance as far as possible. They need the co-operation of state governors of both political parties and of state legislatures that may be dominated by the opposing political party. And Republican presidents, who have almost always faced at least one chamber of Congress with a Democratic majority, could get their legislation through only with the support of conservative Democrats. Bush was the first Republican president since Eisenhower to enjoy Republican majorities in both the House and Senate. He chose to abandon bipartisanship to become an active partisan leader of the Republicans in order to try to establish the party in a permanent majority position (Milkis and Rhodes 2007: 485). President Bush subordinated concern for states' rights to his policy goals, and reversed the policies of his Republican predecessors. In the words of Dale Krane he "pursued policies designed to enhance national government control over domestic policy" (Krane 2007: 407). The consequences for federalism are considerable.

## 3. COERCIVE FEDERALISM

One way of measuring the expansion of the functions of the federal government is the increase in federal spending during the Bush years. Federal government spending as a proportion of gross domestic product (GDP) increased by two percentage points during the Bush years, having fallen by about four points over the preceding two decades. Put differently, federal spending rose from $1.8 trillion in 2001 to $2.9 trillion in 2008, a 33 per cent increase, adjusting for inflation, largely attributable to the wars in Iraq and Afghanistan. It created a fiscal climate in which it became more difficult for the states to levy taxes and thus required an increase in federal grants to the states from $319 billion to $467 billion, an increase after inflation of 18 per cent. The states often had to provide matching funds, however, which imposed yet greater burdens on their budgets.

Federal grants-in-aid were originally devised as a means of encouraging states, through financial incentives, to adopt policies that they might be unable to afford or which they might otherwise choose not to adopt. In principle, a state might choose not to participate in a programme, thus foregoing the federal money on offer, in order to avoid the federal control accompanying the grant of funds. Some states have adopted such self-denying ordinances, but the sheer scale of the federal money on offer, and the prospect of a state's citizens losing out on the benefits of a federal programme, although continuing to pay as much federal tax as the citizens of other states, make refusal politically hazardous.

Federal grant-in-aid programmes can at one extreme be simply a way of ensuring that the states enact a particular programme, leaving them wide discretion in the details of the programme and the levels of state expenditure. This system came to be described in the 1930s and after as co-operative federalism. At the other extreme, the conditions attached to the grants can be designed to ensure a national uniformity of standards, leaving little discretion to the state legislature or to the state bureaucracy. In other words, the federal government issues mandates to which the states must conform. The use of mandates increased significantly during the administration of Lyndon Johnson in the 1960s, and federal power to pre-empt state authority was used extensively in the 1970s and 1980s (Kincaid 1990: 148) leading to the coining of the term "coercive federalism" as a contrast to "co-operative federalism". In the administration of George W. Bush the use of federal mandates became so important in federal–state relations that commentators came to see coercive federalism as its major characteristic (Conlan 2008: 13).

### *a. Education*

The use of mandates to impose federal policy on the states was a feature of the No Child Left Behind (NCLB) Act of 2001. Education is an area in which fear of federal government interference had historically been very powerful, particularly regarding the content of educational programmes and particularly among conservatives. There was no significant federal involvement in education before the 1950s, and it was not until the passage of the Elementary and Secondary Education Act (ESEA) in 1965 that the federal government became closely involved. The ESEA depended upon a complex system of intergovernmental co-operation, however, and the legislation targeted particular groups such as disadvantaged or disabled children. The Bush legislation was very different. It reversed traditional Republican education policies and brought about a significant expansion of federal authority over the programme aspects of education (Wong and Sunderman 2007: 337). NCLB requires that states "adopt content with challenging academic standards in the core subjects of mathematics, reading or language arts, and science" (Parker 2008: 246). Furthermore, the states must regularly test students' achievement in these subjects, every public school teacher must be highly qualified, and schools must meet achievement targets each year, with progressive sanctions applied if they fail to do so.

Opinions on the impact of NCLB on intergovernmental relations vary widely. Some argue it "represents an incremental addition to the direction of federal policymaking that has been occurring for almost half a century. In other words, it is evolution rather than revolution in the context of federalism" (Parker 2008: 242), while others suggest that "The U.S. Department of Education now functions as a national schoolmarm, hovering over state school reform efforts and whacking those states that fail to record satisfactory and timely progress toward federal education goals with financial penalties and mandatory corrective actions" (McGuinn 2005: 68). Wherever the line is drawn between evolution and revolution, it is undeniable that, although the states and districts are still the major players in the field of education policy, NCLB represents an unprecedented level of federal control over education.

### *b. Homeland Security*

After the terrorist attacks of 9/11 the concern to do everything possible to prevent further attacks overrode other considerations. The Patriot Act of 2001 greatly expanded the powers of the federal government in the field of law enforcement, particularly in relation to terrorism and aliens. Congress established a new executive department, the Department of Homeland Security, and President Bush issued directives requiring states to conform to strict standards in the planning and provision of emergency programmes covering a range of natural disasters and terrorist attacks. In 2004 Congress passed the Intelligence Reform and Terrorism Prevention Act which, among other things, directed the Treasury Department to establish federal standards for state-issued driver's licences, so that they would be more effective in establishing identity. The Real ID Act of 2005 meant that driver's licences or state-issued identity cards which did not meet these standards could not be used for identification purposes to board commercial aircraft or to enter any federal facility. The implementation of this legislation caused so much difficulty for the states that in 2008 the deadline for compliance was extended to the end of 2009, which means that the future of this programme will be decided by President Obama.

### *c. Health Care*

Two health-care programmes were introduced by the Social Security Act of 1965: Medicare and Medicaid. Among the groups of people eligible for Medicaid are low-income parents, children, the elderly and people with disabilities. When these two programmes were established there was a degree of overlap, so that some people could be eligible for both programmes. Medicare itself provided prescription medicines only for eligible recipients who were in hospitals or nursing homes, but the states could provide prescription medicines to those people who qualified under both programmes – over six million persons by 2003 (Derthick 2007: 353). In 2003 Congress passed the Medicare Prescription Drug, Improvement and Modernization Act, the largest expansion of the federal role in health care since 1965. The principal purpose of the Act was to expand the federal government's Medicare programme to include coverage of prescription medicines for the elderly and disabled, but it also centralised the provision of medicines for those who had previously been covered by the joint programmes, although it left to the states the option of providing medicines to other recipients of Medicaid. The new regime proved so complex, however, that the states had to step in, albeit in a subordinate role, to protect people who might otherwise have suffered the loss of their former benefits.

The way in which ideology trumped states' rights in the Bush era was well illustrated in 2007 by the process of the reauthorisation of the State Children's Health Insurance Program Act of 1997. The Act provided health insurance for children who would otherwise not be covered, and it operated through a co-operative block grant programme with state governments. As is generally the intention with block grants, the states began to develop a variety of different approaches, some more liberal than others, including extending eligibility to wider groups of children. When it came to the reauthorisation of the Act in 2007, the Republicans wished to restrict state flexibility and standardise requirements, and the Bush administration issued federal guidelines to state officials imposing stricter requirements. Democrats, on the other hand, wished to give greater flexibility to the states in order to expand children's health insurance, and President Bush twice vetoed bills which would have extended the coverage of the programme, so that a temporary reauthorisation was eventually approved without any policy changes. It was Republican ideological perspectives rather than concern with federalism that dominated the president's approach to this programme (Grogan and Rigby 2009: 48, 62).

Bush did preside over one decentralising policy giving greater flexibility to the states in the administration of the Medicaid programme. The Deficit Reduction Act of 2005 gave the states the power to scale back some Medicaid benefits, but the Act also imposed other requirements on the states mandating them to check the citizenship of recipients before providing medical care. Fuelled by conservatives, there has also been a measure of decentralisation of the Medicaid programme through the use of federal waivers, which allow the states to opt out of some of the requirements set by federal legislation and escape to some extent the strict eligibility requirements. The waivers have fostered greater diversity but also inequality between state programmes (Thompson and Burke 2009: 32).

### *d. Elections*

Historically, American electoral law and the machinery for the conduct of elections have been left largely to the states, even for elections to the office of president and Congress. Federal law has been concerned mostly with preventing racial discrimination. The disputed presidential election of 2000, however, caused a crisis of confidence in the American electoral system. There was a dismal daily display on television of the inadequacies of voting machines and electoral procedures generally, and specifically of election clerks in Florida trying to decipher the intentions of voters through the scrutiny of hanging chads (a paper fragment still clinging to the ballot paper as a result of an incompletely punched hole, which rendered the vote choice unreadable). Both political parties knew that something must be done; the result was the Help America Vote Act of 2002. The Act ordered the states to meet federal standards with regard to voting and voter registration in federal elections (Conlan and Dinan 2007: 281) providing for federal funds to improve voting systems and establishing the US Election Assistance Commission to provide guidance to the states on electoral policy.

### *f. Environmental Policy*

Despite early indications that the Bush administration might co-operate effectively with the states in the development and implementation of environmental policy, optimism soon faded (Rabe 2007: 415–16). Environmental policy is an area in which the states have attempted to experiment and develop their own programmes, but state initiatives led to confrontations with a federal government determined to follow policies that favoured energy interests regardless of the consequences for the environment. In California, Republican Governor Arnold Schwarzenegger even went so far as to sign an agreement with British Prime Minister Tony Blair in August 2006 proposing that California join the European Union carbon-trading scheme to reduce greenhouse gas emissions. In September 2006 Governor Schwarzenegger signed into law the California Global Warming Solutions Act, which set gas emissions limits, including limits for new cars and trucks, and gave the California Air Resources Board substantial discretion to establish policies to achieve the target. Twelve other states quickly followed the California initiative and others later passed similar legislation. The California limits for motor vehicles were higher than those set by Congress, however, and required a federal waiver, which the Bush administration refused to grant in spite of appeals by state governors and a lawsuit by Governor Schwarzenegger against the federal Environmental Protection Agency. One of the first things that President Barack Obama did on taking office was to order the EPA to reconsider California's request for a waiver.

### *g. Hurricane Katrina*

Hurricane Katrina was a natural disaster for New Orleans and a political disaster for George W. Bush. It also revealed a great deal about the problems of federalism in coping with large-scale emergencies. Responsibility for disaster planning and the execution of those plans is shared by the federal government, the states and local governments, and success depends upon effective co-ordination of their efforts at all stages. This was sadly lacking in August 2005 when the Category 3 hurricane struck the coast of Louisiana. Divisions and rivalries within and between federal government agencies did not help, and the preoccupation of the Bush administration with the terrorist threat after 9/11 diverted resources away from the preparations for natural disasters (Birkland and Waterman 2007: 694). Federal agencies were slow to provide aid and the president was accused of a lack of concern for the black majority population of New Orleans. There was a breakdown in law and order in New Orleans with outbreaks of looting and violence against the population left behind in the city after the evacuation. There were also significant failures which could be attributed to the federal structure of government. Controversy arose between President Bush and Louisiana Governor Kathleen Blanco about the deployment and control of the Louisiana National Guard. The National Guard is normally under the control of the state governor, other than in the case of an insurrection, and her agreement was necessary if it was to be put under federal command in order to deal with the emergency. As a result of her and other governors' resistance, the Defense Authorization Act was enacted in 2007, giving presidents the power to take control of the National Guard without the permission of a governor in the case of a natural disaster, among other circumstances.

### *h. Other Centralising Policies*

The Bush administration vigorously pursued centralising policies in three other ways. First, problems arise when some states legislate in traditionally state-controlled areas, such as marriage and family law, which particular groups find morally offensive and which might potentially spread to other states. The passage of state laws authorising civil unions or same-sex marriages raised fears in conservative and religious groups that this practice might spread across the nation, fears which were reinforced by the decision of the Supreme Court in the case of *Lawrence* v. *Texas* in 2003, striking down state laws prohibiting consensual homosexual sex (Ashbee 2008: 199). Conservatives in Congress introduced a constitutional amendment to ban gay marriage. The Federal Marriage Amendment won the support of George W. Bush but failed to gain the two-thirds vote necessary to pass the Congress. The federal government did, however, tighten its grip regarding abortion law. Calling on the authority of the commerce clause, Congress passed the Partial-Birth Abortion Ban Act of 2003, making it a crime for a physician to perform the controversial late-term procedure.

Second, when a power is granted to Congress by the Constitution, such as the power to tax or regulate interstate commerce, Congress may allow the states to exercise concurrent power in that area of government activity, or it may specifically exclude them – that is prevent the states legislating on a particular subject. Such pre-emptions of state power by Congress occurred only rarely in the nineteenth century and the early twentieth century but gained pace after 1960 as federal regulatory statutes multiplied (Zimmerman 2007: 436). George W. Bush approved a number of pre-emptive statutes, but few had very far-ranging effects. Two exceptions are the 2007 Internet Tax Freedom Act Amendments Act, which extended the prohibition of state taxes on Internet access first enacted in 1998 under President Clinton, and the 2005 Energy Policy Act in which "nearly a dozen provisions . . . either pre-empt or tightly constrain state authority in a range of areas" (Rabe 2007: 418).

Third, statutes can give rule-making powers to the executive to implement policies laid down in those statutes. The Bush administration made wide use of these powers – reflecting Vice President Cheney's philosophy of the unitary executive, which holds that the president has the same authority to interpret laws relating to the executive branch as the courts – despite considerable opposition from the states. The extent to which Bush used his executive powers to give directions to state policymakers has led to this aspect of American federalism being labelled executive federalism.

> Major programmatic decisions in the 1990s and 2000s emerge to a much greater extent than in previous decades from interactions between the executive branches of the national government and the states during the implementation process . . . What distinguishes the Clinton–G. W. Bush period is the degree to which key decision sites have come to reside in the executive branch at national and state levels rather than in congress and the state legislatures. (Thompson and Burke 2009: 35)

## 4. FEDERALISM AND THE SUPREME COURT

As noted above, the expansion of federal power by the Supreme Court reached a peak with its 1985 *Garcia* v. *San Antonio* decision, which Justice Blackmun authored. "State sovereign interests", noted Blackmun, "are more properly protected by procedural safeguards inherent in the structure of the federal system than by judicially created limitations on federal power." In other words, political safeguards ensure that Congress will not encroach inappropriately on the functions of the states, and it is up to Congress to set the boundaries of federalism.

After the appointment of a number of conservative justices by President Reagan and the elder Bush, however, the Court has since 1992 established a more balanced view of the division between federal and state powers. Unlike George W. Bush, who has resembled a Democrat in his view of the reach of federal power, the conservatives on the Court have taken a more traditionally Republican view of states' rights. From 1992 the Court invalidated a number of acts of Congress on the grounds that they infringed upon the powers of the states. It also took a new attitude towards subjects such as segregation, leaving more latitude to states and localities. During the Bush administration the Court continued its qualified defence of states' rights. Oregon became the first state to legalise assisted suicide in 1994, exempting from civil or criminal liability state-licensed physicians who dispense or prescribe a lethal dose of drugs upon the request of a terminally ill patient. In 2001 the US Attorney General John Ashcroft attempted to overrule the Oregon statute arguing that such behaviour violated the federal Controlled Substances Act. A majority of the Supreme Court concluded, however, that the federal legislation "does not authorize the Attorney General to bar dispensing controlled substances for assisted suicide in the face of a state medical regime permitting such conduct" (*Gonzales* v. *Oregon*, 2006). The Court also rejected the power of the president to direct state courts to follow a decision of the International Court of Justice (*Medellin* v. *Texas*, 2008).

In *FMC* v. *South Carolina Ports Authority*, 2002, Justice Thomas made a pronouncement that could have been made by the Court two centuries earlier: "Dual sovereignty is a defining feature of our nation's constitutional blueprint. States, upon ratification of the Constitution, did not consent to become mere appendages of the Federal Government. Rather, they entered the Union 'with their sovereignty intact'." In a potentially important decision in 2008, *Department of Revenue for Kentucky* v. *Davis*, the Court held that a form of discriminatory taxation employed by forty-one states was "a quintessentially public function" of the states, and therefore not in contravention of the commerce clause.

On the other hand, the Court has upheld the right of the federal government under the commerce clause to prohibit the local cultivation and use of marijuana (*Gonzales* v. *Raich*, 2005); it held that federal power over foreign affairs pre-empted California from requiring information from companies doing business in the state about their activities in Europe during the Nazi period (*American Insurance Association* v. *Garamendi*, 2003); and it upheld under the Fourteenth Amendment the congressional power to require states to provide disabled people with access to state courts through the Americans with Disabilities Act of 1990 (*Tennessee* v. *Lane*, 2004). In three cases in 2008 the Court upheld federal statutes pre-empting state regulatory authority, and in *Gonzales* v. *Carhart*, 2007, the Court upheld the Partial-Birth Abortion Ban Act.

## CONCLUSION

Centralisation is a natural concomitant of the growth of national identity. As people become more aligned with national interests and less aware of local and regional differences, they increasingly demand equal treatment from government. As we have seen, centralisation has been an almost continuous phenomenon in the United States, particularly since the 1930s. The cumulative effect of the centralising policies adopted by the Bush administration is considerable; it has been described as "an administration that has been routinely dismissive of federalism concerns" (Conlan and Dinan 2007: 280).

Of course, centralisation is a relative concept. The United States still has a highly decentralised system of government compared with many other countries, but there has been a number of developments that suggest there might have been a sea change in the nature of American federalism. One explanation is that a number of groups previously considered to be firm defenders of states' rights are now more likely to support federal authority. Republicans and conservatives pursuing more ideological aims have become as determined as

Democrats and liberals to use federal power to achieve those aims. For example, those who see some states as potentially purveyors of dangerously liberal policies – Oregon on assisted suicide, California on carbon emissions or medicinal marijuana and Massachusetts on same-sex marriages, for example – look to the federal government to pre-empt state action. Another explanation is that "the growing independence of presidential and congressional candidates from national, state and local party organizations eroded the party foundations of cooperative federalism, leaving state and local officials feeling like 'just another interest group'" (Kincaid 1990: 149). State and local leaders are aware of the emerging public demands for national policies to solve national problems and are often divided in their response to federal initiatives. Sometimes national mandates are proposed by state political leaders, and states may be more concerned about how mandates are implemented than opposed to them in principle (Posner 2007: 405–6). Yet another explanation is that a number of the Bush administration's centralising policies were passed by bipartisan majorities in a Congress fearful of public condemnation if they failed to act. Whatever the explanation, the outcome is clear: "In essence all levels of government are increasingly engaged in an 'opportunistic federalism' where all actors in the system attempt to use one another to achieve particular policy goals, irrespective of traditional boundaries and authority distributions" (Posner 2007: 409).

In the Bush era, the institutional structure of federalism increasingly became the mechanism through which the politics of pluralism was played out. The decentralised nature of the American party system remains as a bastion of resistance to the kind of centralisation to be found, for example, in Britain, but federalism as an idea has become subordinate to the interests or philosophies of the players in the pluralistic game.

## BIBLIOGRAPHY

Ashbee, Edward (2008), "Gay Rights, the Federal Marriage Amendment, and the States", in Iwan W. Morgan and Philip J. Davies, eds, *The Federal Nation: Perspectives on American Federalism,* New York: Palgrave Macmillan

Birkland, Thomas and Sarah Waterman (2007), "Is Federalism the Reason for Policy Failure in Hurricane Katrina?", *Publius: The Journal of Federalism,* Vol. 37(3)

Conlan, Timothy J. (1998), *From New Federalism to Devolution: Twenty-Five Years of Intergovernmental Reform*, Washington, DC: Brookings Institution Press

Conlan, Timothy J. (2008), "Federalism, the Bush Administration and the Evolution of American Politics", in Iwan W. Morgan and Philip J. Davies, eds, *The Federal Nation: Perspectives on American Federalism*, New York: Palgrave Macmillan

Conlan, Timothy J. and John Dinan (2007), "Federalism, the Bush Administration, and the Transformation of American Conservatism", *Publius: The Journal of Federalism*, Vol. 37(3)

Derthick, Martha (2007), "Going Federal: The Launch of Medicare Part D Compared to SSI", *Publius: The Journal of Federalism*, Vol. 37(3)

Grogan, Colleen M. and Elizabeth Rigby (2009), "Federalism, Partisan Politics, and Shifting Support for State Flexibility: The Case of the U.S. State Children's Health Insurance Program", *Publius: The Journal of Federalism*, Vol. 39 (1)

Kincaid, John (1990), "From Cooperative Federalism to Coercive Federalism", *Annals of the American Academy of Political and Social Sciences*, Vol. 509

Krane, Dale (2007), "The Middle Tier in American Federalism: State Government Policy Activism During the Bush Presidency", *Publius: The Journal of Federalism*, Vol. 37(3)

McGuinn, Patrick (2005), "The National Schoolmarm: No Child Left Behind and the New Educational Federalism", *Publius: The Journal of Federalism*, Vol. 35(1)

Milkis, Sidney M. and Jesse H. Rhodes (2007), "George W. Bush, the Party System, and American Federalism", *Publius: The Journal of Federalism*, Vol. 37(3)

Parker, Jonathan (2008), "No Child Left Behind: Federalism and Education Policy", in Iwan W. Morgan and Philip J. Davies, eds, *The Federal Nation: Perspectives on American Federalism*, New York: Palgrave Macmillan

Posner, Paul (2007), "The Politics of Coercive Federalism in the Bush Era", *Publius: The Journal of Federalism*, Vol. 37(3)

Rabe, Barry (2007), "Environmental Policy and the Bush Era: The Collision Between the Administrative Presidency and State Experimentation", *Publius: The Journal of Federalism*, Vol. 37(3)

Thompson, Frank J. and Courtney Burke (2009), "Federalism by Waiver: Medicaid and the Transformation of Long-Term Care", *Publius: The Journal of Federalism*, Vol. 39(1)

Vile, M. J. C. (2007), *Politics in the USA*, 6th edition, London: Routledge

Wong, Kenneth and Gail Sunderman (2007), "Education Accountability as a Presidential Priority: No Child Left Behind and the Bush Presidency", *Publius: The Journal of Federalism*, Vol. 37(3)

Zimmerman, J. F. (2007), "Congressional Preemption During the George W. Bush Administration", *Publius: The Journal of Federalism*, Vol. 37(3)

# PART II
# FOREIGN POLICY LEADERSHIP

*Chapter 6*

# TO USHER IN A NEW PARADIGM? PRESIDENT BUSH'S FOREIGN POLICY LEGACY

Jason Ralph

Writing about legacies is somewhat speculative. It is an exercise in historical investigation, as we need to know what the subject actually did, but it is also an exercise in forecasting, because we need to say something about the significance of those actions *in* and *for* the future. A perception of what President Bush has bequeathed his successors, for instance, depends on how far one looks into the future. A long-term perspective is needed if one is to claim that his policies are of lasting significance, but the further one looks into the future the less certain one can be that one is seeing the effects of Bush's foreign policy. The exact nature of Bush's legacy, in other words, will be contingent on how his successors react to the policies his administration offered. Even then, however, a legacy is not easy to pin down. Perceptions of the Bush administration's foreign policy will inevitably change in the future because, as E. H. Carr (2001) noted, history tells us more about the time in which it was written than it does about its particular subject. Bush's legacy will be manipulated by future historians to advance or resist various contemporary political agendas. Indeed, the 'Clinton legacy' and, especially, the 'Reagan legacy' were important parts of the political discourse that helped Bush and his supporters define his administration (see Halper and Clarke 2004; Heilbrunn 2007).

Despite these qualifications, there is a clear sense in which the Bush administration has been present at the creation of a new era of American foreign policy. For instance, Luttwak (2008) and Lynch and Singh (2008) draw a direct parallel between the Bush and Truman administrations. Both governed through a time when a new existential threat to the United States emerged, and both were unpopular when they left office because the wars that they had launched in response to that new threat had exacted unexpectedly high costs. Yet according to Lynch and Singh (2008: 3), the parallels do not end there. "Like the Truman doctrine before it", they write, "the Bush doctrine will outlast the president whose name it bears", and just as Truman ushered in the Cold War, so Bush will be regarded as the first president of the "second Cold War". Their implication is that, if future policymakers adopt the framework set out in the Bush doctrine, then the United States will eventually defeat Islamist terrorism just as it prevailed over Soviet communism.

Lynch and Singh therefore offer both an analytical and a normative case for continuity, one that reinforces President Bush's own departing message (2008), which is that his successor needs to understand the lessons of 9/11. There are, of course, many lessons that can be drawn from that tragic event. The lesson that the Bush administration drew was that the United States was not only at war, but that it was engaged in a very different kind of war. In this respect, Lynch and Singh are correct to argue that we may look back on 2001 and see it as a pivotal moment in the same way that we now see 1947. Like the Cold War, the idea of a war on terror simplifies what is inordinately complex and provides a focal point for the public and for policy-makers. Yet to imply that the Bush administration adopted the kind of stance that successfully defeated the Soviet Union is to underestimate the radical nature of the Bush administration's response to the terrorist threat. It is argued in this chapter that there are, of course, elements of continuity with past American foreign policy, but it is also argued that the Bush doctrine involved a fundamental shift in America's relations with its allies and with its enemies. For instance, while Truman oversaw the creation of NATO and the Geneva Conventions, the Bush administration dismissed these institutions as either marginal or irrelevant to the conduct of the war on terror. The Bush doctrine was different from presidential doctrines of the past and this is reflected in the fact that it united liberals *and* realists in opposition to it. Lynch and Singh's case for recognising continuity with the past may have been stronger had realists supported what liberals opposed, but that was not the case with the Bush doctrine. The realist critique did begin to exert influence, particularly in the administration's second term; and one could possibly argue that, by the end of the Bush administration, the United States had adopted a Cold War-type policy, one that was conscious of the limits of American power and understood the importance of human rights in the context of multilateral diplomacy. The ironic fact is that, while this approach may be appropriate for a long war against Islamist terrorism, it is certainly not the same as the Bush doctrine.

## 1. THE "WAR" ON TERROR

Lynch and Singh's argument, that Bush's foreign and security policy is reflective of America's successful past, might have drawn on events preceding the Truman administration. The terrorist attacks on New York and Washington were, of course, compared immediately to the surprise Japanese attack on Pearl Harbor in December 1941. This helped to form the impression that, from 11 September 2001, the United States would be at "war". There are similarities between the two events. On both occasions, the United States had been caught off guard by bolts that came (literally) out of the blue; and on both occasions the surprise, compounded by the sheer horror of the violence, called into question US preparedness. Yet the comparison is also misleading in two significant respects. Firstly, the 9/11 attacks did not change the idea that the United States homeland was protected by its geographical situation between the Atlantic and the Pacific. Pearl Harbor and the Cold War had already done that. The collapse of the Soviet Union had taken away the urgency that had accompanied the nuclear arms races of previous years, but there was no indication, either in the 1990s or in the early part of the Bush administration, that isolationism could ever inform policy in the way it did in the 1920s and 1930s. Indeed, Republicans in the 1990s had advocated national missile defence because they remained convinced that the United States homeland was vulnerable to attack. Secondly, unlike the attack on Pearl Harbor, the 9/11 attacks were not committed by a modern territorial state with conventional armed forces of its own. Rather they were committed by a transnational network of individuals who were difficult to identify. Of course, the al-Qaeda threat, like the Japanese threat, existed before the attack on the United States homeland and both attacks heralded a new world order. But where Pearl Harbor signalled America's undisputed entry into the modern world of great power rivalries, 9/11 signalled America's entry into a postmodern world where the main threats were transnational.

There was no indication that the Bush administration was prepared for the intellectual shift that was required to understand what had happened on 9/11. Foreign policy statements from the campaign trail and from the first eight months of the administration tended to focus on the development of traditional state-based threats which, as noted above, were believed to require greater investment in national missile defence (Rice 2000). The Clinton administration had been chastised for ignoring these realities and for relying too much on the soft power of multilateral diplomacy and not enough on the hard power of America's material might. Its apparent focus on the humanitarian consequences of state failure and its apparent faith that the processes of globalisation would mitigate, and even transcend, great power competition were dismissed as naive in a manner similar to the way Reaganites had attacked the liberal idealism of President Carter. Under President Bush, the United States would instead pay greater attention to managing the renewal and the rise of America's traditional great power competitors, Russia and China, as well as those states that threatened America's regional interests, notably Iraq. It would do this by extending the unipolar moment. It would renew its own strength through an agenda of transforming the military, concentrating not on the peacekeeping, nation-building or humanitarian missions that seemingly dominated the 1990s' agenda, but on emphasising America's comparative advantages in technology and warfare.

Combined with a partisan attitude to foreign policy – the administration reportedly adopted an "anything-but-Clinton" approach (Daalder and Lindsay 2003: 37) – this traditional and statist worldview could only have exacerbated the level of surprise on 9/11. The Clinton administration had been very much aware of this new threat and it had used military force in its response. For instance, the president ordered cruise missile strikes against al-Qaeda bases following the terrorist attacks in Tanzania and Kenya. Yet from the post-9/11 perspective, this seemed tragically ineffective. Indeed, the conservative criticism of Clinton, that he had been too concerned about legitimising American policy in the eyes of the law and international opinion, subsequently translated into an attack on his counter-terrorist policy. His administration's tendency to see counter-terrorism as a law-enforcement issue, and his unwillingness to "take the gloves off" was seen as a reason why al-Qaeda had developed into the threat it now was (Wedgwood 2001; Yoo 2006). From this perspective, Clinton may have had a keen eye for the emerging opportunities of globalisation but his liberal internationalist stance was completely inappropriate to address its problems. The further implication was that, despite its apparent rejection of globalisation's significance, the Bush administration's power-based approach to foreign and national security policy was a much more appropriate response to al-Qaeda. Law enforcement would therefore be replaced by war as the guiding paradigm of counter-terrorism and of national security policy as a whole.

The Bush administration's dilemma was that, as a network of individuals motivated by an idea, al-Qaeda had no territory against which the United States could retaliate. If, as the president insisted, this was a war, where was the battlefield? The answer can be summarised by recalling congressional Joint Resolution 23 which was passed just three days after the attacks and formed the legal centrepiece of Bush's claim to be "a wartime president". It authorised the president to use

> all necessary and appropriate force against those nations, organizations or persons he determines planned, authorized, committed, or aided the terrorist attacks that occurred on September 11, 2001, or harbored such organizations or persons, in order to prevent any future acts of international terrorism against the United States by such nations, organizations, or persons.

Although the significance of this resolution is often overlooked, it is important on several levels. Firstly, it was cited as the source of presidential wartime authority when that was contested in the courts (see below). For Representative Barbara Lee (Democrat, California), the resolution improperly provided the president with open-ended authority. Casting the only vote against it, she compared it to the 1964 Gulf of Tonkin resolution which, of course, laid the foundations for the escalation in Vietnam (Dumbrell 2007: 215). Secondly, by focusing on nations that harboured the terrorists, the resolution territorialised what was otherwise an elusive enemy and it gave the administration a target that could justify action that went beyond Clinton-type cruise missile strikes. The war on terror, in other words, would not only aim to capture or destroy the al-Qaeda network, it would seek to change the regime of those states that provided al-Qaeda with sanctuary and material support. Thirdly, the resolution not only territorialised the war, it in effect created a borderless battlefield, something the president reaffirmed when he famously declared to other nations that they were either with the United States or against it. This might seem uncontroversial given the justness of the American cause but the idea that states no longer had the right to declare neutrality was a fundamental challenge to the Westphalian norms of modern warfare. While the immediate focus for the United States was the Taliban regime in Afghanistan, both the administration and Congress made it clear that the battlefield was not limited to that country. Claiming the authority of Joint Resolution 23 for instance, the president reserved the right to use force within or against any state that refused to co-operate with the United States. Indeed, while the focus of attention was on Afghanistan and later Iraq, the president used military force to target al-Qaeda operatives in Somalia, Yemen, Pakistan and Syria without the prior consent of these governments (Tisdall 2008; Schmitt and Shanker 2008). Again, this might not be controversial given the importance of destroying al-Qaeda but it was clearly a breach of the Westphalian norm that wars have identifiable and set battlefields, and combatants limit themselves to taking action within geographically defined boundaries. The fact that the United States under Bush reserved the right to use force when states were unable or unwilling to counteract the terrorist threat is discussed further in consideration of pre-emption below.

Before that discussion, however, it is worth considering the US war against the Taliban in Afghanistan. The Taliban and al-Qaeda may have appeared to be one and the same thing yet, prior to Operation Enduring Freedom, a separation was evident and possibly exploitable. Certainly, the Taliban were a threat to the liberal agenda of protecting and promoting human, and particularly women's, rights but their existence and de facto control of the Afghani state was not considered a threat to American national interests before 9/11. As noted, Clinton targeted al-Qaeda not the Afghani government and Condoleezza Rice made no mention of the Taliban in her 2000 article "Promoting the National Interest". The fact that the United States adopted a policy of regime change in response to 9/11 has come under criticism from two different directions. From one side, liberals like Helen Duffy (2005: 188–97) suggest that the Taliban may not have been responsible for the actions of al-Qaeda under international law and that its regime therefore should not necessarily have been targeted. She also adds that one can question whether the Bush administration gave the Taliban sufficient time to hand over Bin Laden and other members of al-Qaeda. Despite statements that force would be directed against the same source as the 11 September attacks, she notes that "the military intervention went way beyond the targeting of al-Qaeda operations, to the removal of the Taliban regime" (Duffy 2005: 193). Coming from another direction, realists might also criticise the Bush administration for needlessly turning the Taliban into an enemy. Given the weakness of the Taliban regime, the Bush administration may have adopted a Saudi-type strategy. That is, the United States may have given more time to cultivate a relationship with the Taliban, which would have included handing over Bin Laden and denying the true enemy, al-Qaeda, the sanctuary of Afghani territory (Bush 2001).

Both arguments assume that the Taliban would have co-operated if the United States had invested more time in exploiting differences with al-Qaeda, and any criticism of the Bush administration is weakened by the counterfactual nature of this point. Yet what is certain is that the conflation of the Taliban and al-Qaeda gave the United States a military target. It provided substance to the general impression that the United States was at war, and it perpetuated the Pearl Harbor/World War II analogy. Caught by surprise on 9/11 (Pearl Harbor), the US military would go to the heart of enemy territory, Afghanistan (Japan), indeed to their capital city of Kabul (Tokyo), and would replace an ideologically driven regime with liberal democracy. To be sure, the argument is not that the use of military force in Afghanistan was a war of choice. There was, to repeat, no certainty that the Taliban would have co-operated properly in the extradition of Bin Laden, and a solid consensus supports the view that the use of force was necessary. The strategy guiding the use of force, however, has not escaped criticism.

Perhaps the most telling criticism of the Bush administration's approach to Afghanistan was not that it decided regime change was necessary but that it failed to do that job properly. Indeed, the resurgence of the Taliban during the administration's second term led to what might be seen as an ironic reversal of positions. Towards the end of Bush's second term in office, critics linked together the Taliban and al-Qaeda to suggest that the Taliban's resurgence was a threat to American national security. Led by the then Senator Obama, they berated the administration for "taking its eye off the ball" and advocated reprioritising where military force should be deployed in the war on terror. Elsewhere, a new realism seemed to be entering the policy discourse which called for new attempts to separate the Taliban from al-Qaeda and to co-operate with the former so that it could contribute to a national government that would deny sanctuary to the latter (Winnet 2007; Burke 2008). While publicly the Bush administration continued to insist that the Taliban were terrorists, it was evident from a number of reports that America's allies in Afghanistan were searching for a new strategy, including the possibility of talking to the Taliban. This realist strategy of separating Bin Laden and al-Qaeda from the Taliban was also useful for defending the Bush administration's counter-terrorist record. The Taliban may have been resurgent, but that mattered less than the fact that Bin Laden's al-Qaeda network had not been able to attack the American homeland.

## 2. A DIFFERENT KIND OF WAR

The polarisation of opinion concerning the Bush administration's response to 9/11 centred not on the fact that the United States responded with military force. Rather, the controversy stemmed from the administration's insistence that the war on terror was (as its name suggests) a very different kind of war. The idea that the war in Afghanistan was a new kind of war can be understood at three different levels: political, military and legal. At the political level, the Bush administration made it clear that American forces would not be constrained by what was perceived as the hypersensitivity of traditional allies and international organisations. Guided by the lessons he derived from NATO's action in Kosovo, for instance, Secretary of Defense Donald Rumsfeld spoke for the administration when he insisted the United States would fight the war on its terms. Allies would be welcome but America's mission would determine the coalition; the coalition would not determine the mission (Freedman 2003).

At another level, the conflict would help Rumsfeld demonstrate his vision of a lighter, more mobile and ultimately more efficacious American military. In contrast to Clinton, Bush would put US forces on the ground, but they would still be relatively light and they would work closely with air support and local forces to overthrow the Taliban. This strategy was remarkably successful, at least initially. The United States liberated Kabul and other cities in just over a month. Yet it is fair to say that the Taliban's resurgence during the second term was in great part a consequence of this strategy. Despite NATO efforts to stabilise the country, the Bush administration's assumption that peace building was much easier than war fighting has been proven wrong. Combined with a political eagerness to shift focus to Iraq, the United States left behind a security vacuum that has been occupied, seemingly, by the old enemy. As noted below, the fact that a similar pattern occurred in post-war Iraq suggests that this was a failure of strategy and not simply the fog of war. This aspect of the Bush doctrine may have been new but it was not effective. Its architect, Donald Rumsfeld, ultimately paid for that when he resigned as defense secretary midway through Bush's second term.

The third new aspect of American foreign and security policy after 9/11 involved a controversial legal argument that the Geneva Conventions did not apply to the detainees being held in relation to that conflict. Detainees started to arrive at the camps in Guantánamo Bay in January 2002 and the president surprised many by stating that they would not be granted the privileges of prisoner-of-war status, which would usually include immunity from prosecution (provided they did not commit war crimes) and protections against abuse. Following the Abu Ghraib prisoner-abuse scandal of 2004, documents were released that shed light on how the administration justified this decision (Greenberg and Dratel 2005). It is clear that one aspect of the Bush administration's motivation was to release American officials from their obligations under the Geneva Conventions so that they could use aggressive interrogation techniques on the detainees. As Attorney General Alberto Gonzales (2002) put it, America's new war

> places a high premium on . . . the ability to obtain information from captured terrorists and their sponsors in order to avoid further atrocities against American civilians, and the need to try terrorists for war crimes such as wantonly killing civilians. In my

> judgment, this new paradigm renders obsolete Geneva's strict limitations on questioning of enemy prisoners.

This, of course, was a purely political calculation but it was justified in legal terms by Gonzales and his colleagues at the Department of Justice who noted the unique situation in which the United States now found itself. The United States had been attacked on 9/11 by a transnational network of non-state actors. The president and Congress had authorised a state of armed conflict against this network. The law of armed conflict, however, applied only to states that had consented to be bound by the Geneva Conventions or to state-like actors (such as national liberation movements) that met certain criteria, including wearing uniforms and carrying arms openly. Al-Qaeda fitted neither of these criteria, so the president determined that the Geneva Conventions did not apply to the US–al-Qaeda war.

Ignoring the conventions was a fundamental departure from American practice since World War II and, as noted, diminishes Lynch and Singh's argument that the Bush doctrine had a continuity with the past. The Truman administration may have stepped back from the more liberal elements of Franklin D. Roosevelt's vision for the post-war order but his administration gave impetus to a new era in the laws of war. Even the Reagan administration, which refused to send the Geneva Protocols to the Senate for ratification, did not attack the original 1949 treaty. Bush's decision regarding the Geneva Conventions was new. It was, in fact, a dramatic step away from the Cold War and post-Cold War consensus. But if one did want to make the case for continuity, then it is true that the Bush administration's argument on the laws of war reflects the US approach to frontier warfare which was itself an imitation of European colonial warfare (Grenier 2004). In this type of warfare, there is no normative symmetry between combatants. The modern separation of *jus in bello* from *jus ad bellum*, whereby combatants would act with restraint towards the prisoners of the other side regardless of the injustice of their cause, did not apply to these wars for civilisation. Where warfare between "civilised" states would be restrained by norms and laws that honoured the combatant by not prosecuting or abusing him, wars against "uncivilised barbarians" were not restrained because, for example, the Native American was seen as an obstacle to progress. To be clear, the Bush administration's approach was not motivated by the commercial imperialism that drove many of the wars during the age of empire. The point merely is that the Bush administration's approach to the laws of war reflects that of a previous age when the justness of one's cause was the only consideration in warfare and when just ends legitimised all manner of abuses.[1]

The photographs of prisoner abuse at Abu Ghraib graphically revealed the consequences of such an approach, and the public reaction to such images lent political weight to the legal efforts to check the administration's policy. This was ultimately played out at the level of the Supreme Court which delivered rebuffs to the administration. First, the Court rejected the administration's argument that, because Guantánamo Bay was not United States territory, the US courts had no jurisdiction over this issue.[2] Second, it ruled that the military commissions that the Bush administration had created to prosecute certain detainees with terrorist-related offences were illegal under the Uniform Code of Military Justice. The Court insisted that the security situation was not a state of emergency and the president could not therefore create such tribunals without getting legislative authority from Congress. The administration responded to this by getting congressional authorisation in the form of the Military Commissions Act which enabled prosecutions to go ahead. These trials have been influenced greatly, however, by the third way in which the Supreme Court checked the administration's policy. In its 2006 ruling *Hamdan* v. *Rumsfeld*, the Court ruled that the administration could not simply ignore the Geneva Conventions in its new war. The possibility existed that some of the detainees held at Guantánamo Bay may have qualified as prisoners of war and thus should have been granted the privileges and protections of the third Geneva Convention (Ralph 2007: 181–204). Indeed, this argument was deployed to great effect by Hamdan's defence team, when he became the first of the Guantánamo detainees to stand trial before a military commission. In August 2008, Hamdan was found innocent of conspiring to commit terrorism after his defence team argued that he was a lawful combatant and entitled under the Geneva Conventions to immunity from prosecution. The tribunal did find Hamdan guilty of the lesser offence of providing material support to terrorists (he had been Bin Laden's bodyguard) but the sentence was not as long as the administration had been anticipating (Williams 2008).

While the Guantánamo policy did not deliver the convictions the president anticipated, the administration argued that American detention policy since 9/11 was key to preventing further attacks. Again, this is a counterfactual argument that is difficult to prove, and evidence exists to suggest that, in fact, the intelligence gained was of very little value in the fight against terrorism (Bright 2004). What is certain is that the images associated with Guantánamo Bay, and particularly with Abu Ghraib, did immense damage to America's image in the world and to its claim that the war on terror was also a fight for liberty and human rights. The administration insisted that those who were responsible for the abusive behaviour towards prisoners were punished. Indeed, the reservists who were responsible for the Abu Ghraib photographs were convicted by the Army courts martial in 2005, yet many serious commentators insisted that responsibility for the context in which these abuses took place lay much higher up the chain of command (Hersch 2004; Sands 2008). Calls for war crimes trials, moreover, came from the very heart of the American establishment. For instance, Major General Anthony Taguba, the two-star general who led an Army investigation into Abu Ghraib, openly accused the Bush administration of war crimes and called for accountability (Froomkin 2008).

## 3. A NEW DOCTRINE OF PRE-EMPTION

The transnational nature of the war on terror not only caused Bush administration lawyers to revise, at least in their own minds, the laws regulating the *conduct of* war, it also prompted a rethink of the laws and norms governing when the United States could *resort to* war. For Bush administration officials the attacks could have been much worse. Had al-Qaeda been able to use Weapons of Mass Destruction (WMD) rather than civilian airliners, the casualty levels would have been much higher. The gravest threat to the United States, as the president put it in his West Point speech in June 2002, now lay

> at the crossroads of radicalism and technology. When the spread of chemical and biological and nuclear weapons, along with ballistic missile technology – when that occurs, even weak states *and small groups* could attain a catastrophic power to strike great nations.

This realisation caused a fundamental rethink in American national security policy. The United States would no longer be able to rely on its nuclear deterrent to prevent WMD attacks against its own society and this was, as the National Security Strategy (NSS) of 2002 noted, a key departure from the Cold War consensus. From Truman on, the assumption had been that the United States would be able to deter a WMD attack against the United States because those that had WMD were rational states responsible for the security of their citizens. If the United States was able to achieve the relatively simple task of guaranteeing a retaliatory capability, then other states would be deterred from attacking it. This consensus held for the Cold War. It was challenged only briefly during the early years of the Reagan administration when nuclear hawks argued that the United States had to demonstrate its ability to fight and win a war against the Soviet Union. The attacks on 9/11, however, illustrated that America's enemy was not the rational actor that deterrence theory assumed. It had no territory to target, it was driven by an ideological hatred of the United States rather than by the security of its own people, and it would go to any lengths, including suicide, to achieve its goals. The United States could not deter these enemies; it could only prevent them from getting their hands on WMD. That realisation resulted in a shift in how the Bush administration would relate to "rogue states", which had themselves expressed enmity towards America and had either acquired or intended to acquire WMD. It would also inform a policy shift in how the United States would relate to the laws governing the use of force against states.

As the 2002 National Security Strategy noted, the right of a state to use force in self-defence was enshrined in international law, which included a customary right to use force pre-emptively. It went on, however,

> Legal scholars and international jurists often conditioned the legitimacy of preemption on the existence of *an imminent threat – most often a visible mobilization of armies, navies, and air forces preparing to attack. We must adapt the concept of imminent threat to the capabilities and objectives of today's adversaries*. Rogue states and terrorists do not seek to attack us using conventional means. They know such attacks would fail. Instead, they rely on acts of terror and, potentially, the use of weapons of mass destruction –

> weapons that can be easily concealed, delivered covertly, and used without warning. [emphasis added]

The NSS also noted that the United States had "long maintained the option of preemptive actions to counter a sufficient threat to our national security", a point which Lynch and Singh make to support their continuity thesis. But again this underestimates how the new threat perception changed the way that the doctrine of pre-emption would operate in practice. Where the strictest interpretation of customary law demands a 100 per cent certainty that an attack is imminent, the United States administration it seems reduced this figure to 1 per cent. In the words of Vice President Dick Cheney,

> if there's a one per cent chance that Pakistani scientists are helping al Qaeda build or develop a nuclear weapon, we have to treat it as a certainty in terms of our response . . . It's not about our analysis, or finding a preponderance of evidence . . . It's about our response. (Suskind 2006: 62)

Or, as the Director of Central Intelligence George Tenet reportedly put it, "It is increasingly a matter of intent that we need to be concerned with. If a group, or a state for that matter, *wants* to build a nuclear weapon . . . the President feels the need to act" (quoted in Suskind 2006: 69). Had the United States operated within these margins during the Cold War, it is unlikely that the world would have avoided a nuclear exchange. President Kennedy would have pre-empted a Soviet attack during the Cuban missile crisis, when the possibility of war was much higher than one in a hundred. Instead, as we now know, President Kennedy used a subtle blend of diplomacy and coercion to secure America's interests while avoiding the actual use of force. Again, the Bush doctrine was different, and, in providing the rationale for the invasion of Iraq, it exacted a high cost.

Cheney's 1 per cent doctrine, and the president's emphasis on the enemy's intent rather than capability that Tenet articulated, are the reasons why so many found it hard to believe that self-defence was the motivating factor behind the Iraq war. Opponents of the war generally argued that Saddam Hussein had been contained by the UN sanctions regime. As noted, however, the Bush administration's perception of Iraq changed after 9/11. The threat was not simply that

Iraq itself might use WMD, nor that Saddam might give that technology to terrorists who would not hesitate to use it. Rather the post-9/11 threat was that Saddam *intended* to get WMD for the purpose of harming America and its interests. Certainly, the concerns about Saddam reconstituting a WMD programme were shared by other states, particularly after the UN weapons inspectors left Iraq in 1998. Yet those concerns were mollified when Hans Blix's team of inspectors was given unprecedented access to Iraqi facilities from November 2002. Blix did find Iraq to be in material breach of UN resolutions on disarmament, a fact that American and British lawyers pointed to while claiming the invasion was lawful. He also pointed out, however, that in January 2003 Iraq was dismantling the offending weapons, a fact that tended to undermine the political case for war. If the argument that Iraq had WMD seemed to a majority of the Security Council to be dubious, the possibility that Saddam would give them to terrorists appeared fanciful. For the Bush administration, that was not the point. For them, Saddam's intentions were the issue and that required regime change.

The problem for the administration was that many states did not share this logic and, when the president was persuaded by a combination of British and American State Department lobbying to seek UN authorisation for the invasion of Iraq, the issue became one of *analysis* and not only one of *response* (Ralph 2005). Simply put, the international community had a much higher burden of proof than the Bush administration. The tragedy is that in its efforts to convince the world that Saddam was a threat, the administration politicised and corrupted the intelligence cycle. This intelligence failure in turn had profound implications for its domestic and international image. Again, a comparison with the Cuban missile crisis illustrates the point. Secretary of State Colin Powell's presentation to the UN Security Council, which supposedly set out evidence to prove Iraq had WMD, was no "Stevenson moment", a point that Powell now painfully acknowledges (Weisman 2005).[3] But perhaps the administration's corruption of the intelligence process is best illustrated by the so-called Plame Affair. This involved the leaking of Valerie Plame's identity as a covert CIA agent in an attempt to silence her husband, former ambassador Joseph Wilson. Wilson had become an outspoken critic of the way the administration dealt with intelligence on Iraq, in particular the supposed link between Saddam's WMD programme and uranium in Niger. For attempting to cover up the source of the leak, the Vice President's Chief of Staff Lewis "Scooter" Libby was convicted of obstructing justice and of perjury.

The cost to personal reputations, however, pales in significance next to the national political costs of the 1 per cent doctrine. The failure to find WMD left the administration relying solely on the argument that Saddam *intended* to get weapons of mass destruction which, for many, was an insufficient reason for war. This failure increased the political costs to pro-Bush governments, notably Spain and the United Kingdom, both of which suffered terrorist attacks in part because of their support for the war. These political costs contributed to the reluctance of states to engage in post-war reconstruction efforts, something that was compounded by an almost intolerable security situation in Iraq. Indeed, the UN withdrew its corps of international civil servants following the deadly attack on its headquarters in August 2003. Of course, the primary reason for the post-war chaos lay not in the failure to justify the war in a manner that secured international support. That certainly was a compounding factor but the main reason was a lack of post-war planning which was born of the naive idealism of the Bush doctrine. The costs of a war driven by the 1 per cent doctrine have inspired a shift back to realism when dealing with the question of nuclear proliferation. While the option of a military strike against Iranian nuclear facilities was seemingly never far from the agenda, it was clear by 2006 that it was second best to a diplomatic strategy which involved talking to a regime that the president had once called evil (Kessler 2006; Baldwin and Beesten 2007; Sherwell 2008). By June 2008, moreover, Secretary of State Condoleezza Rice was holding direct talks with the previously isolated North Koreans (Spillius and Blair 2008).

## 4. DEMOCRACY PROMOTION

It should not have been a surprise to see Secretary Rice leading the policy shift away from the Bush doctrine based on pre-emption and regime change and towards a type of Cold War realism. She had served in that most cautious and realist of presidencies, the G. H. W. Bush administration, and had been mentored by Brent Scowcroft who was from the same stable of realist thinker-practitioners as Henry Kissinger. Yet the realist's return late in the second administration *was* somewhat of a surprise because there was a moment when Rice seemed to have accepted the Bush doctrine, in particular the neo-conservative part that believed democracy emerged out of times of political instability. Indeed, when Rice (2005) told her Cairo audience that the United States had pursued stability at the expense of democracy in the Middle East, it could have been interpreted as an attempt to legitimise the invasion of Iraq and as a harbinger of things to come in Iran. Yet the speech itself was careful not to endorse a policy of regime change through military force, and while her departing article in *Foreign Affairs* was strong on the need to promote democracy, this too stressed a gradual, bottom-up approach. Thus, President Musharraf's regime in Pakistan was neither celebrated nor demonised. It was recognised as being necessary for stability in the region but the United States, Rice argued, helped provide the foundations for civil society with a $3 billion investment in health, education, judiciary development and humanitarian relief programmes (Rice 2008).

The United States chose not to adopt this approach towards Afghanistan and Iraq. Policy was instead guided by an assumption that constitutional democracy would naturally follow on from regime change. The rights and wrongs of regime change can be judged on the merits of the security rationale that drove policy. Yet what is clear is that the assumption that democracy would easily replace the Taliban and the Baathist regimes was wrong. What made the policy based on that assumption irresponsible, particularly in the case of Iraq, was the apparent failure to challenge sufficiently its ideological underpinnings. There was ample warning within the policymaking community, particularly from the CIA and the State Department, that the transition from tyranny to constitutional democracy would not be easy. There was also warning from within the Pentagon that the troop levels were insufficient to provide the stability that political reform required.[4] The neo-conservative faith in the idea that history was on democracy's side, and that American military power could accelerate that process by overthrowing entrenched dictators, was held with such conviction that the Bush administration did not even ask to see such assessments. Not only did this faith contribute to a lack of commitment to the post-war security situation, it informed decisions that compounded the initial error. The policy of de-Baathification may have fitted nicely with a World War II-type narrative but, together with the decision to disband the Iraqi army, it exacerbated instability and contributed to a chronic state of insecurity.

By the end of the second Bush administration, the security situation in Iraq had been transformed by a combination of the "surge" in American troop numbers and the changing nature of Sunni politics. Announced by the president in January 2007, the surge involved the deployment of an additional 20,000 troops. This bold decision was 180 degrees removed from the withdrawal option advocated by some Democrats who, as a party, by then controlled Congress. It also seemed to be a rejection of the policy set out by the Iraq Study Group, a bipartisan commission that included G. H. W. Bush-era realists like Lawrence Eagleburger and James Baker. The group's report called for new and enhanced diplomatic and political efforts in Iraq and in the region that would enable the United States to start a responsible withdrawal of its forces (Baker and Hamilton 2006). The group's strategy would have meant a less ideological and less hostile approach towards Iran and Syria. Yet the president chose a plan that was more consistent with that espoused by neo-conservative think tanks like the American Enterprise Institute (Kagan 2007). This might suggest that the supposed shift towards realism in the second administration had its limits. It would be wrong, however, to draw this conclusion. The increase in troop numbers represented recognition of a fundamental realist principle, that ends must be matched to means (and vice versa). Unfortunately, for the Iraqi people and for thousands of American service personnel, the realisation that more troops were needed to meet America's political goals came several years too late. It would be incorrect, moreover, to conclude that an increased military commitment delivered success in Iraq by itself. As noted, the United States downgraded, if not dropped, its confrontational stance towards Iraq's neighbours and it started a diplomatic process under the stewardship of Rice. Inside Iraq as well, it abandoned the tendency to link the nationalist resistance with al-Qaeda, and it integrated the former (under the banner of "the Awakening") into the new security strategy (Thorold 2008). If anyone were to go so far as to call US policy in Iraq a success, they must conclude therefore that it was a consequence of a new-found realism. They must also acknowledge that the ideological underpinnings of the Bush doctrine both delayed and increased the costs of that success.

## CONCLUSION

> A doctrine is something that pins you down to a given mode of conduct and dozens of situations which you cannot foresee, which is a great mistake in principle. When the word "containment" was used in my "X" article, it was used with relation to a certain situation then prevailing, and as a response to it. (George Kennan quoted in Eisele 2002)

Reading Lynch and Singh's case for continuity at the end of the Bush administration, one is reminded of Winston Churchill's famous quip that we can rely on America to do the right thing once it had exhausted the alternatives. The Bush administration may have found appropriate policies on the treatment of terrorist suspects, the proliferation of WMD and the insurgency in Afghanistan and Iraq, but only after the Bush doctrine had been checked by the realities of domestic and international politics. It is only because Lynch and Singh underestimate the extent to which the Bush doctrine was new, and only because they ignore the checks that it came up against, that they can claim that it has provided the foundations for future policy. Their portrayal of realism as amoral is inaccurate and misinterprets the realist tradition in American foreign policy, and especially the thoughts of thinker-practitioners like Henry Kissinger and, above all, George Kennan. This misinterpretation is strange because, of course, at the centre of Lynch and Singh's thesis is the argument that the Bush administration has laid the footings for a doctrine that imitates containment, a policy that Kennan is said to have fathered. If we look closely at Kennan's philosophy and to the thoughts that lay behind containment, we find major differences with the Bush administration, differences that are based on varying understandings of hard power. "I would submit", Kennan wrote in stark contrast to the neo-conservative influences on the Bush administration,

> that we will continue to harm our own interests almost as much as we benefit them if we continue to employ the instruments of coercion in the international field without a better understanding of their significance and possibilities. It is essential to recognize that the maiming and killing of men and the destruction of human shelters and other installations, however necessary it may

> be for other reasons, cannot in itself make a positive contribution to the democratic purpose. (Kennan 1952: 89)

Kennan opposed the Vietnam war on these grounds. He is reported to have opposed the Iraq war, prophetically warning that American history taught that "you might start in a war with certain things on your mind as a purpose of what you are doing, but in the end, you found yourself fighting for entirely different things that you had never thought of before" (quoted in Eisele 2002).

These sentiments speak to Kennan's wider concern that the United States policymaking community was almost addicted to doctrines at the expense of realistic policies. His famous attack on the legal and moral foundations of liberal internationalism should not disguise the fact that he was against doctrines of any kind. His preference for stability, moreover, should not be characterised as amoral. It may sometimes come at the expense of democracy, as Rice reminds us, but it is rarely, as Kennan's words illustrate, the consequence of amoral reasoning. Furthermore, a policy that promotes stability may sometimes be the most appropriate strategy for promoting democracy, and here Lynch and Singh misread the way the Cold War against the Soviet Union ended. The end of the Soviet Union may have become apparent during the Reagan administration but its weaknesses and demise were foreseen by Kennan back in 1947. The democratic movements that emerged to replace communism, moreover, were born in the period of détente, inspired by the Helsinki Final Act and the need to hold governments to their human rights and treaty commitments (Thomas 2001). This is the true historical legacy of containment and the Cold War. International stability can facilitate democratisation. The Bush administration may have realised this by the end of its term of office and, if that is its legacy, then it is one worth keeping. It is unfortunate, however, that the administration had to discover that by a costly process of trial and error.

## NOTES

1. Calls to revise the laws of war so that a just cause could legitimise unrestrained warfare did exist prior to 9/11 but only on the margins of policy discourse (see Carvin 2008).
2. Guantánamo Bay was only leased from Cuba which is, under the terms of

the agreement, "the ultimate sovereign".

3. Powell sought to achieve the same effect as President Kennedy's UN Ambassador Adlai Stevenson, which was to convince the Security Council that the Soviets were stationing missiles in Cuba (Borger 2003).
4. On CIA and State Department assessments of post-Saddam Iraq, see Pillar 2007 and Byrne 2005. For criticism of the war planning, in particular that of General Shinseki, see Woodward 2004.

## BIBLIOGRAPHY

Baker, James A. and Lee H. Hamilton (2006), *The Iraq Study Group Report,* at http://www.usip.org/

Baldwin, T. and R. Beesten (2007), "Progress as Rice talks to Syria and chats with Iran", *The Times,* 4 May

Borger, J. (2003), "Was it an Adlai Stevenson moment? Powell did not even come close, says UN veteran", *The Guardian,* 6 February

Bright, M. (2004), "Guantanamo has failed to prevent terror attacks", *The Guardian,* 3 October

Burke, J. (2008), "Why the West thinks it's time to talk to the Taliban", *The Observer,* 28 September

Bush, George W. (2001), "Bush rejects Taliban offer to hand Bin Laden over", *Guardian.co.uk,* 14 October

Byrne, M. (2005), "State Department experts warned CENTCOM before Iraq war about lack of plans for post-war Iraq security", *National Security Archive Electronic Briefing Book No. 163* at http://www.gwu.edu/~nsarchiv/

Carr, E. H. (2001), *What is History?,* Basingstoke: Palgrave

Carvin, S. (2008), "Linking Purpose and Tactics: America and the reconsideration of the Laws of War during the 1990s", *International Studies Perspectives* 9 (2)

Daalder, I. H. and J. M. Lindsay (2003), *America Unbound: The Bush Revolution in Foreign Policy,* Washington, DC: Brookings Institution Press

Duffy, H. (2005), *The 'War on Terror' and the Framework of International Law,* Cambridge: Cambridge University Press

Dumbrell, J. (2007), "The Iraq and Vietnam Wars. Some Parallels and Connections", in John Dumbrell and David Ryan, eds, *Vietnam in Iraq. Tactics, Lessons, Legacies and Ghosts,* London and New York: Routledge

Eisele, A. (2002), "George Kennan Speaks Out About Iraq", History News Network, George Mason University, at http://hnn.us/articles/997.html

Freedman, L. (2003), "America Needs a Wider Coalition However Difficult", *The Independent,* 29 March

Froomkin, D. (2008), "General Accuses White House of War Crimes", *Washington Post,* 18 June

Gonzales, A. (2002), Memo 7, Memorandum for the President, Decision Re Application of the Geneva Convention on Prisoners of War to the Conflict with Al Qaeda and the Taliban, from Alberto R. Gonzales, 25 January 2002, in Greenberg and Dratel, eds (2005), *The Torture Papers. The Road to Abu Ghraib*, Cambridge: Cambridge University Press

Greenberg, K. J. and J. L. Dratel (2005), *The Torture Papers. The Road to Abu Ghraib*, Cambridge: Cambridge University Press

Grenier, J. (2004), *The First Way of War. American War Making on the Frontier, 1607-1814*, Cambridge: Cambridge University Press

Heilbrunn, J. (2007), "A Uniter, Not a Decider", *The National Interest*, 90, July/August

Hersch, S. (2004), *Chain of Command: The Road from 9/11 to Abu Ghraib*, London: Allen Lane

Kagan, F. W. (2007), "Choosing Victory: A Plan for Success in Iraq", *American Enterprise Institute*, http://www.aei.org/

Kampfner, J. (2004), *Blair's Wars*, London: Simon and Schuster

Kennan, G. (1952), *American Diplomacy, 1900–1950*, London: Secker and Warburg

Kessler, G. (2006), "Rice Key to Reversal on Iran", *Washington Post*, 4 June

Luttwak, E. (2008), "A Truman of Our Times", *Prospect*, 149, August

Lynch, T. J. and R. Singh (2008), *After Bush. The Case for Continuity in American Foreign Policy*, Cambridge: Cambridge University Press

Pillar, P. R. (2007), "The Right Stuff", *The National Interest*, 91, September/October

Ralph, J. (2005), "Tony Blair's 'new doctrine of international community' and the UK decision to invade Iraq", *POLIS Working Paper*, August

Ralph. J. (2007), *Defending the Society of States. Why America opposes the International Criminal Court and its Vision of World Society*, Oxford: Oxford University Press

Rice, C. (2000), "Promoting the National Interest", *Foreign Affairs*, 79 (1) January/February

Rice, C. (2005), Remarks at the American University in Cairo, June, at http://merln.ndu.edu/archivepdf/NEA/State/48328.pdf

Rice, C. (2008), "Rethinking the National Interest: American Realism for a New World", *Foreign Affairs*, 87 (4) July/August

Sands, P. (2008), *Torture Team: Rumsfeld's Memo and the Betrayal of American Values*, New York: Palgrave Macmillan

Schmitt, E. and T. Shanker (2008), "Officials Say U.S. Killed an Iraqi in Raid in Syria", *New York Times*, 27 October

Sherwell, P. (2008), "Condoleezza Rice Wins Battle for George W Bush's Ear Over Iran Talks", *The Daily Telegraph*, 21 July

Spillius, A. and D. Blair (2008), "Condoleezza Rice Holds Nuclear Weapons

Talks with North Korea", *The Daily Telegraph*, 23 July

Suskind, R. (2006), *The One Per Cent Doctrine: Deep Inside America's Pursuit of Its Enemies Since 9/11*, London: Simon and Schuster

Thomas, D. (2001), *The Helsinki Effect: International Norms, Human Rights, and the Demise of Communism*, Princeton: Princeton University Press

Thorold, C. (2008), "Securing Baghdad with Militiamen", BBC, 27 August, at http://news.bbc.co.uk/

Tisdall, S. (2008), "Bush Secret Order to Send Special Forces into Pakistan", *The Guardian*, 12 September

Wedgwood, R. (2001), "The Law at War: How Osama Slipped Away", *The National Interest*, Winter

Weisman, S. R. (2005), "Powell Calls His U.N. Speech a Lasting Blot on His Record", *New York Times*, 9 September

Williams, B. G. (2008), "Defending Hamdan: The Capture and Defense of Bin Laden's Driver", at http://www.terraplexic.org/

Winnet, R. (2007), "Government Backs Taliban Talks", *The Daily Telegraph*, 13 December

Woodward, B. (2004), *Plan of Attack*, London: Simon and Schuster

Yoo, J. (2006), *War by Other Means: An Insider's Account of the War on Terror*, Atlantic Monthly Press

*Chapter 7*

# REFORMING THE NATIONAL SECURITY APPARATUS

Steven Hurst

Before 11 September 2001 the United States's homeland defence policy focused on threats from state, rather than from non-state, actors. With little history of domestic terrorism and few attacks from terrorists originating abroad, however, limited attention was paid to these potential dangers. In December 2000, the Gilmore Commission reported that "the organization of the Federal Government's programs for combating terrorism is fragmented, uncoordinated, and politically unaccountable" (Advisory Panel 2000: v). Despite that warning, the administration of George W. Bush paid little attention to the terrorist threat before 11 September. Since that date, in contrast, the Bush administration engaged in the biggest governmental reorganisation in half a century in an effort better to protect the United States from terrorist attack.

Is the United States now better protected against terrorism as a result? That, unfortunately, is a difficult question to answer. On the one hand, at the time of writing, the United States has not been attacked again and the Bush administration claims to have disrupted several terrorist plots (White House 2005). On the other hand, according to one official involved in homeland security, the Department of Homeland Security (DHS), the centrepiece of George W. Bush's organisational reforms, is "so dysfunctional, and so destructive to agency functions, that it should be dismantled" (Stockton and Roberts 2008: 1). The United States General Accounting Office (GAO) recently determined that, of fourteen key areas for homeland security, the DHS had made substantial progress in just one (GAO 2007).

The divergence thus highlighted demonstrates the problematic nature of any assessment of homeland security policy. What, in the first place, is an appropriate measure of success? The presence or absence of attacks is the obvious indicator, yet an absence may be the result of factors other than policy efficacy. Alternatively, one can follow the approach of the GAO which focuses on tangible measures of preparedness (the existence of plans, availability of equipment, training and so on). Yet this also has obvious shortcomings. In crude terms the problem is sufficiently new, and the policy environment sufficiently uncertain, that no one can be confident what the right measures of efficacy actually are (Caudle 2005). The GAO evaluates the extent to which the DHS has achieved goals based on legislation, presidential directives and DHS strategic-planning documents. It openly admits, however, that its "assessments of progress are not indicative of the extent to which DHS's actions have made the nation more secure in each area" (GAO 2007: 1). The GAO evaluates whether targets have been met; it does not question the relevance of the targets.

Even if we grant that many of the measures used by the GAO are plausible enough, this merely raises the problem of appropriate standards for judgement. According to the United States Comptroller General, it takes five to seven years for the problems resulting from mergers between private-sector organisations to be overcome. Public-sector transformations, he added, are even more problematic because the organisations involved must contend with more, and competing, power centres and stakeholders, have less management flexibility, and are under greater scrutiny (GAO 2004a: 13). The last governmental reorganisation comparable in scale to the creation of the DHS was the establishment of the Department of Defense (DOD) in 1947, and in the view of many observers the DOD still does not work properly. In short, while we may, at this point, offer an evaluation of the efficacy of the Bush administration's homeland security policies and identify failings therein, we must do so with a degree of caution, recognising that those policies are still in the relatively early stages of implementation, and that significant weaknesses are only to be expected at this stage.

The difficulties with which homeland security policy must contend can be roughly categorised under two headings: political and organisational. Efforts to secure the homeland are affected by precisely the same kinds of political factors that have an impact on any other area of domestic policy, namely ideological considerations, interest-group pressures, executive–legislative power struggles and pork-barrel politics where members of Congress seek to bring home to their districts as much federal money as possible. In addition, however, homeland security policy has to contend with challenges that are largely absent from more established policy areas, namely those of ensuring that a whole new set of institutions and processes functions in an effective and co-ordinated fashion. Such a distinction is, of course, artificial to some degree. The fact that the United States is a federal republic with extensive devolution of political authority, for example, has profound ramifications for the organisational dimension of homeland security policy, as will be demonstrated below. Nevertheless, for the purposes of analysis the distinction serves a useful purpose and will be employed here.

The two terms concept, in contrast, is not employed in this chapter to structure the narrative to any significant degree, though there are differences between the two terms which are worthy of note. Bush's first term was characterised by organisational upheaval and transformation and his second by more prosaic matters of bedding in the transformed institutions. Some of the political aspects of homeland security policy were also more prominent in the first term than in the second. Nevertheless, the factors shaping homeland security policy, particularly those relating to organisational matters, are ongoing across both terms in a manner which makes distinguishing between the two a distraction.

## 1. TRANSFORMING THE HOMELAND SECURITY BUREAUCRACY

Before evaluating the effectiveness of the Bush administration's efforts to improve homeland security, it is necessary first to provide a brief description of those efforts.

On 8 October 2001 Bush appointed Pennsylvania Governor Tom Ridge to the post of Assistant to the President for Homeland Security and Director of the Office of Homeland Security (OHS). On 26 October Congress passed the USA Patriot Act which, in addition to establishing new internet surveillance and wiretap rules, empowered the president to make fundamental changes to the FBI and CIA. On 19 November Congress passed the Aviation and Transportation

Security Act, creating the Transportation Security Administration (TSA) and federalising airport security provision.

Having initially opposed the idea of creating a new government department for homeland security, Bush announced in mid-2002 that he wanted legislation to create a new DHS by the end of the year. His proposal called for the merger of twenty-two agencies and 170,000 staff, amounting to the most significant government transformation in nearly fifty years. Shortly thereafter, the administration revealed its *National Strategy for Homeland Security*, which outlined three principal objectives: preventing terrorist attacks within the United States; reducing American vulnerability to terrorism; and minimising damage and recovering from attacks that do occur (DHS 2002).

Congress passed the Homeland Security Act on 2 November 2002, establishing a DHS which was to come into being on 1 March 2003 with Ridge as the new secretary. The department was composed of five directorates: Management; Science and Technology; Information Analysis and Infrastructure Protection (IAIP); Border and Transportation Security (BTS); and Emergency Preparedness and Response. In addition, there were some twenty-four other agencies which reported directly to the secretary, including the Coast Guard and the Secret Service (GAO 2007: 7).

As well as creating the DHS, the Bush administration also sought to reform the intelligence agencies that had so conspicuously failed before 9/11. In January 2003 Bush announced the establishment of a Terrorist Threat Integration Center (TTIC), amalgamating the terrorist-related intelligence gathering and analysis efforts of the CIA, FBI and DHS. Further changes followed the 9/11 commission's recommendations that a Director of National Intelligence (DNI) be created with control over the budgets and personnel of the whole intelligence community, and that a National Counterterrorism Center be created to enhance intelligence-sharing and be responsible for counter-terrorism planning (National Commission 2004). Both recommendations were included in the Intelligence Reform and Terrorism Prevention Act of 2004, and John Negroponte was appointed as the first DNI.

After the 2004 elections, Ridge was replaced as DHS Secretary by Michael Chertoff, who immediately announced a second-stage review of DHS organisation and activities. This produced four main changes: the establishment of a policy office; efforts to improve management of intelligence and information-sharing; the formation of a new operations co-ordination office and a consolidation effort to integrate preparedness work; and, lastly, the abolition of the Border and Transportation Security directorate and its replacement by the TSA and the Customs and Border Protection Bureau (DHS 2005).

## 2. THE POLITICS OF HOMELAND SECURITY

Homeland security has proved to be as vulnerable to the vicissitudes of day-to-day politics as any other policy area, as the process that led to the establishment of the DHS demonstrates.

Initially, Bush appointed Ridge to the position of White House Assistant within the Executive Office of the President (EOP). Congressional critics, however, argued that Ridge's status did not give him the authority necessary to be effective, and demanded the consolidation of the relevant programmes and responsibilities in a new department. According to one of Ridge's aides, however, at this point "there was zero interest in the White House in setting up a new department" (Glasser and Grunwald 2005). Officials argued that reorganisation would take time and attention away from the real job of protecting Americans.

While the argument was thus framed in terms of effectiveness, political considerations were at the heart of this confrontation. By making Ridge part of the EOP, Bush sought to minimise congressional control over homeland security policy. As Donald F. Kettl noted, however, if Congress "could pass legislation authorizing the office, setting out its powers . . . and controlling the department's budget, they could dramatically shift the balance of power". Bush's congressional critics were thus not just concerned about effectiveness, they "saw this as one of the biggest new initiatives in decades, and they wanted to ensure that they could control its direction" (Perrow 2006: 9). Nor was it lost on Democrats that, by arguing that a mere White House Assistant was insufficient for the task at hand, they could seize the political high ground on homeland security.

On 2 May 2002, with popular momentum strongly in his favour, Senator Joseph Lieberman introduced legislation calling for the creation of a DHS. Faced with the seemingly inevitable, Bush reversed himself, announcing his own plan on 6 June. There is little reason to believe, however, that this decision had anything to do with choosing the best solution for homeland security. Bush found himself faced with a situation where he risked having a DHS designed by Congress imposed upon him and where he appeared to be opposed to efforts to improve homeland security. With congressional elections less than six months away and the administration planning to make national security the centrepiece of the Republican campaign, it could not afford to be outflanked by the Democrats on this issue (Becker 2002). When Bush announced his proposal for the DHS, therefore, he did so not because he was convinced of the merits of the idea so much as to neutralise a potentially troubling political problem. In addition, and for good measure, he took the opportunity to deflect attention from growing criticism of his administration's previous failures by announcing the plan on the same day that FBI agent Colleen Rowley testified to Congress on her agency's pre-9/11 errors (Lindsay 2003).

Homeland security has also fallen prey to other aspects of what might be termed politics as usual, such as pork barrelling, whereby congressional politicians seek as much funding as possible for their district or state, regardless of need. Most homeland security funds are disbursed to the states through the Homeland Security Grant Program, amounting to some $1.6 billion in 2006 (DHS 2007). The majority of that funding was initially shared out under a long-established formula that favoured the smaller states (which had the majority in the Senate to block changes). That formula mandated that each of the fifty states receive a minimum of 0.75 per cent of the total funds. Forty per cent of funds were thus divided up equally between the states regardless of size, population or likelihood of terrorist attack. Moreover, although the DHS had discretion in spending the other 60 per cent, in 2002–4 it simply shared it out according to population. As a result, of the top ten states in terms of per capita spending in 2003, only Washington DC was also in the top ten at risk of attack (O'Beirne 2003; Ripley 2004; Roberts 2005).

In 2004 the administration began to press Congress to change the formula to emphasise risk, but the Senate Homeland Security Appropriations Subcommittee killed the plan (Ripley 2004). Widespread criticism in the media and White House pressure eventually forced some changes, however. The Homeland Security Appropriations Act of 2006 altered the formula for two grant programmes (the State Homeland Security Program and the Law Enforcement Terrorism Prevention Program), retaining the 0.75 per cent base share but distributing the remaining 60 per cent according to risk. This left one programme (the Citizens Corps Program) operating under the old formula and a fourth (the Urban Areas Security Initiative), distributed solely on the basis of risk (DHS 2006). According to the Office of Management and Budget, in fiscal year 2007 more than half of all funds flowing to state and local government was, for the first time, disbursed on a risk-assessment basis (D'Arcy et al. 2006: xi).

Homeland security has also been vulnerable to interest-group pressures. Within months of 9/11, the private sector was busily positioning itself to secure a slice of the money pouring into homeland security. Four of Ridge's original senior staff at the OHS left to work as lobbyists, and the number of registered lobbyists who mentioned homeland, security or terror on their forms grew from 157 at the beginning of 2002 to 569 by April 2003 (Perrow 2006: 18). Some of the resulting pressures have served to undermine efforts to protect the American homeland. For example, one of America's major vulnerabilities to terrorist attacks is the chemical industry which is not well protected despite the fact that, according to the Environmental Protection Agency, over a hundred chemical plants could each endanger up to a million lives if attacked in the right way. After 11 September, Senator Jon Corzine introduced the Chemical Security Act to Congress, seeking to establish statutory security standards and ensure safer transport of dangerous materials. In response, the US chemical industry launched a sustained lobbying effort to kill the bill, claiming it would have a disastrous economic impact. The White House and congressional Republicans subsequently withdrew their support and the bill died (Brzezinski 2004).

The reluctance of the Bush administration to impose regulations on the chemical industry was also a reflection of its broader laissez-faire attitude to governing and economics, a philosophy that is in tension with the goal of promoting homeland security. Left to its own devices, the private sector may not take the necessary actions to reduce vulnerabilities if economic logic dictates otherwise. If one firm spends millions to protect against a small risk and their competitors do not, then the former puts itself at a competitive disadvantage (Orszag and O'Hanlon 2006: 75–7). Without regulations that impose the same standards on all firms within vulnerable sectors, therefore, nothing will be done. Three-and-a-half years after 9/11, the CBO found "little evidence that firms have been making additional investments since

September 11 to improve their security and avoid losses" (CBO 2005: 13).

## 3. ORGANISATIONAL CHALLENGES

"The homeland security challenge is primarily a challenge of interagency and intergovernmental affairs", argued Donley and Pollard (2002: 138). Most of the information needed to prevent the events of 11 September was in the possession of American government agencies but the absence of communication and co-ordination between them meant that no one put the pieces together (National Commission 2004). The rationale advanced by those who supported the establishment of the DHS was that merging key agencies within a single department would facilitate such co-ordination. Similarly, they argued that giving the DHS secretary a statutory basis in legislation would give him or her the power to enforce co-ordination across government on homeland security issues. The reality, however, has proved to be less straightforward.

In fact, some organisation theorists have even questioned the creation of the DHS. The problems created by terrorism fall into the category known to organisation theory as "wicked problems" – that is, "problems with no solutions, only temporary and imperfect resolutions" (Harmon and Mayer 1986: 9). Traditional bureaucratic organisations, however, are designed to cope with "tame" problems with neat, technical solutions. Therefore, it is argued, the "adoption of standard, rational, hierarchical designs and practices is likely to be particularly unsuitable for organizations that are expected to operate in complex, unstable environments", such as that presented by counter-terrorism. Instead, such organisations need to adopt structures as complex as the environments in question and to decentralise authority because a changing environment requires rapid, flexible responses (Wise 2002: 132–3). Similarly, Charles Perrow argues that the policy co-ordination supporters of the DHS hope to achieve through centralisation can be thus realised only in small and medium-sized organisations. Huge organisations, he argues, require decentralisation because of the sheer magnitude and diversity of the tasks involved. Such organisations can work only by giving individual agencies a significant degree of autonomy to achieve clearly defined and communicated missions. Despite his many criticisms of the organisational changes, Perrow believes that the Bush administration's initial appointment of Ridge as a White House Assistant was likely to have been the best approach, precisely because the focus was on co-ordination rather than on centralisation (Perrow 2006: 6).

Whatever the validity of that argument, it is undoubtedly the case that, by following the departmental route, Bush initiated a mammoth organisational task that may take decades to be effected properly. The twenty-two agencies incorporated into the new department had different cultures, practices and missions. Some had never had contacts with each other before. Many have had to learn new roles, and all have their own jurisdictions, interests and autonomy which they are reluctant to surrender (Perrow 2006: 12–14). Even relatively mundane tasks, such as establishing common management, personnel and information technology systems, presented time-consuming challenges. The Department's Office of Personnel Management had to try to integrate "15 basic pay systems, 12 special pay systems, 10 hiring methods, eight overtime pay rates, seven payroll and benefit systems, five locality pay systems, and 19 performance management systems" (Relyea 2005: 10).

Alongside the technical problems of integration there have been other difficulties. An almost inevitable consequence of major organisational reform is to produce bureaucratic turf wars as agencies struggle to retain their existing prerogatives. One of the stated purposes in creating the DHS was to provide a single agency, in the form of the IAIP directorate, which would serve as the core agency for intelligence on homeland security and integrate the intelligence from other agencies in order to identify and assess the terrorist threat. In practice, however, the existing agencies within the intelligence community have fought fiercely and successfully to retain their autonomy and prerogatives, with the support of the White House which has decided that the FBI and CIA will continue to have primacy in this area. Even before the DHS was up and running, the IAIP was undercut by Bush's announcement of the creation of the TTIC, which integrated FBI and CIA counter-terrorism intelligence work and was based at CIA headquarters. Moreover, the FBI and the Department of Justice have generally defended their turfs with vigour against the perceived threat of the DHS which has been forced to cede important tasks, such as tracking terrorist funding, to them. As a result, rather than effectively drawing all terrorist-related intelligence together, the DHS has actually found itself to be a marginal player in the intelligence community, with little more than the right to sit on various co-ordinating committees (Perrow 2006: 22).

Nor does the bureaucratic conflict end with resistance to encroachments by the DHS. Intelligence reform in general has been plagued by it. The FBI's increased focus on counter-terrorism since 9/11 has meant that it and the CIA have been working on each other's turfs, and thus treading on each other's toes more than ever. The FBI has increased its activities overseas, often failing to inform the CIA that it is doing so. There have also been conflicts between the CIA and the DOD as the latter has begun to expand its human intelligence operations both at home and abroad. And the most fundamental objective of intelligence reform, the improved sharing of intelligence across government, has been undermined by bureaucratic self-interest. Analysts at the NCTC cannot divulge information to anyone outside the organisation without the permission of the originating agency (Steinberg 2006: 20–1).

The 9/11 commission recommended the creation of the position of DNI precisely in order to overcome these kinds of problems but the post and its prerogatives were themselves the subjects of fierce bureaucratic struggles. The DOD, in particular, fought to protect its turf with great success (Steinberg 2006: 19) and there is little evidence thus far that the DNI has been able to exert significant co-ordinating authority over the intelligence community, with the Pentagon, CIA and FBI conducting business more or less as before (Fessenden 2005; Jehl 2005). The fact that the first holder of the job, John Negroponte, chose to leave a cabinet-level post in favour of being Deputy Secretary of State gave some indication of the limitations imposed on the role.

Perhaps the biggest organisational challenge of all, however, is intergovernmental co-ordination. Here problems of organisation meet with, and are compounded by, the exigencies of the American political system. Extensive devolution of political power to state and local governments means that American federalism poses some difficult problems for homeland security policy.

Federal agencies take the lead on most tasks related to homeland security but those federal agencies must also co-ordinate their actions with state and local governments. The FBI has just 15,000 agents nationwide in comparison to 800,000 state and local police officers. Similarly, the Federal Emergency Management Agency has a mere 2,600 employees, so the primary burden of responsibility for disaster response falls on state and local agencies and so-called first responders – the police, fire and medical services (O'Hanlon 2006: 122; Lehrer 2004). State and local government agencies must therefore play a central role in homeland security but they also need help because the new counter-terrorism agenda imposes demands on them that they are often untrained and unequipped to meet. Federal agencies thus have a crucial role in such areas as developing a national homeland security plan, communicating intelligence and providing expertise and guidance, but require the support and co-operation of state and local agencies whose activities they do not direct (though those agencies must obey national laws). Above all, therefore, the federal government needs to develop an effective partnership with state and local agencies based on genuine co-operation and mutual participation in policy planning and in implementation.

One of the problems that the United States faces in this regard is that by 9/11 the era of expanding federal funding for, and extensive intervention in, state and local affairs was over. In its place has come a policy of benign neglect and/or the less benign policy of imposing federal mandates without the funds to pay for them. As a result, the federal government "was no longer predisposed or well-positioned to lead and support a close intergovernmental partnership" (Eisinger 2006: 537–8).

Initial policy developments seemed to bear this out. When Bush set up a Homeland Security Council (HSC), no representatives of state and local governments were invited to join. The latter also complained that initially they were left to invent their own homeland security priorities and responsibilities and expected to bear the fiscal burden of increased security. When funds did start to flow, local and state governments complained about the constraints imposed on their use (restricted to training, equipment and planning), which prevented them from using the money to pay for overtime or new personnel (Eisinger 2006: 540–1). On the other hand, a GAO analysis found that some local government units delayed voting to accept grants because they did not know what to do with them (GAO 2004b).

Intergovernmental intelligence-sharing has proved to be a particular bone of contention, in part because of the tension between secrecy and the need to share knowledge. The more widely intelligence is shared, the greater the danger of leaks and the compromising of operations. Moreover, many state and local government officials lack the training or security clearance for intelligence work, making federal agencies reluctant to share classified information. While the FBI has increased the number of Joint Terrorism Task Forces, bringing together federal, state and local officials, the last complain that most of the sharing that goes on is one way. In response, an increasing number of local law enforcement agencies have established their own intelligence operations and liaison with each other and even with foreign governments. For example, the New York Police Department has seven officers posted abroad. Such actions have often been taken without consulting federal agencies which complain in turn that they simply add to the intelligence confusion (Steinberg 2006: 19–20, 36; Stockton and Roberts 2008: 6).

Of course, as with any policy innovation, teething problems are to be expected. More worrisome is the fact that, years on from 9/11, significant problems of intergovernmental co-ordination remain. During the course of 2007 the DHS drafted a National Response Framework to replace the existing National Response Plan. Representatives of state and local government were involved in the drafting process but found that, when the draft was published in August, several of their main recommendations had been excluded. While some were restored in the final version, this experience appears to be fairly typical. Participants in a homeland security forum convened in late 2007 recounted a litany of similar complaints. One claimed there had been a "steady deterioration" in relations between the DHS and state and local government over the past three years, another that the DHS was "locking them out of decision-making", while others argued that the DHS "just pays lip service" to the importance of state and local input (Stockton and Roberts 2008: 5–6).

## CONCLUSION

The United States is almost certainly better protected against terrorist attack today than it was before 9/11. Among other developments, there have been real improvements in aviation safety, border controls, identifying potential terrorist targets and intelligence-sharing. Nevertheless, as we have seen, problems remain. Some potential targets in the private sector remain vulnerable because of the combined impact of industry lobbying and the Bush administration's laissez-faire ideology. Bureaucratic politics significantly undermined the crucial effort to reform intelligence, and intergovernmental co-ordination remains a major problem. The DHS itself is far from functional. In a 2007 report the GAO stated that the "DHS's management systems and functions are not yet fully integrated and wholly operational" and that the DHS has "not yet developed performance measures or established structures to ensure effective pursuit of missions" (GAO 2007: 4–5).

With regard to the latter, one of the most troubling, though essentially unprovable, criticisms of the Bush record is that the creation of the DHS itself was unnecessary. None of the improvements listed above, it can be argued, required the establishment of a giant new bureaucracy (Perrow 2006), a bureaucracy, moreover, that is absorbing vast amounts of time, money and other resources simply to get it to function and which might have been better expended elsewhere. The fact that Bush's decision to support the creation of the DHS was driven by short-term political calculations is potentially all the more damning in the light of these arguments.

That aside, the report card on the efforts of the Bush administration should probably read "could do better". Some problems were inevitable but others, such as its ideological blinkers and failure to impose coherent and effective intelligence reform, were not. Nevertheless, for all the evident problems and failings, and as was emphasised in the introduction, it would be a mistake to condemn homeland security policy as a disaster just yet. Progress has been made, and given the scale of the task involved, further progress is bound to be slow and problems to abound. Less than a decade on from the events of 9/11, it is still too early for definitive answers.

## BIBLIOGRAPHY

The Advisory Panel to Assess Domestic Response Capabilities for Terrorism Involving Weapons of Mass Destruction (Gilmore Commission) (2000), "Toward a National Strategy for Combating Terrorism", 15 December, www.rand.org

D'Arcy, Michael, Michael O'Hanlon, Peter Orszag, Jeremy Shapiro and James Steinberg (2006), *Protecting the Homeland 2006/2007*, Washington, DC: Brookings Institution Press

Becker, Elizabeth (2002), "Big visions for security post shrink amid political drama", *New York Times*, 3 May

Brzezinski, Matthew (2004), "Red Alert", *Mother Jones*, 1 September, www.motherjones.com

Caudle, Sharon (2005), "Homeland Security: Approaches to results management", *Public Performance and Management Review* 28: 3, pp. 352–75

Congressional Budget Office (2005), "Federal terrorism reinsurance: An update", January, Washington, DC: Congressional Budget Office

Donley, Michael B. and Neal A. Pollard (2002), "Homeland security: The difference between vision and wish", *Public Administration Review*, 62, pp. 138-53

Eisinger, Peter (2006), "Imperfect federalism: the intergovernmental partnership for homeland security", *Public Administration Review*, July/August, pp. 537–45

Fessenden, Helen (2005), "The limits of intelligence reform", *Foreign Affairs* 84: 6, pp. 106–20

Glasser, Susan B. and Michael Grunwald (2005), "Department's mission was undermined from the start", *Washington Post*, 22 December

Harmon, Michael M. and Richard T. Mayer (1986), *Organization Theory for Public Administration*, Glenview: Scott, Foresman and Co.

Jehl, Douglas (2005), "Little authority for new intelligence post", *New York Times*, 14 October

Lindsay, James M. (2003), "Deference and defiance: The shifting rhythms of executive–legislative relations in foreign policy", *Presidential Studies Quarterly*, 33: 3, pp. 530–47

National Commission on Terrorist Attacks upon the United States (9/11 Commission), (2004), *The 9/11 Commission Report: Final report of the National Commission on Terrorist Attacks upon the United States*, New York: W. W. Norton

O'Beirne, Kate (2003), "Introducing Pork-Barrel Homeland Security: a little here, a lot there", *National Review*, 11 August

O'Hanlon, Michael (2006), "The Roles of DOD and First Responders", in D'Arcy et al., *Protecting the Homeland*, pp. 113–28

Orszag, Peter and Michael O'Hanlon (2006), "Protecting infrastructure and providing incentives for the private sector to protect itself" in D'Arcy et al., *Protecting the Homeland*, pp. 73–95

Perrow, Charles (2006), "The disaster after 9/11: The Department of Homeland Security and the intelligence reorganization", *Homeland Security Affairs*, 2: 1, pp. 1–32

Relyea, Harold C. (2005), *Homeland Security: Department Organization and Management – Implementation Phase*, CRS Report for Congress, 3 January

Ripley, Amanda (2004), "How we got homeland security wrong", *Time*, 20 March

Roberts, Patrick S. (2005), "Shifting priorities: congressional incentives and the homeland security granting process", *The Review of Policy Research*, 22: 4, pp. 437–49

Steinberg, James (2006), "Intelligence Reform" in Michael D'Arcy et al., *Protecting the Homeland*, pp. 17–46

Stockton, Paul N. and Patrick S. Roberts (2008), "Findings from the forum on Homeland Security after the Bush administration: Next steps in building unity of effort", *Homeland Security Affairs*, 4: 2, pp. 1–11

United States Department of Homeland Security (2002), *National Strategy for Homeland Security*, July 2002

United States Department of Homeland Security (2005), "Secretary Michael Chertoff, US Department of Homeland Security Second Stage Review Remarks", Ronald Reagan Building, Washington, DC, 13 July

United States Department of Homeland Security (2007), *Overview: FY 2007 Homeland Security Grant Program*, www.dhs.gov

United States, General Accounting Office (2004a), *The chief operating officer concept and its potential use as a strategy to improve management at the Department of Homeland Security*, 28 June, Washington, DC: GAO

United States, General Accounting Office (2004b), *Emergency preparedness: Federal funds for first responders*, Washington, DC: GAO

United States, General Accounting Office (2006), *FY 2006 Homeland Security Grant Program*, www.ojp.usdoj.gov

United States, General Accounting Office (2007), "Department of Homeland Security: Progress report on implementation of mission and management functions", Statement of Comptroller General David N. Walker before the Committee on Homeland Security and Governmental Affairs, US Senate, 6 September, Washington, DC: GAO

White House (2005), Bush speech at the National Endowment for Democracy, 6 October. www.whitehouse.gov

Wise, Charles R. (2002), "Organizing for Homeland Security", *Public Administration Review*, 62, 2, pp. 131–44

# *Chapter 8*

# BUSH AND EUROPE

David Patrick Houghton

It is hard to generalise about United States–European relations, not least because Europe is a collective of many disparate, strong, individual nations. Nevertheless, because this chapter requires a good deal of generalisation about the relationship between the Bush administration and Europe during the former's two terms in office, a good place to start is with a book which was often taken as emblematic of contemporary neo-conservative thinking about transatlantic relations. In his slim but fascinating 2003 volume, *Of Paradise and Power*, Robert Kagan claims that a permanent rift has developed between the United States and Europe, based on gaping power differentials in the wake of the Soviet Union's demise:

> It is time to stop pretending that Europeans and Americans share a common view of the world, or even that they occupy the same world. On the all-important question of power – the efficacy of power, the morality of power, the desirability of power – American and European perspectives are diverging. Europe is turning away from power, or to put it a little differently, it is moving beyond power into a self-contained world of laws and rules and transnational negotiation and co-operation . . . The United States, meanwhile, remains mired in history, exercising power in the anarchic Hobbesian world where international laws and rules are unreliable and where true security and the defense and promotion of a liberal order still depend on the possession and use of military might. That is why on major strategic and international questions today, Americans are from Mars and Europeans are from Venus: they agree on little and understand one another less and less. (Kagan 2003: 3)

Kagan sees the development over time of a United States impatient with diplomacy, increasingly unilateralist and viewing the world in the strict categories of good versus evil. Europeans, on the other hand, see various shades of grey, are increasingly multilateralist, prefer negotiation and persuasion, and turn to international law far more readily than military force. Kagan traces the causes of this supposedly permanent shift to changes in relative power between the two, with the balance of power moving dramatically in favour of the United States. The behaviour of states, he argues, is determined by their power. Thus, the United States argued for multilateralism and the sharing of power when it was weak. Now it is powerful, it behaves as powerful nations do, or as the Europeans used to behave, while the Europeans have taken the positions always advocated by the weak. World superpowers do not willingly give up decision-making powers to international bodies, for instance, while weaker powers have less to lose and tend to favour such bodies. Added to this power differential, Kagan says, has been the emergence of a genuine belief within the European Union in a postmodern world. Europe has convinced itself that realist balances of power and the use of military power are now obsolete and has taken a long "holiday from strategy". Stunned by two world wars, Europe has created a new system in which war between its members is simply inconceivable.

It would be a dangerous exaggeration to see the intellectual Kagan and the dominant foreign-policy decision-makers within the Bush administration as entirely synonymous. It is unlikely, for instance, that George W. Bush ever intellectualised issues to the extent that more thoughtful commentators like Kagan did. Like practically all former state governors, Bush came to office with virtually no foreign-policy experience, which was exacerbated by an apparent lack of interest in the world outside the fifty states. Nevertheless, Kagan's ideas – represented also in his equally influential 1998 article "The Benevolent Empire" – represent a powerful current of thinking that ran through both terms of the Bush administration.

That there were important transatlantic differences in outlook between the Bush administration and many of America's European allies is impossible to deny. They differed on a whole range of issues, including international trade, climate change and human rights and, of course, most visibly on the Iraq war. Nevertheless, this chapter argues that the divisions were predominantly the product of the Bush administration's beliefs, and that there is nothing unusual in the history of transatlantic relations about such disputes. An examination of the record demonstrates that the extensive degree of transatlantic conflict between 2001 and 2009 stemmed not from permanently conflicting interests or power imbalances, however, but from the policy choices made by political leaders, particularly George W. Bush.

## 1. THE INITIAL RIFT

The Bush administration began its first term expressing disdain for the very idea of an international community. As the prominent European observer Harald Muller put it,

> from the law of the seas to the Kyoto protocol, from the biodiversity convention, from the extraterritorial application of the trade embargo against Cuba or Iran, from the brusque calls for reform of the World Bank and the International Monetary Fund to the International Criminal Court: American unilateralism appears as an omnipresent syndrome pervading world politics. (quoted in Nye 2002: 155)

The trend towards unilateralism did not begin with George W. Bush, since it was Bill Clinton who had refused to place the Kyoto and International Criminal Court (ICC) treaties before the Senate during his final days in office. But Clinton's reluctance to do this was mostly a matter of domestic politics, rather than stemming from any kind of ideological motive.

What was immediately apparent about the Bush administration was that it had fundamental ideological objections to international laws, condemning what it saw as Clinton's squandering of America's vast and overwhelming power. Instead, the Bush administration asserted forcefully that international commitments and treaties should never be permitted to infringe upon US sovereignty or America's right to embrace whatever foreign policy positions it saw fit. The trend towards unilateral ventures greatly alarmed Europeans who, as Kagan correctly observed, had been moving in the opposite direction. In this new climate, transatlantic relations began to deteriorate swiftly. Though Kagan's assertions that the differences are permanent and attributable mostly to power differentials are highly debatable, it is clear that

Europe embraced multilateralism and diplomacy at a time when the Bush administration turned decisively against it.

During its first term, in particular, the Bush administration showed a strong disinclination to consult its allies in Europe. A commitment to unilateralism was embedded in the famous Bush doctrine, known more formally as the *National Security Strategy of 2002*, which clearly stated the administration's willingness to go it alone where America's allies were unwilling or unable to act. The document baldly asserted that the United States would support international bodies like the United Nations and treaties like the ICC only when they promoted America's vital interests, as perceived by Bush officials. While President Clinton had signed the ICC treaty, the Bush administration theatrically announced in 2002 that it was "unsigning" it, much to the amazement of many in Europe. Similarly, Bush's rejection of the painstakingly negotiated Kyoto Protocols on the environment "created a veritable uproar on the continent", as Alexander Moens notes. The president seemed to care not a whit about Europeans' concerns, and the price paid in terms of transatlantic relations was a high one (Moens 2004: 114). More generally, this behaviour fuelled the feeling that the hegemon wished to place itself above the law, free from international restrictions and multilateral agreements of any kind. But if United States–Europe relations were tense during early 2001, there was far worse to come: the issue of Iraq would stretch the transatlantic relationship to breaking point.

## 2. THE SCHISM OVER IRAQ

It has become a rather commonplace truism to assert that a vast reservoir of goodwill towards the United States was forged by the events of 9/11 but the observation is no less true for being so often repeated. It is equally well established that it was the American response to 9/11 that substantially depleted this reservoir and powerfully contributed to the divisions during Bush's two terms in office. Bush's rhetorical response to the attack on America, while perhaps understandable initially, was overstated. The president alarmed Europeans with his talk about an axis of evil composed of Iran, Iraq and North Korea, which sounded very much like a military "to do" list. The sabre-rattling rhetoric alone was bound to dismay the Europeans who, historically, prefer the more realist language of balances of power and a less Manichean conception of good and evil. Moreover, Bush's new doctrine of pre-emption – asserting the right to strike first at any and all threats to American security – probably engendered more unease in Europe than in Baghdad, Pyongyang or Tehran. What was Europe's old ally up to? Did Bush really mean what he was saying?

The case of Iraq saw a unilaterally minded president prepared to go to war, with or without America's allies, pitted against an overwhelmingly unwilling international community which included most of Europe. For largely political reasons, the United States and Britain went to considerable effort to draft a final resolution that would lend United Nations support to the invasion of Iraq. On 8 November 2002, three weeks after the US Congress approved the Iraq resolution authorising military action, the UN Security Council unanimously passed resolution 1441, which found Iraq in "material breach" of its previous resolutions. It gave Iraq "a final opportunity" to disarm but required both that UN inspectors be given full and immediate access to all sites deemed possible locations for the concealment of weapons of mass destruction and a full written account within thirty days of its chemical, biological and nuclear weapons programmes. The desire to appear to be acting multilaterally was driven mainly by British Prime Minister Tony Blair. As Bob Woodward suggests, a major consideration in pursuing a second UN resolution was to provide political cover for leaders who were paying a heavy domestic price for their support of American plans, among them Spain's Jose Maria Aznar and Blair himself. "At the core of the dithering over the UN's resolutions", Woodward explains, "was Blair's fate. It was very much on Bush's mind. If Blair's government fell, it would be a real disaster, they all agreed" (Woodward 2004: 341). In March 2003, Britain, Spain and the United States drafted another resolution condemning Iraq for non-compliance with previous resolutions and also giving the UN's official imprimatur to an invasion. Disagreement within the United Nations Security Council about the extent of the threat posed by Saddam stalled the resolution, however, and the Bush administration announced that it would proceed without broad European or international support (Woodward 2002: 365).

This is not the place to speculate upon the precise point at which Bush decided to invade Iraq but it is clear that the Bush administration ignored the protestations of its traditional allies in Europe when making that decision. Apart from one or two countries pulled along in America's wake, the invasion was a more or less unilateral action opposed by the vast majority of members of the European Union. Neo-conservatives, both inside and outside the administration, thought that European support for their initiatives was desirable but far from necessary.

Neo-conservatives were not the only voices in the Bush White House, however. From the very start, the neo-cons tussled with traditional realists over control of foreign policy. Represented in the first term most clearly by Deputy Secretary of Defense Paul Wolfowitz, the neo-cons enjoyed the upper hand after 9/11, while traditional realists like Colin Powell increasingly were isolated. One often overlooked fact about this division, however, is that both camps questioned European motives in opposing the Iraq war. Neo-cons like Kagan suggested that Europeans opposed the invasion primarily because it was an affront to the viability of the European project which was based on a Kantian rejection of brute unilateralism and a search for perpetual peace. Realists like former National Security Advisor Brent Scowcroft insisted in private that the crisis over Iraq was really about the competition between France and Britain for leadership of the European Union. Paraphrasing Scowcroft, Sarwar Kashmeri argues that "the French saw that European public opinion was *strongly* opposed to what America wanted to do in Iraq, and they thought this was their chance to get out ahead, lead European public opinion, and get the United States out of Europe". The British, on the other hand, took the position that they could lead Europe by providing a natural bridge between the United States and the continent (Kashmeri 2007: 10–11).

Neo-conservatives and realists aside, there was also a widespread and rather cynical tendency in the United States to denigrate any state opposed to the war by claiming that supposedly critical trade linkages with Iraq were the true motivations behind its actions. France's opposition in particular was often explained away as selfish realpolitik. German Chancellor Gerhard Schroeder's opposition to the war, on the other hand, was portrayed as pandering to domestic political opinion. Yet clashing psychological perceptions of reality – not simply economic interests, domestic politics or internal European Union power plays – were arguably critical to the rift over Iraq, and Europeans were outraged to have their objections to the war dismissed so lightly.

## 3. THE SECOND BUSH TERM: PAPERING OVER GIANT CRACKS

In transatlantic terms, the tale of Bush's second term was in large part the story of America's and Europe's mutual attempts to patch up the damage that the rift over Iraq had caused. As Elisabeth Bumiller notes, "Mr. Bush began changing [the] tone in the first days after his re-election, when Condoleezza Rice, then his national security adviser and now his secretary of state, presented him with a lengthy memorandum telling him that improved relations with Europe had to be his foreign-policy priority in the second term" (Bumiller 2005a). In selecting Rice as his new Secretary of State, Bush seems to have intended that the administration should return to a more traditional form of diplomacy towards Europe and other regions of the world. Despite her apparent support for the chest-thumping unilateralism of Bush's first term, Rice was by instinct a realist and possessed a less strident or ideological image than most advisers surrounding Bush. It came as no surprise, then, when Rice embarked on a major fence-mending tour of Europe at the beginning of her term in office (Bumiller 2005b). The president himself set off in February 2005 on a four-day trip to Belgium, Germany and Slovakia in which he sought to "sell himself to Europe as a new man with open arms" (Bumiller 2005a). While Bush offered no substantive changes in American foreign policy, the trip was clearly intended to promote a change in style. "It's got to be the beginning of a thaw", commented US Ambassador to Belgium Tom Korologos. "It's like a family that got a divorce. You have to kiss before you go to sleep" (Bumiller 2005a: 11). Speaking in Brussels, a location deliberately chosen because it is the headquarters of NATO, the European Union and the European Commission, Bush echoed Rice's comments, assuring his audience that "the alliance of Europe and North America is the main pillar of our security in a new century . . . no temporary debate, no passing disagreement of governments, no power on earth will ever divide us" (Bumiller 2005b). Most surprisingly of all, even the combative Donald Rumsfeld made light of his infamous remarks about new and old Europe, in which he contrasted the staid, ancient backward-looking nations of north-west Europe with the emerging, dynamic nations in southern and eastern Europe. "When I first mentioned I might be traveling in France and Germany, it raised some eyebrows", Rumsfeld joked in a February 2005 speech. "One wag said it ought to be an interesting trip after all that has been said. I thought for a moment and then I replied, 'Oh, that was the old Rumsfeld'" (Sciolino 2005: 1).

## 4. THE TORTURE QUESTION

The charm offensive by Bush, Rice and Rumsfeld seemed to work, at least in the sense that it restored a measure of civility to transatlantic relations. The Democratic Party's victory in the 2006 congressional mid-term elections and the replacement of Donald Rumsfeld as Secretary of Defense with the more realist Robert Gates seemed to improve matters further. Nevertheless, the same core disagreement over the status of international law persisted. The war on terror presented the Bush administration with the difficult political and military issue of what to do with prisoners captured on the battlefield. Vice President Cheney and others argued that the detainees were uniformly terrorists and members of al-Qaeda. While the United States has been a signatory to the Geneva Conventions since 1949, Cheney saw no reason to include under its provisions members of an organisation that did not itself honour the conventions. In a controversial 2002 decision, the Bush administration classified those captured not as prisoners of war, which would give them full rights under the Geneva Conventions, but as enemy combatants. Guantánamo Bay and various prisons in Iraq were used to house the prisoners, including the Abu Ghraib facility which became notorious in 2004 after evidence of torture and other human rights abuses was uncovered. The definition of torture was also changed in internal government documents effectively to allow its use, and was even openly advocated by the vice president, despite being prohibited by international law.

All this created further strains in the transatlantic alliance. Many Europeans were surprised and outraged that the legal principles of war were being undermined by a nation they had come to think of as their leading defender and upholder. To make matters worse, it emerged that some of the enemy combatants denied access to human rights in Guantánamo were, in fact, European nationals, which soon created enormous pressure for the return of these citizens to the host countries involved. It became increasingly clear over time, moreover, that at least some of those in Guantánamo, or Gitmo as the US military called it, had been imprisoned mistakenly in the absence of meaningful evidence against them. Further dissensus within the transatlantic alliance was created with the widespread publicising of CIA rendition, the practice of transporting terror suspects for interrogation in countries that legally allow torture. On another visit to Europe in December 2005, Rice claimed that "at no time" had the Bush administration sanctioned acts of torture but, on her return to Washington, she left behind

> the skeptical Europe of the media and much of the public, those still inclined to feel that Ms. Rice papered over some specific, nasty truths about the abuse of American power – and, more generally, that the United States is an out-of-control superpower whose abuses are widespread and deeply troubling. (Bernstein 2005)

Rumours persisted that both Poland and Romania, part of Rumsfeld's new Europe, had provided rendition sites where terror suspects had been interrogated (Bernstein 2005).

## 5. MARS AND VENUS TALK AGAIN, WITHOUT REALLY CHANGING

By early 2007, the United States and Europe again professed to be on friendly terms. But, diplomatic hyperbole aside, neither side changed its policy positions in any appreciable way during the last two years of the Bush administration. The United States did not shift its stance towards the International Criminal Court, did not re-sign the anti-ballistic missile treaty, and remained committed to the notion of missile defence which was seen in many European capitals as a dangerous act of nuclear destabilisation. Despite the occasional nod in Bush's speeches towards the idea of global warming, the administration offered no meaningful new environmental initiatives. And, most tellingly, the administration steadfastly refused to discuss a timetable for withdrawal from Iraq. Indeed, in what could be construed as an escalation of the war, the administration ordered a surge in troop numbers, a move ostensibly designed to hold the line temporarily in a war that most Europeans, now joined by many Americans, saw as unwinnable. True enough, Bush officials made it clear that they had no plans to invade Iran, and eventually conceded to demands for diplomatic talks (which included European states) on the issue of Iranian nuclear proliferation. This seeming about-face was less a concession to Europe, however, and more a response to mounting political pressure at home. It also represented the realisation that a third front was militarily impractical, with the jobs in Afghanistan and Iraq still unfinished.

The Europeans did not change significantly either. They toned down their earlier rhetoric and even agreed, rather surprisingly, not to block the controversial appointment of Paul Wolfowitz, a leading architect of the Iraq war, as president of the World Bank in 2005. Most European leaders remained unwilling, however, to put their own troops in harm's way to help the Bush administration extract itself from what they saw as a needless war of choice in Iraq. Gerard Baker noted that, at its fiftieth birthday celebrations in April 2007, the European Union had also failed to address issues like the rise of radical Islamic fundamentalism and the spread of terrorism, and most European states refused to send troops to stem the radical Islamist tide in Afghanistan. That this occurred despite the departure of Jacques Chirac in France and Gerhard Schroeder in Germany – both replaced by more Atlanticist rivals – spoke volumes about the refusal of Europe to alter its priorities to fit those of the United States (Baker 2007).

## 6. "YO, BROWN"?

The electoral defeat of Jose Maria Aznar's party in Spain in 2004, widely attributed to his support of the Iraq venture, robbed Bush of a key friend and ally in Europe. Perhaps more significantly, Tony Blair's resignation in June 2007 removed a critical advocate for the president's preferred brand of foreign policy. British commentators correctly speculated that the ascendancy of Gordon Brown would have a further dampening effect on transatlantic relations. Blair was derided in Britain as Bush's poodle, and his seeming submissiveness to American wishes during the Iraq war – symbolised perhaps most tellingly when Bush was unwittingly caught by an open microphone addressing the British prime minister with the words "yo, Blair" – had become a crippling political liability in Britain. The political lessons were not lost on Blair's replacement (Serfaty 2007: 75). Somewhat colder and more analytical in demeanour than his predecessor, Brown's relations with Bush looked much more like the polite distance between George H. W. Bush and John Major than the warm embrace of Ronald Reagan and Margaret Thatcher.

Speculation that there would be real policy changes on Iraq under a Brown government proved well founded and readily observable. While the widely predicted British troop withdrawals from Iraq did not happen as swiftly as some expected, most British forces were soon reassigned to a non-combat role and, in July 2008, Brown signalled that Britain's 4,000 troops would leave by early 2009 (Summers and Wintour 2008). Even before taking office, Brown stressed that Britain's national interest would govern its transatlantic relations under his prime ministership, and so low key was an official meeting at the White House between Brown and Bush on 10 May 2007 that the former tried later to imply that their encounter had been accidental.

The election of Nicholas Sarkozy in May 2007 was generally assumed to herald better times for the Bush administration (Hoagland 2007; Murphy 2007) after United States–France relations had plumbed new depths during the onset of the Iraq war when fast food vendors in America, including in the US Congress, had even begun to sell "freedom fries" rather than French fries. Certainly, Sarkozy was widely regarded as more amenable to American leadership than some of his predecessors. On a trip to New York and Washington DC in September 2006, before he became president, he expressed his profound admiration for the United States and stunned audiences on both sides of the Atlantic by railing against "French arrogance" over the war in Iraq. Calling for a "new era in transatlantic relations", he even suggested that his country's opposition to the war stemmed from French envy of America's position, arguing that it is "unthinkable for Europe to forge its identity in opposition to the United States" (Pedder 2007: 122). In truth, however, Sarkozy's ascendancy towards the end of Bush's second term came too late to effect a radical change in the bilateral relations between the two countries. The new French administration's focus on human rights issues continued to generate tension with the United States over the torture question, and Sarkozy's repeated and insistent statements about global warming and climate change, as well as German Chancellor Angela Merkel's continued commitment to the same issue, left the Bush administration as much at odds with Europe as it was before Sarkozy took office (Sciolino 2007).

## CONCLUSION: A PERMANENT DIVIDE?

While George W. Bush's relations with Europe over the course of his two terms in office were often difficult and tense, there is probably nothing permanent about United States–European conflict, and hence no reason why the Obama administration cannot mend the fences trampled during Bush's first term and repaired only superficially in his second. For an astute American, Robert Kagan is ironically on a surer footing describing the Kantian policy views of Western Europe, which seem unlikely to change any time soon, than analysing the supposedly permanently Hobbesian United States (Kagan 2003). Kagan's leading error was to treat the policy preferences of the Bush administration as a lasting policy shift (along the lines, say, of the Truman Doctrine) that future administrations would be compelled to follow, an error others have made as well (Lynch and Singh 2008). But just as American politics shifted considerably after Vietnam and Watergate, strong domestic disapproval of Bush's policies during his second term suggests that his odd blend of table-thumping foreign-policy adventurism, Machiavellianism and ideologically driven unilateralism is not likely to survive a change of administration.

In addition to the obvious case of Iraq, to the end of his administration Bush and his European counterparts remained seriously divided over the issues of the International Criminal Court and environmental degradation. These two debates seem likely to continue to bedevil the transatlantic relationship no matter who the American president is; the global warming debate affects critical economic interests, for instance, and is therefore particularly intractable. But most other issues that divided the United States and Europe during the Bush years seem far less permanent. Strong Democratic majorities in the House and the Senate after the 2008 elections made it more likely that the United States would move closer to Europe on a host of foreign policy issues. One source of division, as we have seen, was the Bush administration's approach to human rights. Guantánamo Bay, torture, rendition and the American position on the rights of non-American citizens generally were still sources of enormous disagreement within the transatlantic alliance as Bush left office in January 2009. But these reflected temporary differences of opinion between the Bush administration and various European governments. Barack Obama announced during his first week in the White House that

Guantánamo Bay would be closed. At the time of writing, the new Democratic administration seemed likely to embrace some form of post-Clintonian liberal internationalism, recognising that incidents like the Abu Ghraib scandal have squandered America's soft power (Nye 2005).

Judged on its own merits – that is, strictly in terms of what the Bush administration seems to have been trying to achieve – its policy towards Europe might be regarded as a success of sorts in its first term; after all, Bush seems to have regarded Europe as much as a strategic rival as an ally during that period. If the strategy intended to create colder relations between the United States and Europe, then it clearly succeeded in doing so. By more conventional diplomatic standards, however, it probably damaged American and European interests alike. Moreover, it clearly failed on its own terms in Iraq and Afghanistan where it became clear that the United States could not go it alone without becoming heavily overstretched in military and strategic terms.

In March 2009 there were already signs that relations between the new Obama administration and Europe were improving. Obama's evident popularity in Europe during his July 2008 pre-election trip there – including a well-attended and warmly received speech in Berlin recalling John Kennedy's famous *Ich bin ein Berliner* oration over forty years earlier – stood in sharp contrast to the angry protests and heightened security that greeted Bush during his rare European visits. Moreover, Obama's professed commitment to greater multilateralism promised a return to the warmer relations that have traditionally characterised the transatlantic alliance.

## BIBLIOGRAPHY

Baker, Gerard (2007), "Continental Drift: Europe Gets Even Less Serious", *The Weekly Standard*, 19 March

Bernstein, Richard (2005), "Rice's Visit: Official Praise, Private Doubts", *New York Times*, 11 December

Bumiller, Elisabeth (2005a), "Bush Seeks to Begin a Thaw In a Europe Still Cool To Him", *New York Times*, 20 February

Bumiller, Elisabeth (2005b), "Bush is Expected To Express Support For A Strong Europe Today", *New York Times*, 21 February

CBS News (2004), "Bush Sought 'Way' To Invade Iraq?" at http://www.cbsnews.com/

Clarke, Richard (2004), *Against All Enemies: Inside America's War on Terror,* New York: Free Press.

Hoagland, Jim (2007), "For Bush, a Gift From Paris", *Washington Post,* 24 June

Kagan, Robert (1998), "The Benevolent Empire", *Foreign Policy,* 111, pp. 24–35

Kagan, Robert (2003), *Of Paradise and Power: America and Europe in the New World Order,* York: Vintage Books, 2003

Kashmeri, Sarwar (2007), *America and Europe After 9/11 and Iraq: The Great Divide,* Westport, CT: Praeger

Lynch, Timothy and Robert Singh (2008), *After Bush: The Case for Continuity in American Foreign Policy,* Cambridge: Cambridge University Press

Moens, Alexander (2004), *The Foreign Policy of George W. Bush: Values, Strategy and Loyalty,* Burlington, VT: Ashgate

Murphy, Kim (2007), "New Face of Old Europe Gives US Reason to Smile: Leadership Changes Bring a Pro-American Tilt That Could Revive the Atlantic Alliance", *Los Angeles Times,* 1 June

Nye, Joseph (2002), *The Paradox of American Power: Why the World's Only Superpower Can't Go It Alone,* New York: Oxford University Press

Nye, Joseph (2005), *Soft Power: The Means To Success in World Politics,* New York: Public Affairs

Pedder, Sophie (2007), "Atypically French: Sarkozy's Bid to Be a Different Kind of President", *Foreign Affairs,* 86: 3, May/June

Sciolino, Elaine (2005), "New Rumsfeld Is Seeking Stronger Ties With Europe", *New York Times,* 13 February

Sciolino, Elaine (2007), "A Confident Sarkozy Talks Foreign Policy", *New York Times,* 5 June

Serfaty, Simon (2007), *Architects of Delusion: Europe, America and the Iraq War,* Philadelphia: University of Pennsylvania Press

Summers, Deborah and Patrick Wintour (2008), "Brown Signals Iraq Troops Withdrawal", *The Guardian,* 22 July

Suskind, Ron (2004), *The Price of Loyalty: George W. Bush, the White House and the Education of Paul O'Neill,* New York: Simon and Schuster

Woodward, Bob (2002), *Bush At War,* New York: Simon and Schuster

Woodward, Bob (2004), *Plan of Attack,* New York: Simon and Schuster

*Chapter 9*

# INTERNATIONAL TRADE POLICY UNDER GEORGE W. BUSH

Nitsan Chorev

Trade policies, particularly laws and regulations that affect the price of imports entering the country, have always been bitterly contested in the United States. On the one hand, local manufacturers who cannot compete internationally strongly oppose imports which would reduce their share of the domestic market, as do workers who are employed by those manufacturers. On the other hand, American manufacturers who can compete internationally welcome easier access to foreign markets and strongly advocate the reduction of trade barriers in the United States as a way to induce trade liberalisation in other countries. Recently, these traditional interests have been joined by new voices concerned with consumer protection in the United States and with the labour and environmental conditions where imports come from.

While the Republican Party is considered the party of free trade and the Democratic Party the party more anxious to limit imports to preserve jobs, it is also the case that presidents from both parties have been generally supportive of expanding trade relations with other countries while members of Congress – Democrats primarily, but also Republicans representing industrial regions – have always been more reluctant in opening the American market to international competition. Hence, like most recent Republican and Democratic presidents, George W. Bush came to office with an ambitious free-trade agenda but without clear congressional support for it. After eight years in office, what did President Bush accomplish? Initially, the Bush administration engaged in a great flurry of activity, including successfully launching a new round of multilateral trade negotiations.

By 2008, however, hardly any progress had been made at the multilateral negotiations, and other relatively ambitious regional plans failed to materialise. Additionally, the Bush administration had great difficulties convincing Congress to ratify those agreements that had been signed by the president.

What was the cause of such modest achievements? Observers rightly point to the growing rift between the Bush administration and Congress as the main source of political paralysis. Indeed, Congress was uncharacteristically confrontational, seeking revisions of already-signed trade agreements and refusing to ratify others, to the great frustration of the Bush administration. But why the growing tensions between the White House and Congress? Some observers point to an alleged increase in protectionist sentiments, especially among the newly elected Democrats in 2006 (Hitt and King 2006), but members of Congress did not act on behalf of protectionist interests during the Bush years any more zealously than in the past. In fact, Congress followed conventional, rather than overtly confrontational, strategies when dealing with trading partners, even in the relatively contentious case of China. Others argue that the administration's confrontation with Congress was an outcome of Bush's overt partisanship (Stokes 2004). Although the Bush administration had little interest in Democrats' concerns about workers' rights and environmental standards, after the Democrats gained a majority in Congress the two parties reached an agreement that would allow congressional ratification of some of the bilateral and regional trade agreements that had been signed by the Bush administration.

Thus, between 2001 and 2008, Congress was not exceptionally protectionist and the administration was not particularly partisan (at least in the realm of trade). Instead, this chapter demonstrates that what made it difficult for the Bush administration to advance its version of trade liberalisation was Congress's unprecedented opportunity to make its voice heard. In particular, the Bush administration's handling of multilateral trade negotiations during his first years in office had the unintended consequence of providing Congress the means to play a relatively active role in trade policy in later years, making the Bush administration relatively vulnerable to Congress's position.

## 1. TRADE POLICYMAKING IN CONGRESS AND THE EXECUTIVE

The United States Congress has the constitutional authority to raise and lower tariffs, making it the ultimate site for disputes over trade policy. Since the 1930s, however, Congress's monopoly over trade policymaking has eroded quite substantially and executive capacity to enter trade agreements without congressional intervention has strengthened greatly. This was the result of three important legal changes (see Chorev 2007). First, in 1934, Congress more or less gave up its widely used practice of increasing tariffs unilaterally by delegating its authority to regulate tariffs to the president. Second, in 1974, Congress established a "fast-track" procedure allowing the executive, with only limited congressional intervention, to negotiate with trading partners both the reduction of tariffs and non-tariff barriers to trade, such as subsidies. Finally, in 1994, the contracting parties to the General Agreement on Tariffs and Trade (GATT) created the World Trade Organization (WTO). One of the major differences between the original GATT and the new WTO was that the latter had much improved dispute settlement mechanisms. Consequently, trade disputes between the United States and its trading partners were handled at the multilateral level, without much congressional input.

The legal changes in 1934, 1974 and 1994 shifted radically the balance of influence between Congress on the one hand and the executive and the WTO on the other. Trade policy was largely formulated at the WTO in rounds of multilateral trade negotiations, where American negotiators offered to liberalise American trade policy in return for trade liberalisation in other markets. Congress was left only with the veto function: it could refuse to grant a president fast-track trade-promotion authority and could later refuse to ratify signed trade agreements, but had no power to change unilaterally the terms agreed by American negotiators because under the fast-track procedure Congress cannot amend bills implementing international trade agreements.

The diminished involvement of Congress in trade issues, however, depended on the ability of the executive to reach agreements at the multilateral level and on the type of trade agreements the executive reached. The most useful predictor for Congress's reaction to international trade agreements is not the number of Democratic votes relative to Republican votes but, rather, the number and size of interest groups in favour of a given agreement relative to the number of interest groups opposed. In general, as United States negotiators well know, the more ambitious a trade agreement is – that is, the more issues and topics covered under the agreement – the more contentious it might be but also the more likely it is to get enough interest groups to lobby enough members of Congress ultimately to pass the implementing bill. As a result, a *multilateral* trade agreement negotiated under the auspices of the WTO's 153 members would be more palatable to Congress than *regional* agreements, which cover only a small number of trading partners, or *bilateral* agreements, which regulate trade relations with only one country. It also follows that when regional or bilateral agreements are considered, the more ambitious the agreement is, the greater support it would get in Congress.

It is for exactly this reason that the Bush administration's first priority was to secure fast-track trade-promotion authority from Congress and to launch a new round of multilateral trade negotiations. When multilateral negotiations proved difficult to conclude, however, the Bush administration responded by disengaging itself from multilateral efforts and adopting a strategy of "competitive liberalisation" which focused on negotiating regional and bilateral agreements instead. Many of these agreements were of little economic consequence for internationally competitive business. Paradoxically, this provided Congress with leverage, which it would not normally have, to become an active – and from Bush's point of view, distracting – player in trade policies. In short, it was the opportunity to discuss a large number of relatively insignificant bilateral and regional trade agreements that provided Democrats in Congress a stage they would not normally have enjoyed.

The remainder of this chapter describes how the shift in Bush's strategy away from multilateral negotiations provided Congress with the opportunity to get actively involved, ultimately resulting in nominal accomplishments compared to Bush's original agenda.

## 2. ROUND 1: 2001–4

### *a. Preparing for the Multilateral Front*

As discussed above, Bush's first trade-policy priority was to gain fast-track trade-promotion authority which would allow him to revive multilateral trade negotiations. The authority had lapsed during the Clinton administration in 1994 because of Republican opposition to Democratic demands that trade agreements should include certain labour and environmental standards. Similar disagreements emerged in 2001 but Democrats failed to block the Republicans in the way the latter had done seven years earlier. The new fast-track rules said that trade pacts should include requirements that countries enforce their own labour laws vigorously but the executive avoided having to impose trade sanctions, or even monetary fines, as mechanisms for enforcing such labour provisions.

With the trade promotion authority that Bush had gained, the executive could launch a new round of multilateral trade negotiations. To help to win the support of developing countries, the round was called the Doha Development Round and promised to address development needs. Less encouraging for developing countries was the United States farm bill, passed just a few months after the Doha Round got under way, which committed $173.5 billion in agricultural subsidies over ten years. The bill was justified, at least in part, as a necessary concession to win farm states' support for the fast-track authority. Still, this was a quite provocative action, as developing countries had agreed to participate in the trade negotiations mostly to get the United States and Europe to lower their tariffs on agricultural products and to reduce their trade-distorting subsidies for domestic farmers.

### *b. The Doha Round of Multilateral Trade Negotiations*

The WTO Bush inherited was almost paralysed since the anti-globalisation demonstrations in Seattle in 1999, with deep divisions between rich and poor members. Although the United States and the European Union (EU) offered developing countries sufficient concessions to agree to launch a new round of multilateral trade negotiations, the negotiations promised to be particularly contentious.

The first ministerial meeting after launching the new round of negotiations took place in Cancún, Mexico, in September 2003. As expected, agricultural issues took centre stage, ultimately leading to the collapse of the meeting and a serious rupture between North and South. Responding to an earlier Bush-administration abandonment of a subsidies-cutting proposal in favour of a more watered-down compromise with the EU, Brazil put together a coalition of large, resource-rich nations from the South – the Group of 20 or G20 (not to be confused with the similarly named group of the world's twenty largest national economies) – to demand stronger commitments from rich countries on agriculture and other issues, and West African countries pleaded for WTO members to end cotton subsidies. The conference was finally halted by a coalition of mostly African and Caribbean countries that felt disenfranchised and ignored.

This was hardly the first time the United States government encountered difficult trade negotiations – the previous round had taken eight years before it was successfully concluded. Unlike the conciliatory tone state representatives usually take after unsuccessful economic negotiations, however, the Bush administration responded harshly, threatening withdrawal. As in its refusal to engage constructively at the international level in other realms – such as the build-up to the war in Iraq and the Kyoto environmental negotiations – here, too, the Bush administration rejected multilateralism in favour of an "us versus them" attitude. American officials even borrowed phrases from the war on terrorism to describe the administration's position in the trade negotiations, including a reference to a "coalition of the willing". In statements following the collapse of the Cancún talks, US Trade Representative Robert Zoellick blamed the impasse on Brazil and the G20 countries. Accusing them of making demands on rich countries without being willing to make any concessions in return, he complained, "Many countries just thought this was a freebie . . . and now they will have to face the cold reality of going home with nothing" (King and Miller 2003). Zoellick didn't hesitate to use overt threats, suggesting that the deadlock at Cancún might leave the United States with no choice but to achieve free trade through other deals and warning that "as WTO members ponder the future, the US will not wait: we will move towards free trade with can-do countries" (Zoellick 2003). Zoellick's warnings were soon followed by an array of bilateral and regional negotiations.

### *c. Bilateral and Regional Talks*

Hence, in response to the impasse at the multilateral negotiations, the Bush administration adopted the unprecedented and rather confrontational strategy of "competitive liberalisation" (Destler 2005), where the United States entered bilateral and regional trade agreements with "willing" countries. Focus on bilateral and regional free-trade agreements was justified on the theory that if the United States struck free-trade deals with countries that were enthusiastic about open markets, then the excluded countries would be more willing to accept the big deals at the multilateral level for fear of losing out to their competitors in the giant American market.

The Bush administration's strategy of competitive liberalisation concentrated on Latin America and the Middle East, the latter mostly for geopolitical reasons. Of the greatest economic importance to American business was the Free Trade Agreement of the Americas (FTAA). A regional agreement formally proposed in 1994, the FTAA aimed to unite the Americas in a gigantic, duty-free zone. Disagreements between the two countries with the largest economies, the United States and Brazil, were difficult to overcome, however. Brazil demanded greater access to the US market for its sugar, steel and orange juice, and wanted the United States to revise its anti-dumping statutes. The United States government insisted, however, that farm subsidies and anti-dumping laws had implications that went beyond trade relations in the region and should therefore be dealt with only in the context of global trade talks. After Cancún, US promises to address these issues at the Doha Round lost any credibility. In return, Brazil refused to discuss any of the top US priorities, including investment rules, intellectual property rights and government procurement. The only way out of this impasse was to reduce the scope of the agreement so that it would not include any of the issues opposed by any of the countries but this also minimised the motivation to reach an agreement, and no serious negotiations followed after November 2003 (Stokes 2001; Lindsey 2003).

With the FTAA negotiations on hold, the United States government focused instead on the Central America Free Trade Agreement (CAFTA), a regional agreement with Costa Rica, El Salvador, Guatemala, Honduras, Nicaragua and later also the Dominican Republic, as well as on individual agreements with Chile, Peru, Panama, Colombia, Bolivia and Ecuador. The goal was to establish a coalition, which would exclude Brazil but cover almost half the US trade with the region not already covered by the North American Free Trade Agreement (NAFTA) with Canada and Mexico. Owing to United States insistence, none of these negotiations addressed farm subsidies or anti-dumping issues.

Bush also launched a ten-year effort to form a United States–Middle East Free Trade Area, in an attempt to project "soft" power to accompany the wars in Iraq and Afghanistan (Allen and DeYoung 2003). At the time the initiative was launched, only Israel and Jordan had signed free-trade pacts with the United States, and the agreement with Jordan had not yet been ratified. During Bush's first term, the administration concluded negotiations with Morocco and Bahrain, talks started with Oman and Egypt, and five other countries in the Middle East – Saudi Arabia, the United Arab Emirates, Kuwait, Qatar and Yemen – reached trade and investment framework agreements with the United States. The Bush administration also successfully negotiated agreements with Singapore and Australia.

International trade agreements signed by the executive had then to be ratified by Congress. The first free-trade agreement to be considered was with Jordan, and the debate that ensued was a sign of things to come. The agreement with Jordan had been signed by the Clinton administration and its provisions called for each country to enforce its labour and environmental laws, and made labour obligations subject to sanctions. To reassure reluctant Republicans who opposed the use of trade sanctions for enforcing labour standards, United States Trade Representative Robert Zoellick and Jordanian Ambassador Marwan Muasher exchanged letters that said that the two countries did not intend to resolve trade disagreements by resorting to formal dispute-settlement procedures. This satisfied enough Republicans to allow Congress narrowly to approve the pact – the first trade agreement with a Muslim country – in 2001.

As with Jordan, the trade agreements negotiated by the Bush administration with Chile and Singapore included basic labour provisions although, this time, sanctions were authorised only for failure to enforce one's own labour laws and only if this failure had an effect on trade. These agreements, as well as the agreement with Australia, largely maintained existing restrictions on imports of commodities such as sugar, beef and dairy products, and they were ratified quite easily in Congress. The agreements with Morocco and Bahrain, mostly with symbolic rather than economic consequences, were similarly approved although Senate Democratic Leader Harry Reid saw the Bahrain initiative as an act of "fiddling while Rome is burning". In his opinion, it demonstrated the administration's flawed trade priorities, ignoring China while focusing on significantly less important nations, such as Bahrain, which accounted for just $^{3}/_{100}$ of 1 per cent of US trade. Reid also criticised the agreement for not providing adequate labour provisions.

Democrats' concern with including enforceable labour and environmental standards in trade agreements became a major source of contention, starting with the debate over CAFTA. Pointing at a long history of suppressing unions and denying workers the right to organise, bargain collectively and strike in some of those countries, Democrats wanted to introduce into the trade agreement provisions requiring the governments to enact and enforce international labour standards and allowing for trade sanctions to ensure compliance. Democrats' opposition stopped Bush asking for a vote before the November 2004 elections, even though CAFTA members had already signed the agreement in May.

### *d. Unilateral Initiatives*

If free-trade agreements serve to open markets to imports, other trade-policy measures often restrict access. During the Bush era, one of the most controversial issues was the administration's decision to raise unilaterally tariffs on steel. In March 2002 the Bush administration responded positively to a petition made by the steel industry and decided unilaterally to impose safeguard measures – tariffs of nearly 30 per cent – on certain steel imports. The affected countries, however, filed a complaint against the United States at the World Trade Organization which found that the measures imposed were inconsistent with international rules. Complying with the ruling had a potentially high domestic political price because several states with influential steel interests, including Ohio, Pennsylvania and Michigan, were considered pivotal for the forthcoming 2004 presidential election. The WTO granted the European Union permission to impose sanctions on American imports worth $2.2 billion, however, and the EU shrewdly aimed its proposed sanctions on commodities produced in other states considered pivotal in the elections, including Florida, Michigan and Wisconsin. Eventually, the Bush administration decided to comply with the WTO decision and lifted the tariffs on imported steel. A *New York Times* reporter commented:

> For the first time in his nearly three years in office, the president, who has often reveled in the exercise of American power, finally met an international organization that had figured out how to hit back at the administration where it would hurt. (Sanger 2003)

In the case of China, where the United States was an alleged victim of another government's protectionism, the multilateral venue again ultimately prevailed over unilateral action. For example, to protect the interests of the US semiconductor industry, the Bush administration filed a complaint at the WTO over China's tax on imported semiconductors. To avoid a negative WTO decision, Chinese officials agreed to phase out the rebate system, which was the source of the dispute.

A more complex issue was China's currency policy. Some members of Congress complained that Chinese authorities were artificially deflating the value of the yuan, thereby making Chinese imports to the United States unfairly cheap and US exports to China expensive. During Bush's first term, the administration avoided diplomatic confrontation, with the Treasury Department using "quiet diplomacy" to try to convince China that a flexible currency regime was in its best interest (Alden et al. 2005).

## 3. ROUND 2: 2005–8

In Bush's second term, the administration's enthusiasm for bilateral and regional agreements waned and trade officials instead focused on convincing Congress to ratify already signed pacts before the president's trade promotion authority expired. After Democrats took control of Congress in the 2006 mid-term elections, however, the possibility of ratification became even more challenging than before. Some of the newly elected Democrats were conservative on issues such as gun ownership, abortion and taxes but quite populist on trade issues. While trade issues were not prominent in the campaign, some Democratic candidates promised to block future trade deals, and were looking for opportunities to confront Bush on this issue (Hitt and King 2006). Democrats' concern with labour standards in particular turned into a major source of conflict.

### *a. Another Failed Chance for the Doha Round*

After the collapse of the meeting in Cancún, the Development Round talks revived only slowly. In the ministerial meeting in Hong Kong in December 2005, the United States and the European Union faced an alliance of 110 countries, uniting middle-income economies, such as Brazil and India, with less developed countries. The talks made some progress, including agreements to eliminate subsidies for exported farm goods by 2013 and to end cotton subsidies even earlier. A US-promoted initiative to eliminate industrial nations' tariffs and quotas on almost all exports from the world's poorest countries also won support but other contentious issues, such as the question of domestic agricultural subsidies, were left untouched.

After the Hong Kong session, talks stalled. On the one hand, the United States and the European Union could not agree over the level of cuts in trade-distorting farm subsidies; on the other, the US and the EU joined forces against India and Brazil, insisting on cutting tariffs on manufactured goods. A subsequent meeting in Geneva in June 2006 collapsed and, when another in July 2006 also failed, WTO Director-General Pascal Lamy declared a suspension of the round.

Congress added obstacles to Bush's ability to revive the multilateral trade negotiations. First, when trade promotion authority expired at the end of June 2007, Congress did not extend it. Then, in May 2008, Congress passed a new farm bill that included nearly $300 billion worth of subsidies over five years, some of which would be directed to the cotton farmers in defiance of a WTO ruling that US cotton subsidies violated its international obligations. Bush, who found the subsidies fiscally irresponsible, vetoed the bill but Congress overrode it.

### *b. Bilateral and Regional Talks*

To assure the ratification of CAFTA, the Bush administration made some significant concessions in the agreements that managed to pacify the textiles industry and the sugar sector. In contrast, the only concession offered to organised labour, which opposed the relatively weak labour provisions merely requiring countries to enforce their own laws, was a promise to increase foreign aid funding for enforcement of labour and environmental laws in CAFTA countries. This was not enough to mollify labour or its Democratic supporters, who angrily denounced the agreement, warning that CAFTA would allow "mega-corporations [to] get all the breaks by breaking the backs of workers on both sides of the continent" (Smilowitz 2005). While Congress eventually approved the agreement in July 2005, the vote represented a clear partisan division, winning the lowest number of Democratic votes for any free-trade agreement in the House. Arguably, the relatively inconsequential economic benefits from the trade agreement made it easier for Democrats to support labour's pleas, as they were not confronted with opposite appeals from business. As former Representative Cal Dooley suggested, "The fact that this wasn't an agreement that was going to have a significant impact on our economy made it easier for some members to give greater consideration to a political agenda" (Vaughan 2005).

As part of the Middle East agenda, trade negotiations with Oman were concluded in January 2006. With Oman accounting for less than 0.5 per cent of all US trade in goods, the agreement was of little economic importance but supporters of the deal portrayed the sultanate as a US ally in the war on terror. Some of the opposition, too, was based on national security sentiments. In addition to arguments regarding labour rights and other provisions favouring multinational corporations – the opposition referred to the agreement as a "NAFTA–CAFTA clone" – criticism also came from lawmakers anxious about a provision protecting Oman's right to manage operations, including ports, in the United States. The agreement was presented to Congress not long after the uproar following a sale of port management businesses in major United States seaports to Dubai Ports World, a company based in the United Arab Emirates. Critics warned that the agreement with Oman would similarly compromise US national security. Congressman Mike Michaud, a Democrat from Maine, stated,

> It is bad enough that we are asked to support agreements that will ship more jobs overseas, that undermine our environmental standards, and that ask us to stick our head in the sand over serious human rights violations – but it is simply unacceptable to ask this Congress to support legislation that could potentially undermine the security of our nation. (Congressional Record, 20 July 2006)

After several months of heated debate, Congress voted barely in favour of the agreement and with hardly any Democratic support.

During the first half of its second term, the Bush administration also completed negotiations over free-trade agreements with Peru (signed in April 2006), Colombia (November 2006), Panama (June 2007) and South Korea (June 2007). Following the 2006 elections, however, Bush could not possibly win their ratification without Democratic support. In a compromise agreement between the Democratic leadership and the administration, the latter agreed to amend already-signed agreements so that trading partners would no longer be required merely to enforce their own laws, as was Bush's preferred formula. Rather, new provisions would require the implementation and enforcement of multilateral environmental agreements and the adoption and maintenance of their own labour laws as well as the five core standards of the International Labour Organization (ILO). Those standards bar forced labour, child labour and discrimination in the workplace while protecting the rights of workers to organise unions and bargain collectively. The new guidelines applied to labour standards the same enforcement mechanism that governed other areas of dispute, potentially resulting in punitive tariffs rather than mere fines. The compromise indicated that the labour provisions in those agreements were not reciprocal and could not apply to the United States, since Republicans worried that such standards would allow countries to challenge the United States's own labour laws which are not compatible with ILO principles. Other terms of the compromise ensured that foreign investors did not enjoy greater investment protections than US citizens and provided guarantees of access to affordable prescription drugs (Goodman and Montgomery 2007).

A few months after reaching that compromise, tensions arose again when congressional Democrats asked that Peru and Panama enact the promised legal changes renegotiated by the White House before Congress acted (Hitt 2007). Bypassing official channels controlled by the executive, Democratic leaders took the rare step of negotiating the issue directly with foreign leaders. House Ways and Means Committee Chairman Charles B. Rangel reached an agreement with Peruvian President Alan Garcia, which satisfied the Democrats, leading to a vote ratifying the agreement (Meyerson 2007). No such compromise was reached with Panama, and Congress did not vote on the agreement during Bush's presidency.

Colombia presented an even more complicated matter. The deal signed in November 2006 was of minor economic significance – two-way trade with Colombia is less than 1 per cent of total US trade – and the Bush administration celebrated its geopolitical implications rather than economic effects. Supporters of labour rights, however, strongly opposed the agreement given their concern over Colombia's human rights record. The agreement had amendments addressing workers' rights and the environment, but AFL-CIO President John Sweeney said in a statement that "there is no labor language that could be inserted into the US-Colombia FTA that could adequately address the extraordinary – and unpunished – violence confronting trade unionists in that country" (Ukman 2007). In spite of the strong opposition, Bush decided to force a vote on the agreement in Congress in April 2008. However, House Speaker Nancy Pelosi, a California Democrat, made an *ex post facto* change to House rules which postponed action on the trade pact indefinitely. In addition to Panama and Colombia, Bush also left the White House without getting Congress to vote on the signed agreement with South Korea, which would be the world's largest bilateral free-trade pact.

### *c. Restrained Unilateralism*

The United States government continued experimenting with unilateral and multilateral means to persuade China to strengthen its currency, adopting an increasingly more confrontational approach in response to the failure of two years of quiet diplomacy. Senators Schumer, Democrat of New York, and Graham, Republican of South Carolina, devised a "nuclear option", an across-the-board punitive tariff of 27.5 per cent on Chinese imports if China did not substantially raise the value of the yuan (Blustein 2006). China responded by announcing it would increase the value of the yuan and abandon its decade-old fixed exchange rate to the US dollar in favour of a link to a basket of world currencies. While this represented China's first concrete move towards a free-floating currency, the re-evaluation amounted to just a 2.1 per cent increase against the US dollar, far less than the 10 per cent demanded by Congress. Nonetheless, China's actions encouraged Schumer and Graham to drop their bill and formulate more moderate legislation.

Arguably, one reason for the active congressional involvement is that currency is an issue not regulated by a multilateral organisation. In other cases, the United States government chose multilateral channels over unilateral action. The United States complained in one WTO case about the high import tariffs that China levied on foreign-made car parts; another case involved China's alleged use of government support and tax policies to bolster local companies in competition with foreign firms; and in a third case the United States tried to force China to crack down on copyright piracy by filing complaints regarding the sale of American books, music and films. While this list of complaints implies an antagonistic, even hostile, attitude, multilateral WTO procedures represent a legitimate form of contestation, relative to traditional unilateral measures.

## DISCUSSION

In the realm of trade policy, President Bush's two terms in office were evidently stormy but little progress was made on his original agenda of trade liberalisation. The origins of Bush's difficulties lie at the multilateral level, with the inability of the United States and Europe to address the fundamental needs of developing countries, particularly in the area of agricultural subsidies and tariffs. Bush was not the first US president to be confronted with difficult international trade negotiations but he was quite original in his harsh public criticisms of those countries that did not succumb to US pressure. Also unique was his strategy of competitive bilateralism which turned the United States government away from multilateralism in favour of negotiating agreements with individual nations.

The original expectation that regional and bilateral agreements would lure some countries and force others into meaningful concessions at the multilateral level failed to materialise. The United States executive's choice of partners for bilateral agreements contributed to divisions among the G20 – American pressure was responsible for Colombia, Costa Rica, Ecuador, Guatemala and Peru defecting from that group (Smith 2003) – but bilateral negotiations failed to soften countries' positions in the multilateral negotiations.

As significantly, the bilateral agreements themselves caused major political headaches for the Bush administration. As we saw, the Bush administration launched a large number of negotiations and signed many agreements but struggled to win ratification in Congress, especially after the 2006 elections. This was not because Congress was uncharacteristically protectionist, or because Bush was exceptionally partisan. Rather, Bush's own strategy of preferring bilateralism to multilateralism gave Congress ample opportunities to play hard. Each bilateral or regional agreement provided a stage for critics and allowed Congress to confront the administration with demands for concessions. Somewhat ironically, therefore, a bilateral strategy provided greater leverage to domestic actors who seized the opportunity to slow down Bush's agenda.

Democrats' willingness to support labour and environmental interests was also the result of Bush's choice of partners for the trade agreements, which was driven heavily by non-economic concerns, and the war on terror in particular. Geopolitical logic was certainly behind the plans for a Middle East Free Trade Area and the United States government delayed signing an agreement with Chile for more than six months to show its disappointment at Chile's reluctance to support its Iraq policy at the United Nations. As a result of such priorities, the trade agreements had few economic consequences for those American interest groups that would normally support them, and Democrats could take a more pro-environmental and pro-labour position without it having a negative impact on their relationships with business.

Given the Democrats' position, Bush's initial success in winning back trade promotion authority was followed by major difficulties ratifying signed agreements. In some cases Bush won congressional approval only with great difficulty and small margins; in other cases, he was forced to modify quite substantially the labour and environmental provisions before submitting the implementing bill to Congress; and in yet other cases, Congress simply refused to vote on the bill.

The fate of the unilateral initiatives taken by the United States government, including against the European Union and China, offers additional support for the argument that, unlike bilateralism, multilateralism reduces the active role of domestic actors. Countries could transform US unilateral measures into multilateral debates by filing complaints at the WTO. In this way, countries bypassed congressional authority and could force the United States government to reverse its original policies.

In short, the Bush administration's difficulties with Congress were largely an outcome of its non-conciliatory competitive liberalisation strategy combined with the administration's choice of partners. The preference for bilateralism over multilateralism led to the unintended consequence of allowing Congress to play a more active role in pursuing interests very much in conflict with Bush's own.

The preference for bilateralism over multilateralism also, of course, negatively affected US trading partners' bargaining leverage. Even agreements with little economic consequence to American business could still have grave economic consequences to the trading partner. For example, while the United States government grudgingly agreed to support a multilateral declaration regarding public health and international property rights, it introduced provisions to many of the bilateral trade agreements that obliged signatories to support a much more rigid intellectual property regime. Similarly, while countries fought at the Doha Round against including investment provisions in the trade agreement, bilateral agreements often contained investment clauses that granted greater access for the American service sector (Abbott 2004). With a Democratic majority in Congress, the Obama administration may be able to gain trade promotion authority and relaunch multilateral negotiations. To secure a stable and fair multilateral trading system, the new administration needs not only to revive multilateralism but to do so in a way that genuinely addresses the needs of poor and middle-income countries.

## BIBLIOGRAPHY

Abbott, Frederick M. (2004), "The Doha Declaration on the TRIPS Agreement and Public Health and the Contradictory Trend in Bilateral and Regional Free Trade Agreements", Occasional Paper 14, Quaker United Nations Office

Alden, Edward, Andrew Balls and Mure Dickie (2005), "Foreign exchanges: the American diplomacy behind China's revaluation", *Financial Times,* 25 July

Allen, Mike and Karen DeYoung (2003), "Bush Calls Trade Key To Mideast", *The Washington Post,* 10 May

Blustein, Paul (2006), "Senators Withdraw 'Nuclear' Bill in Trade Fight", *The Washington Post,* 29 September

Chorev, Nitsan (2007), *Remaking U.S. Trade Policy: From Protectionism to Globalization,* Ithaca: Cornell University Press

Destler, I. M. (2005), *American Trade Politics,* 4th ed., Washington, DC, Institute for International Economics

Goodman, Peter S. and Lori Montgomery (2007), "Path Is Cleared For Trade Deals", *The Washington Post,* 11 May

Hitt, Greg (2007), "Bipartisan Trade Harmony Imperilled by New Demand", *Wall Street Journal,* July 2007

Hitt, Greg and Neil King (2006), "Slow Track: Democratic Gains Raise Roadblocks To Free-Trade Push", *Wall Street Journal,* 11 November

King, Neil and Scott Miller (2003), "Trade Talks Fail Amid Big Divide Over Farm Issues", *Wall Street Journal,* 15 September

Lindsey, Brink (2003), "Americas: The Miami Fizzle – What Else but Cancun Redux?", *Wall Street Journal,* 28 November

Meyerson, Harold (2007), "Why the Rush on Trade?", *The Washington Post,* 7 November

Sanger, David E. (2003), "A Blink From the Bush Administration", *New York Times,* December 2003

Smilowitz, Elliot (2005), "Unions Blast CAFTA", *United Press International,* 11 May

Smith, Tony (2003), "Argentina and Brazil Align To Fight U.S. Trade Policy", *New York Times,* 21 October

Stokes, Bruce (2001), "Brazil's Brush-Off", *National Journal,* 33(15), p. 1096

Stokes, Bruce (2004), "Partisanship Trumps Protectionism", *National Journal,* 36(4), pp. 250–1

Ukman, Jason (2007), "Rights Cases Threaten To Derail Trade Pact", *The Washington Post,* 5 May

Vaughan, Martin (2005), "K Street Struck Out With Dems On CAFTA", *National Journal,* 37(32), p. 2532

Zoellick, Robert B. (2003), "America will not wait for the won't-do countries", *Financial Times,* 22 September

# PART III
# DOMESTIC POLICY LEADERSHIP

*Chapter 10*

# PRESIDENT BUSH AND THE ECONOMY

Graham Wilson

President George W. Bush left office with the United States and world economies in catastrophic condition. Millions of Americans lost their homes in mortgage foreclosures, the stock market fell by 40 per cent, unemployment rose rapidly and a full-scale recession threatened. In the largest extension of government ownership of business in American history, financial institutions, such as the mortgage giants Fannie Mae and Freddie Mac, the insurance giant AIG and nine major banks passed into total or majority government control. Even before the 2008 crash, many middle- and working-class Americans had seen their real wages stagnate. Most of the benefits of the modest levels of American economic growth over the two Bush terms went to the top 5 per cent of wage earners. Despite Republican rhetoric about small government and balanced budgets, government spending rose by 4 per cent of gross domestic product, the budget deficit doubled and the national debt surged to $11 trillion.

Bush's public reputation declined with the economy. By mid-2008, only 20 per cent of Americans approved of his performance on economic policy (May *Quinnipiac* poll), and three-quarters thought that Bush's policies had made the United States worse off (June *LA Times/Bloomberg* poll). In November 2008, Bush's approval ratings hit a record low of 20 per cent (*New York Times/CBS* poll). Economic conditions and Bush's low rating probably doomed the chances of any Republican candidate winning the presidency in 2008 (Lewis-Beck and Tien 2008) and contributed powerfully to the Democrats' gains in the House and Senate. Events called into question not only the policies of the administration but also the intellectual trends that, since the late 1970s, had fostered faith in markets and scepticism about government and its regulatory role. Bush's economic record thus damaged not only his party but also undercut the neo-liberal agenda he had supported throughout his political career. Even worse, some believed that the crash marked a permanent decline in the United States's position in the world.

## 1. THE PRESIDENCY AND ECONOMIC POLICY

The American public retains confidence in the ability of government to control the American economy (Pew 2008) but most experts disagree, contending that globalisation has reduced the degree to which any government or even a number of governments working together can influence the economy (Strange 1996; Held 2005). Nevertheless, the United States enjoys a special position in the international economy. Perhaps because the dollar has remained the basic unit of international exchange or because of the size of its economy, the United States is able to borrow money overseas more easily than other countries. A theoretical limit must exist beyond which the United States is unable to borrow but it was not reached during Bush's two terms. It is likely that countries that have loaned heavily to the United States, especially China, cannot afford to create a currency crisis by stopping current lending because a collapse in the value of the dollar would place their past investments at risk. In this sense, some countries therefore cannot afford *not* to lend the United States money. In consequence, US presidents continue to enjoy unusual freedom to sustain deficits in both the balance of payments and the government's own budget on a scale that would have prompted immediate crises for other nations.

United States presidents do, however, face greater institutional constraints in making economic policy than leaders of most advanced industrial nations do. Congress has the final say on expenditure and taxes, and thus controls the purse-strings. The Federal Reserve Board, or the Fed as it is widely known, controls monetary policy. It alone sets interest rates and is responsible for controlling inflation. It is one of the most autonomous and powerful of the world's central banks. There is a well-developed mechanism for consultation between the Treasury Department and the Fed but this in no way guarantees that the Fed will listen to the president's preferences.

While the nature of US institutions complicates and constrains the president's power over, and responsibility for the state of, the economy, the chief executive is still the leading figure in federal economic policymaking. Presidents propose budgets to Congress, have an opportunity mid-term to replace the chair of the Fed, and usually define the policy agenda. Trade policy is addressed in detail elsewhere in this volume, but fiscal policy, monetary policy and regulation during the Bush years are discussed below.

### *a. Fiscal Policy*

The area in which it is clearest that Bush had a decisive impact is fiscal policy. Bush pushed through Congress two of the three largest tax cuts in the nation's history. The first, in particular, was a major legislative accomplishment, given that Bush won 500,000 fewer popular votes than his Democratic opponent, Al Gore, in the 2000 election, and given that the Republicans held the Senate by only one vote where sixty are usually required to secure passage of most controversial legislation through the upper chamber. The Republicans actually lost control of the Senate in May 2001 when Republican Senator Jim Jeffords (Vermont) defected to the Democrats. Before he did so, however, the new Bush administration manoeuvred adroitly around the obstacle of Senate resistance by using budget reconciliation procedures that cannot be filibustered and therefore require only fifty-one, not sixty votes. Bush signed the tax cut, worth about $1.3 trillion, into law on 7 June 2001.

While they comprised a political triumph, it is debatable whether the tax cuts represented sound economic policy. Traditional conservative Republicans in the administration argued that the economy, even after the economic disruption wrought by the 9/11 attacks, did not need such a large stimulus and that the tax cuts would transform for the worse the government's finances. The question at the end of the Clinton presidency of how to use the government's growing budget surpluses was replaced with the much more familiar problem of how to contain ballooning budget deficits. Bush raised total government debt to more than double its highest point since World War II, but advocates of tax cuts in the administration, including Vice President Dick Cheney, argued that deficits were not important. Though the government's debt was lower as a percentage of gross domestic product (GDP) than government debt in some other OECD

(Organization for Economic Cooperation and Development) countries such as Italy, the absolute size of the debt was enormous. In summer 2008 the administration projected that Bush would leave his successor a deficit of $482 billion but even this figure was probably too low as it did not account fully for the cost of the wars in Iraq and Afghanistan. Before tallying in the extra borrowing to finance the bail-out of financial institutions in the autumn of 2008, the budget deficit was equal to 3.3 per cent of GDP. Attempts by Bush, and later President Barack Obama, to deal with the crash would more than double this figure. Moreover, Bush must face additional criticism for his handling of the economy because deficits during times of full employment are less justifiable economically than deficits during economic downturns, in part because they are unnecessary and actually constrain policy choices when times are bad.

Bush argued that if only Congress had cut expenditures, the deficits would not have been so large. This argument ignores the considerable increases in expenditure that occurred at the president's instigation. As noted above, some of the increase reflected the costs of responding to the 9/11 terrorist attacks and the two subsequent wars but, as conservatives lamented, much was unrelated to either terrorism or war. For example, and rather oddly, Bush was responsible for the single most expensive new domestic entitlement programme in decades, the prescription drug benefit for recipients of Medicare, the government health plan that covers all older Americans. Administration claims that it was trying to make expenditure cuts to balance its tax cuts are unconvincing. United States government expenditure was noticeably higher as a proportion of GDP at the end of Bush's White House tenure (38.3 per cent) than at the beginning (35.3 per cent), according to OECD data.

A more plausible defence of the administration is that it was making tax cuts on the basis of Keynesian economic theory. This defence is ironic, however, because Keynesian economics had been pronounced outmoded particularly, but not only, by conservatives. That it is ironic does not necessarily make it untrue. In the aftermath of the 9/11 attacks and during the recession following the sub-prime mortgage crisis of 2008, the administration did, indeed, employ a variety of remedies, including classic Keynesian fiscal measures, to stimulate demand. One trite but nonetheless symbolically important example is Bush's advice to patriotic Americans post 9/11 to go shopping. Keynes in the afterlife must have been recalling his adage in his *General Theory* that "Practical men, who believe themselves to be quite exempt from any intellectual influences, are usually the slaves of some defunct economist." If the administration was influenced consciously or unconsciously by Keynesianism, however, it was a one-sided distortion of Keynes by the very vote-anxious politicians who had themselves done much to discredit his work. In other words, the administration proved willing to cut taxes to stimulate demand when necessary early in the first term but did not act to restore them when the economy improved between 2002 and 2007. The deficits created during prosperity were an unhelpful backdrop to, and a constraint on, the large deficit spending that most economists felt was essential to combat the consequences of the later crash.

### *b. Monetary Policy*

United States presidents have a modest ability to influence monetary policy. Their primary means of influencing interest rates and the rate of inflation is through appointing or reappointing the chair of the United States central bank, the Fed, which itself controls monetary policy. Through careful institutional design, presidents have to wait two years into their first term to change the Fed chair. Bush inherited Alan Greenspan, gave him another four-year term in 2002, and appointed Ben Bernanke in 2006.

Greenspan was a major and respected figure in the United States government – referred to as "the maestro" and the "oracle" – but his reputation is unlikely to withstand the crash of 2008. Greenspan, perhaps inappropriately credited with engendering the prosperity of the 1990s, used his popularity to promote conservative economic causes in general. Such was his prestige that a Democratic president, Bill Clinton, did not feel able to displace him. Greenspan's successor, Bernanke, was also in the conservative monetarist tradition, an admirer of that icon of right-wing economists, Milton Friedman. Unlike Greenspan, Bernanke did not aspire to use his position to promote the conservative agenda in general and limited his public comments to issues connected with his responsibilities. Moreover, faced with the danger of financial meltdown in 2008, Bernanke was surprisingly flexible, departing easily from conservative nostrums on the role of government. As Wall Street tottered, Bernanke was a generous provider of welfare for capitalists, propping up the merchant banks that had made disastrous purchases of derivatives based on sub-prime mortgages. In one of the largest government acquisitions of financial institutions in United States history, Bernanke helped arrange the government takeover of Fannie Mae and Freddie Mac, the privately owned but government-created traders in mortgages. Deeply aware of the errors of monetary policy that contributed to the Great Depression, Bernanke cut interest rates aggressively, offered to swap US treasury bonds for worthless junk bonds held by banks, and expanded the money supply by buying back treasury bonds – not conventional conservative monetary policies.

In addition to the limited and delayed power of appointment, presidents can also try to influence monetary policy through persuasion. There are deeply institutionalised weekly conferences between the Fed and the Treasury, and the administration also makes its views known on what interest rates and monetary policy should be. No doubt it is wise for a chair of the Fed seeking reappointment to pay attention to the president's views. Although the Fed is supposed to be autonomous, Greenspan in practice was part of the inner sanctum of the Bush administration's economic policymakers, sharing views on policy as though a member of the administration, not the leader of a supposedly independent agency (Suskind 2004). In general, Greenspan was consciously and openly a supporter of the conservative cause, facilitating co-ordination between the Fed and the administration. Although worried about the effect of Bush's major tax cuts on government debt, Greenspan remained loyal to the conservative cause and did not voice his doubts in public about lax fiscal policy or balance it with a tougher monetary policy. There are therefore real questions about whether the independence of the Fed was compromised by Greenspan's close association with the administration. Bernanke consciously avoided being drawn so deeply into the inner circle of administration policymaking (Harris 2008).

### *c. Regulation*

Government in the United States pursues many of its objectives through the regulation of many aspects of American life, often in excruciating detail and with a legalistic, adversarial approach to enforcement. While liberals and the Clinton administration explored innovations in regulation intended to overcome these problems, conservatives sought to minimise or repeal regulations, particularly those focused on environmental or consumer protection that are unwelcome to business and that they contended impeded economic growth.

Bush pursued the conservative, anti-regulatory agenda assiduously, right up to the administration's end when he issued a spate of deregulations, such as a reduction in emission standards for power plants. His refusal to ratify the Kyoto accords on global warming symbolised his antipathy to environmental regulation. Similarly, not until the price of fuel started to escalate rapidly in 2007 did the administration agree to raise the mileage requirements for new vehicles. For most of Bush's presidency, the new car market was dominated by inefficient vehicles such as sport utility vehicles (SUVs) and pick-up trucks. The symbol of the era and an environmental disaster was the Hummer, a civilian version of a military vehicle that achieved spectacularly poor fuel consumption.

In general, and probably not without justification, Republican administrations have thought of social regulatory agencies – in the environmental field, for example – as being staffed by civil servants who are enthusiastic about their agencies' regulatory missions. The challenge for the Bush administration was how to rein in these regulators. Its answer was to use central agencies such as the Office of Management and Budget (OMB) and to appoint anti-regulatory conservatives to key positions within agencies. The OMB has long had the power to control the development and issue of new regulations, a power now exercised by the Office of Information and Regulatory Affairs (OIRA) which is part of OMB. Previous Republican presidents insisted on proposed new regulations passing cost-benefit analyses that tended to emphasise costs over benefits. The OIRA gave the Bush administration greater capacity to block proposed new regulations, a capacity that was used effectively. One well-known example was the use of the OIRA to delay a regulation designed to protect migrating whales by slowing ships entering Boston Harbour; in doing so, the OIRA deferred to the wishes of shipping interests and the anti-regulatory sentiment of the president. The ships continued full steam ahead. The OMB and OIRA also frequently prevented the release of scientific papers written by agency staff when the papers' conclusions did not match administration goals.

The administration was also determined in using the power to make political appointments to strengthen its control over regulatory agencies. The number of political appointees increased significantly, and changes in the senior bureaucracy – such as the creation of the Senior Executive Service (SES) – also expanded opportunities for political control, in part because the new appointees have less job security than traditional positions. As Lewis (2008) shows, Bush also proved adroit at using tactics that would undermine the supposedly secure position of regular civil servants, forcing them out and filling their positions with an SES or political appointee. Civil servants naturally resented these tactics as well as the administration's willingness to disregard scientific evidence that did not support its cause.

The major exception to the administration's deregulatory zealotry was the adoption of the Sarbanes–Oxley accountancy regulations. Sarbanes–Oxley imposed much more stringent, possibly overly stringent, accounting procedures on American corporations and their overseas subsidiaries. Sarbanes–Oxley resulted from the Enron scandal which broke early in Bush's first term; the supposedly highly profitable giant proved to be a facade, disguising dubious accountancy procedures. Bush, a friend of Enron CEO Kenneth Lay – whom the president referred to as "Kenny Boy" – was not in a position to resist calls for reform.

Sarbanes–Oxley excepted, the Bush years were a golden age for business lobbyists. The administration was eager to please them and, on a number of occasions, provided business with exclusive opportunities to shape its thinking. Vice President Cheney's taskforce on energy policy typified the administration's values. Shielded from public scrutiny, it allowed almost no input from environmental groups but very considerable input from energy corporations. The OIRA similarly worked closely with business lobbyists. Ironically, this anti-regulatory zeal would allow the crash of 2008 that was such a blow to American business in general. Before discussing the crash in detail, one other aspect of Bush's economic record requires review.

### *d. Growth and Equality*

It is often said that Americans do not object to income inequality as long as everyone's income is increasing. As Bartels (2008) shows, however, there are strong reasons to dispute this piece of conventional wisdom: Americans do care about equality.

For the first seven years of the Bush administration, the United States economy grew by an average of 2.2 per cent a year. The results of this growth were very unequally distributed. The top 5 per cent of wage earners saw their real incomes rise by 1.2 per cent over the first seven of Bush's eight years in charge, and the top 20 per cent by 1.6 percent. In contrast, those in the middle of the income distribution saw their incomes stagnate and those at the bottom actually saw their incomes fall (Bernstein 2008). Far from a rising tide raising all boats, the higher paid benefited from a wave of income growth and the lower paid were, at best, stuck in slack water.

This pattern of increasing inequality is not unique to the United States. Many OECD countries saw widening gaps between the incomes of the highest paid and other workers. The causes are much debated but certainly did not begin in 2001 with the inauguration of Bush. It is clear, however, that the Bush administration not only failed to counteract the trend but actively accentuated it through its taxation policies. Its tax cuts are not only open to criticism as bad fiscal policy but were also heavily skewed in favour of higher-income groups. In contrast, as Alesina and Glaeser (2004) show, other advanced industrialised countries offset the trends towards inequality caused by structural economic conditions, but the Bush administration chose not to.

## 2. COMING HOME TO ROOST: THE BUSH RECORD AND THE CRASH OF 2008

The United States economy initially seemed to show resilience during the first years of the twenty-first century. Despite a limited recession in early 2001, the economic and psychological shock of the 9/11 attacks did not trigger deeper economic troubles; the economy achieved modest growth for most of Bush's tenure, and unemployment remained low until the end of 2008. The United States did somewhat better in economic policy than the Euro area and slightly less well than the OECD as a whole, and retained its position as the wealthiest of the advanced economies. The unequal distribution of the gains from growth seemed to be the only major blemish on what had been, for most of the administration's tenure, a record of moderate success.

The modest successes of the first seven years were eclipsed, however, by the dramatic crash of 2008. The relationship between the administration and the downturn can be analysed at three levels: its responsibility for the underlying conditions that led to the crash; its handling of events as the crash unfolded; and the long-term consequences of its actions.

### *a. Responsibility*

How far was Bush to blame for the economic catastrophe? No doubt the causes of the crash and the degree of the administration's responsibility for it will be debated by historians with as much fervour as today's historians debate the causes of the Great Crash of 1929. Five aspects command particular attention.

First, the administration's decisions to pursue tax cuts and accept the cost of increased dependence on borrowing, especially from China, may have produced an inherently unstable situation. Owing to its ability to borrow overseas, the United States avoided the economic constraints that deficits in government budgets and balance of payments customarily impose on other countries. Yet this borrowing introduced vast quantities of low-cost capital into the American economy. The dollar's overvaluation made it unprofitable to invest in manufacturing, so capital flowed into ever riskier investments including the bonds based on the now notorious sub-prime mortgages (Judis 2008).

Second, the administration's commitment to deregulation made it highly unlikely that any of the multiple regulatory agencies with some capacity to prevent risky behaviour by financial institutions would, in fact, do so. Large profits in financial circles are often the result of potentially risky innovations. While innovation is the lifeblood of successful market systems, regulators should watch for innovations where risk might destabilise the financial system and thereby the economy. Trading in bonds linked to mortgages, including bonds based on high-risk or sub-prime mortgages, was one such innovation. Creating and selling sub-prime mortgages was such a highly profitable activity that any financial institution that did not take part seemed to neglect their shareholders' interests. As events were to prove, however, these bonds were based on assets of dubious worth. Mortgages had been issued to home buyers far in excess of those buyers' capacity to pay and, when these mortgages had been repackaged into complex derivatives, it was virtually impossible to calculate their value. Ideally, regulators should have stepped in to end this practice but the administration's choices for key regulatory positions made it unlikely that necessary new regulations would be forthcoming. For example, Christopher Cox, the conservative former Republican member of the House of Representatives, who was appointed to lead the Securities and Exchange Commission (SEC), could be counted on to discourage innovative regulation. Nor was Ben Bernanke, the president's choice as Fed chair, a vigorous regulator. The administration's antipathy to regulation made the creation of new regulations to deal with risky financial innovations unlikely but not all the blame can be pinned on it. Opposition to regulation certainly was not confined to the administration. Republican Senator Phil Gramm of Texas, for example, took the lead in the Senate in the late 1990s in insisting that the financial derivatives at the heart of the 2008 crisis should not be regulated (Lipton and Labaton 2008). Nor was there much enthusiasm for regulation in the Clinton administration, especially from Secretary of the Treasury Robert Rubin. Leading congressional Democrats with close ties to Wall Street, such as Senators Charles Schumer (New York) and Christopher Dodd (Connecticut), were also active in opposing stricter regulation. Nonetheless, the primary responsibility lies with the Bush administration. Risky behaviour by financial institutions grew dramatically under Bush, and his administration failed to respond.

Third, the determined ideology of the president and his administration made it reluctant to recognise the instability that the markets were producing. Markets are supposed to produce optimal outcomes, and it was a deep shock to conservatives such as Greenspan that markets were not self-balancing.

Fourth, the quality of the administration's economic policymaking can also be questioned. The primary discussions of economic policy within the executive branch take place between the Treasury, the OMB and the Council of Economic Advisers (CEA). The secretary of commerce is also part of the economic policy group, particularly when trade issues arise. Inevitably, the White House staff is a key participant in major policy decisions. The key actors in the Bush administration initially were Bush's economic aide in the White House, Larry Lindsey, CEA Chair Michael Bosworth, Fed Chair Alan Greenspan, Secretary of the Treasury Paul O'Neill and OMB Director Mitch Daniels. The administration's early years produced what could have been an interesting struggle for ideas between traditional conservatives, such as O'Neill and Greenspan, and tax cutters such as Lindsey. Indeed, presidential scholars often argue that such a diversity of opinions within an administration is useful (Campbell 1986; Porter 1982) but this did not prove to be the case for the Bush administration.

O'Neill was quickly marginalised and discovered some general characteristics of policymaking in the Bush administration. He thought somewhat naively that policy would be decided in debate between the economic policy principals with close attention to, and appropriate respect for, the economic analyses and facts provided by the relevant government departments, including the Treasury. He soon saw that debate was limited or avoided altogether, that ideological purity carried more weight than analysis, and that, as noted above, the administration tended to discount information and advice from civil servants and the relevant government departments. The administration committed itself to tax cuts and did not worry overly about their impact on the deficit, despite undoubtedly being aware of the experts' concerns.

Finally, Bush's personality also made it difficult to foster effective debate. It was difficult to involve Bush in a detailed debate on policy. Arguments for organising the presidency on the basis of recruiting advisers with differing opinions generally assume that the president is capable of resolving the clash of opinions. Bush was unwilling, and perhaps unable, to perform this role. Uninterested in policy details and used to the hierarchical decision-making models of the business world, Bush did not want to debate options and was even less keen to read conflicting memorandums. Preferring to delegate complex, though crucial, decisions to others, the president apparently took little part in deciding what the role of the federal government should be in rescuing collapsing financial institutions in the late summer of 2008. Making this problem worse, the administration also had rapid turnover in its key economic positions. Bush went through four OMB directors (Mitch Daniels, Josh Bolten, Rob Portman and Jim Nussle) and three Treasury secretaries (O'Neill, John Snow and Henry Paulson), for example.

In sum, the administration did not develop an advisory system that was well placed to question its assumptions about economic policy. The president chose not to think in these broad terms, often disengaging from the issues. The predominance of ideology rendered the administration less capable of recognising the signs of the on-coming crisis. Nor was the administration well served by the rapid turnover in its leading staff.

### *b. Handling the Crisis*

Despite the criticism of the administration's economic policymaking process outlined above, the Bush team's response to the crisis showed surprising flexibility. As the administration neared its end, the ideological disputes of the early Bush years between more traditional, deficit-averse conservatives and more radical tax cutters were resolved in favour of the former. Bernanke, though a conservative monetarist, was more restrained in offering policy opinions and more willing to act pragmatically than his predecessor, Alan Greenspan. Both, however, were willing to accept – perhaps had no alternative than to accept – that the dire economic situation of 2008 demanded government intervention and nationalisation that would have been regarded as extreme liberalism in a Democratic administration.

Bailing out failing companies, such as Bear Stearns, Fannie Mae and others, stood in sharp contrast to the advice that the United States had freely offered to other countries: no company is too big to be allowed to fail. Yet in 2008 the Bush administration uncertainly and unpredictably operated on precisely the grounds that some financial institutions were too big to be allowed to fail. This was not the only departure from the Washington consensus in 2008. The Treasury secretary in a conservative Republican administration called in nine major banks and demanded that they sell stock in their businesses to the government. It is equally astounding that a conservative Republican administration took two of the world's largest mortgage companies, Fannie Mae and Freddie Mac, and one of the world's largest insurance companies, AIG, into government ownership. Anyone who had predicted these events immediately after Bush's re-election in 2004, or even in spring 2008, would have been suspected of living in the realms of fantasy. Even the $750 billion bail-out of financial institutions in autumn 2008 involved a significant break with orthodoxy. Risking rewarding "moral hazard", the government sought the money to buy up the "junk bonds" or "toxic assets" created through irresponsible lending. Breaking dramatically with the Republican tradition of opposing the extension of government power, the administration successfully sought almost unlimited discretion for the secretary of the Treasury in spending the bail-out funds.

The case of the American car makers was rather different. Ford, General Motors and Chrysler requested subsidised loans of $25 billion for research and retooling to compensate for their failure to invest in fuel-efficient cars. It soon became apparent that much larger subsidies were necessary if General Motors and Chrysler were to survive. Although such subsidies were incompatible with supposedly core American beliefs in free markets, Michigan, home of the industry, had the advantage of being viewed as a battleground in the 2008 elections. Both parties thus rushed to endorse the economically questionable loans. Bush could at least claim that in abandoning free-market principles he was approaching the crisis with flexibility and pragmatism. Unfortunately the administration's pragmatism was tempered by an odd and destabilising free-market fundamentalism in its decision to allow the major investment bank, Lehman Brothers, to go bankrupt in mid-September 2008. The stock market declined by 40 per cent in the weeks that followed as faith in financial institutions in the United States and around the world crumbled. Lehman Brothers' failure was the definitive event in the crisis becoming global. Lehman Brothers was probably no less deserving of help than institutions that were rescued, such as Bear Stearns, and its fall prompted both questioning of the future of all investment banks and their ultimate absorption by the commercial banking industry.

As the crisis escalated, major banks and insurance company AIG passed in large part into government ownership – an ironic, unintended consequence of free-market fundamentalism. Critics of the administration contended that the assistance to the financial sector did nothing to address what might be regarded as the root of the problem: the rising tide of mortgage foreclosures and the collapse of house prices. In this view, government aid should have been targeted on homeowners struggling to pay their mortgages, not on financial institutions owning securities based on the value of those mortgages.

Increasingly isolated within his own party, Bush was highly dependent on congressional Democrats to secure passage of the bank bail-out. In the House, the bail-out failed initially on a 228 to 205 vote, with Republicans casting 133 of the no votes. A catastrophic day on the stock market followed and the bail-out was revived seventy-four to twenty-five in the Senate, with Democrats providing slightly more of the yes votes (thirty-nine) and Republicans slightly more of the no votes (fifteen). The politics in the House was complicated not only by the antagonisms both of conservative Republicans to government intervention and of liberal Democrats to bailing out the bankers who had caused the crisis but also by Democrats determined not to be held largely responsible for an unpopular if vital measure. Speaker Nancy Pelosi and her lieutenants were determined that a significant number of Republicans support the measure. Ultimately this was arranged and the bailout cleared the House by 263 to 171. Nonetheless, Republicans cast the vast majority (108) of the no votes. While it is not unprecedented for a president to be so reliant on the votes of the opposing party, presidents rarely find their own party in Congress so antagonistic in a time of crisis. It was a striking measure of Bush's low standing.

## CONCLUSION: THE ECONOMIC CONSEQUENCES OF PRESIDENT BUSH

George Bush's economic legacy will be defined by the length and depth of the recession that began towards the end of his administration. If it is long and deep, the perception that George W. Bush was one of the worst presidents in American history is likely to be cemented.

At least four consequences of the 2008 crash were clear at the end of Bush's term. First, the crash changed the structure of the American financial system. The disappearance of investment banks as separate entities was perhaps the clearest aspect of this change, with familiar and long-established names in American finance, such as Lehman Brothers, vanishing from Wall Street altogether.

Second, the dominance of the Washington consensus public policy discourse of faith in markets, deregulation and a minimal role for government is over. Even Greenspan felt obliged to express doubts about the degree to which market forces operated as beneficently as he had assumed. While the American public's attachment to capitalism was unshaken, there was considerable anger at corporate executives, stoked by a degree of banker insouciance reminiscent of the French aristocracy on the eve of the revolution. No sooner had AIG been rescued by the taxpayers, for example, than some of its executives flew off to Britain for an expensive shooting holiday paid for by the firm. Later, and to a chorus of public and political disgust, some of its traders, including those in the division most responsible for the corporation's huge losses, were awarded large bonuses. The extent and form of reregulation of the financial sphere were necessarily left to the Obama administration but even right-wing commentators suggested that government aid for companies be accompanied by a stipulation that no corporation receiving it should pay its executives a salary higher than the president. Perhaps of more enduring consequence was the widespread feeling that markets needed to be guided by a firmer hand from government.

Third, the success of the financial sector in obtaining help from the United States government – and the absence of onerous conditions such as limits on paying dividends and bonuses while receiving aid – encouraged other industries to ask for assistance. If bankers could be bailed out, why not the American car industry and others? Again, the Obama administration would be required to decide where to draw the line.

Fourth, measures to combat the crash added significantly to government debt. Some accounts suggested that the government budget deficit was likely to be equivalent to 5 per cent of GDP. Few thought it desirable to cut expenditure or increase taxes during the recession that followed the crash but it remained an open question whether the extent of government borrowing would have important consequences in terms of America's power in the world or the affordability of new policy initiatives by the Obama administration.

In sum, the Bush administration changed the United States economy and American economic thinking significantly but it did not accomplish this deliberately or bring about changes that it would have desired. Bush had a profound impact but one opposite to the one he would have wished.

## BIBLIOGRAPHY

Alesina, Alberto and Edwin L. Glaeser (2004), *Fighting Poverty in the US and Europe: A World of Difference,* Oxford: Oxford University Press

Bartels, Larry (2008), *Unequal Democracy: The Political Economy of the New Gilded Age,* Princeton: Princeton University Press

Bernstein, Jared (2008), "Median Income Rose as did Poverty in 2007",

*Economic Policy Institute,* 26 August, at http://www.epi.org/

Campbell, Colin (1986), *Managing the Presidency: Carter, Reagan and the Search for Executive Harmony,* Pittsburgh: University of Pittsburgh Press

Harris, Ethan (2008), *Ben Bernanke's Fed: The Federal Reserve After Greenspan,* Cambridge, MA: Harvard Business Press

Held, David and Anthony Barnett, eds (2005), *Debating Globalization,* Cambridge: Polity

Judis, John B. (2008), "Debt Man Walking", *The New Republic,* 3 December, pp. 19–23

Lewis, David E. (2008), *The Politics of Presidential Appointments: Political Control and Bureaucratic Performance,* Princeton: Princeton University Press

Lewis-Beck, Michael and Michael Tien (2008), "The Job of the President and the Jobs Model Forecast", *PS,* pp. 687–90

Lipton, Eric and Stephen Labaton (2008), "The Reckoning: A Deregulator Looks Back Unswayed", *New York Times,* 17 November

Pew Research Center (2008), "Inflation Staggers Public But Economy Still Seen as Fixable"

Porter, Roger (1982), *Presidential Decision Making: The Economic Policy Board,* Cambridge: Cambridge University Press

Strange, Susan (1996), *The Retreat of the State: The Diffusion of Power in the World Economy,* Cambridge: Cambridge University Press

Suskind, Ron (2004), *The Price of Loyalty: George W. Bush, the White House and the Education of Paul O'Neill,* New York: Simon and Schuster

*Chapter 11*

# THE POLITICS OF AGING

Alex Waddan

As the Bush administration drew to a close, the president seemed marginalised from events. This made it easy to forget just how ambitious President Bush's White House had been in its earlier years as it sought to redraw the contours of domestic policy. The tax cuts of 2001 and 2003, the No Child Left Behind (NCLB) education reform and the appointment of conservative judges to federal courts all marked significant political victories. Furthermore, the administration had embarked on major legislative efforts to reform the United States's two biggest public policy programmes, Medicare, which provides health care for the nation's seniors, and Social Security, the public pension scheme. These were both bold political advances on to terrain normally occupied by the Democratic Party. Hence, examining these two reform efforts provides an instructive account of the Bush presidency and its capacity to impose its political will.

As it was, the attempts to reorganise Medicare and Social Security had quite different outcomes that provide a startling illustration of the contrasting fortunes of President Bush's domestic policy agenda in his first and second terms. In 2003 President Bush, with great fanfare, signed into law the Medicare Modernization Act (MMA), but in 2005 the plan to transform the Social Security system made no legislative progress, despite the elections of 2004 confirming unified Republican government. As will be detailed below the MMA was an ideologically hybrid package and many Republicans later lamented their support for the bill; critically, however, the final passage of the Act showed just how decisively, and indeed brazenly, the White House and the Republican leadership in Congress were prepared to act in order to get their way. In contrast the legislative efforts in 2005 were badly mishandled, with the White House unable to impose partisan discipline for what would have been a landmark reform of the country's biggest social policy programme. In hindsight it is evident that the effort to reform Social Security was a grave political miscalculation that undermined Republican and conservative optimism in the wake of the 2004 elections. Moreover, opposition to Bush's plan partially to privatise the public pension system provided a rallying point for dispirited congressional Democrats. Hence this failed policy initiative did much to set the political tone for Bush's second term.

Integral to President Bush's agenda was to build on the conservative foundations laid by Ronald Reagan in the 1980s; one of the chief targets of Reagan's rhetoric was the welfare state. In this context, reform of Medicare and Social Security, the bulwark programmes of the American welfare state, would be a signature achievement and cement Bush's place as a landmark conservative president. In reality, Reagan himself had not really taken on this task. Reagan's complaints about the size of government were consistent and a number of discretionary programmes were cut back (Davies 2003) but his efforts at a conservative reform of Social Security barely amounted to a skirmish and, as he retreated from that policy battlefield, he ended up signing legislation that increased the Social Security payroll tax and more generally reinforced the existing structures and principles of that programme (Light 1995). In the 2000 campaign, however, Bush promised both Medicare and Social Security reform with the latter particularly designed to push the Reagan revolution beyond what had proved possible in the 1980s. This chapter examines the ideological implications of these reform efforts and analyses why there was such a difference in the final outcomes across policy areas and between Bush's first and second terms.

## 1. MEDICARE REFORM

The story behind the enactment of the MMA of 2003 is a complex one both in terms of its legislative progress and its political development. The headline aspects as the bill was enacted were twofold. First, with regard to process, were the extraordinary scenes as the House voted on the final conference version of the bill. In an unprecedented manner, the House Republican leadership kept the vote open for three hours as they worked to overturn an initial 219 to 215 defeat into a

220 to 215 victory. During that three-hour period, Speaker Dennis Hastert and Health and Human Services Secretary Tommy Thompson patrolled corridors through the night seeking to persuade reluctant Republicans (Pear and Toner 2003). Bush's legislative affairs director David Hobbs awakened a jet-lagged president at 4.00 a.m. so that he could talk to those still wavering (Draper 2007: 280). Second, the policy headline was an apparently very unconservative expansion of Medicare, as a benefit providing subsidised prescription medicines for seniors was added to the programme. In order properly to understand why the vote on the bill was so close amid much partisan rancour and to explain why unified Republican government produced a bill that, on the face of it, was ideologically counter-intuitive, it is necessary to go back to the final months of the Clinton administration. It is also important to take note of the considerable small print of the MMA that included a number of clauses and provisions that were much more in tune with conservative sentiment than the principle of the prescription medicine benefit itself (Hacker and Pierson 2005: 85–93; Jaenicke and Waddan 2006).

The idea of adding a prescription medicine benefit to Medicare was thrust into the political spotlight by President Clinton in his 1999 State of the Union address. Clinton was then able to suggest that this new benefit would be paid for out of the projected budget surpluses (Clinton 1999). The rationale for the initiative was that many seniors were paying considerable amounts of their own money for their prescribed medication. When Medicare was established in 1965, the programme paid for in-hospital medicines but did not pay for outpatient prescription medicines. At that time this seemed a satisfactory arrangement for patients since most drugs were administered in hospitals. As an increasing number of medicines became available for outpatients, however, so this gap in Medicare's coverage became increasingly significant. By the early 1990s the nation's seniors were spending as high a proportion of their income on health care as they had before the Medicare programme was established, with the cost of prescription medicines an important contributory factor (Hacker 2004: 253). As it was, Clinton's proposals made little progress but the issue remained on the political agenda into the 2000 presidential election campaign. At this stage, embracing the principle of expanding Medicare coverage sat more comfortably with the Democratic candidate Al Gore than with his Republican opponent. As the campaign developed it became evident that the question of providing prescription medicines for the nation's elderly was an issue of the "first-order" (Oberlander 2003: 189). Candidate Bush felt compelled to respond in order to at least have a plan on the table. Hence he declared that he, too, would provide a new benefit and that this would be a top priority (Carey 2000: 2084). Gore still comfortably won among the 7 per cent of voters who named Medicare and a prescription medicine benefit as the most important issues of the election (NEP Exit Poll 2000) but the new President Bush had made a headline commitment that would prove hard to ignore.

For the first two years of the Bush administration the question of how to design a prescription medicine benefit for the elderly was kicked around by congressional Republicans and Democrats in a noisy, but unproductive, game of political football. Critically, however, the game continued even as forecasts of budget surplus turned into the reality of fiscal deficits, in part a consequence of Bush's fiscal policies and his tax cuts in particular. Congressional Democrats consistently offered up more generous packages to seniors than the Republican Party, and with no legislation on the books by the time of the 2002 mid-term elections the Democrats emphasised their credentials as the party that was committed to expanding access to health care. This perception was confirmed by polls reinforcing the view that the public trusted the Democrats emphasised their opponents on the prescription medicines issue (Serafini 2002). It is ironic, therefore, that the advent of unified Republican government in Washington DC was the prelude to legislative action on the issue. This was because Republican control of all the levers of legislative and executive power meant that partisan lines of responsibility were much more clear cut. Blame for further policy inaction would lie firmly with the White House and the Republican leadership in Congress. Moroever, enacting legislation to provide a new drug benefit would give the opportunity for the Republicans to claim political credit in a policy domain that normally favoured the Democrats.

The determination of the White House to act decisively was therefore not surprising but it is still worth reflecting on how far the administration shifted from its original proposals. Upon taking office the president put forward a plan that would have distributed $48 billion in block grants to the states over four years to fund a drug benefit for the nation's seniors on a means-tested basis. In December

2003 President Bush signed into law a bill with estimated costs of $410 billion over ten years. Furthermore, there was a significant philosophical change from the nature of the proposals in January 2001 to those enacted in late 2003 as the White House acknowledged that any new benefit would need to be available to all Americans rather than being means tested. Importantly this meant that any new benefit would, like the wider Medicare system, be a social insurance entitlement rather than a residual safety-net arrangement.

Shortly after the bill was signed it emerged that the administration had been prepared to pay an even higher price to get the legislation passed than it had admitted at the time. Within two months of President Bush signing the law the estimated cost had risen to $534 billion over ten years. Even more remarkably it then became clear that the administration had deliberately kept the latter figure suppressed during the final stages of debate about the MMA in order not to frighten fiscally conservative Republican members of Congress. As Aberbach explains that was a prime example of the strong-arm tactics, even deceit, used by an administration determined to get its own way (Aberbach 2005: 141). Moreover, a year later the ten-year cost of the bill was estimated at $724 billion. As many in Congress railed at this increase the president insisted he would veto any attempt at scaling back the benefit as he continued to hail it as a "landmark achievement" (Pear 2005). Some Republicans nevertheless expressed buyer's remorse. Senator Trent Lott, for one, regretted: "I think I made a big mistake . . . That's one of the worst votes I've cast in my 32 years in Congress" (Carey 2005: 726). In September 2005 Senator John McCain suggested that the law be reversed: "I'm saying cancel it. It was a bad idea to start with" (cited in Bartlett 2006: 80). Conservative commentators and pundits also expressed their discomfort (Bartlett 2006; Moore 2004: 105). Yet, for all the anguish about the cost of the drug benefit, it was far from comprehensive in terms of the coverage that it offered to seniors. For example, the law contained a so-called doughnut hole, meaning that once an individual's annual medication bill hit $2,250 they would not receive any more assistance until it increased beyond $3,600 per annum.

According to Democratic critics of the bill, one reason why it was so expensive without being comprehensive was that the administration had deliberately not flexed all the muscles of government. Critically the law prohibited Medicare from using its buying power as a lever to negotiate with the pharmaceutical companies for cheaper medicines, even though this was already the practice of the Veterans Administration. The law also stipulated that the benefit be provided by private insurers rather than directly through the Medicare programme. The emphasis on delivery through private insurers and minimal state intervention in price setting reflected conservative preferences. Several other aspects of the MMA package also reflected a conservative socio-economic outlook. One element that caused particular fury on the Democratic side was the inclusion of a clause expanding the availability of Health Savings Accounts (HSAs). HSAs, which had previously been available only to limited numbers on an experimental basis, are tax-privileged savings accounts that can be used to pay for health care. Supporters of these accounts see them as a means of increasing choice to individuals by giving people greater opportunity to find a health insurance plan tailored to their needs, particularly with regard to plans with high deductibles, where people trade off cheaper insurance packages against higher fixed initial payments on any claim. Opponents see HSAs as a means of further dividing the insurance market to the benefit of the healthy and wealthy since they should be more willing to take the risk of paying a higher deductible. Individuals likely to require medical treatment could continue with more traditional insurance packages but possibly at a higher premium since they would be unattractive customers for insurance companies. Former Speaker of the House Newt Gingrich was so enamoured of HSAs that he rallied those congressional Republicans who had their doubts about the MMA. Calling HSAs "the single most important change in health care policy in 60 years", Gingrich urged passage of the MMA despite its cost (Dreyfus 2004: 26). Gingrich's claim about the impact of HSAs was an exaggeration but the capacity of these accounts to change the nature of the health insurance market received very little attention during the public debate about the MMA legislation.

It is also worth reflecting on the extensive interest-group activity focused on the new benefit. The Pharmaceutical Research and Manufacturers of America (PhRMA), while not in principle opposed to the new benefit, lobbied hard to ensure that it came with as little government regulation as was possible. On the other hand, pressing for as extensive a benefit as possible at the lowest cost was the powerful seniors' organisation, the American Association of Retired

Persons or AARP (Stone 2002). As it was, PhRMA largely got its way but, to the surprise and frustration of many Democrats, the AARP also endorsed the final version of the MMA.

Despite being enacted in 2003 the plan was not in fact scheduled to come into effect until 1 January 2006. As that date neared it was evident that there would be many different packages offered by insurance companies with a whole range of premiums and co-payments for Medicare beneficiaries to choose from. It was also evident that the rules governing the new benefit were so complex that even the government advice to seniors was at times misleading. Furthermore, there were various teething problems as some insurers restricted access to some medicines or imposed onerous requirements before they would pay for them (Pear 2005, 2006). There was disagreement over how effective the new benefit was proving to be. Administration officials proclaimed success, maintaining that there were more plans with lower costs to beneficiaries than anyone had predicted in 2003. Michael Levitt, the Secretary of Health and Human Services asserted: "The Medicare drug benefit is saving seniors an average of $1,200 a year" (Pear 2007). On the other hand a *New York Times* investigation found that "Tens of thousands of Medicare recipients have been victims of deceptive sales tactics and had claims improperly denied by private insurers that run the system's huge new drug benefit program" (Pear 2007). At the close of the Bush era, government spending on the new benefit was lower than anticipated. In the fiscal year ending 30 September 2008, the government's spending on the drug programme had declined by 12 per cent over the previous year. This was largely because of the use of cheaper generic medicines. On the other hand, the cost to seniors rose as insurers raised premiums and co-payments (Appleby 2008).

## 2. SOCIAL SECURITY

Given the steadfast opposition of most Democrats, and uncertainty among Republican ranks, it was a mark of the Bush administration's political willpower that it forced the MMA through Congress. One consequence of that victory and the capacity to push through the controversial tax cuts of 2001 and 2003 was to convince key figures in the White House, notably Chief of Staff Andrew Card, that the administration could win on the even bigger issue of Social Security reform (Draper 2007: 294). Social Security, established in 1935, is the most significant social policy programme in the United States, covering over 95 per cent of American workers. It is the primary source of income for many elderly Americans and is critical in reducing the poverty rate among retirees. One analysis demonstrated that, between 2000 and 2002, Social Security benefits on average lifted the annual incomes of thirteen million seniors above the federal poverty line. Without those benefits, 46.8 per cent of the country's elderly would have had incomes below the poverty line but, after Social Security payments, this number stood at 8.7 per cent (Sherman and Shapiro 2005). Unlike welfare programmes for working-age Americans, Social Security is seen as a legitimate reward, an entitlement, for those who have entered retirement and is hugely popular. Moreover, the programme has a powerful constituency of supporters that, through the AARP, has a clear political voice.

Nevertheless, the administration felt that it had a political opportunity to challenge the fundamental tenets of the Social Security programme. From a conservative perspective, Social Security reform was the holy grail of politics as it offered the chance to undermine one of the fundamental building blocks of New Deal liberalism. That is, successful pension reform *might* have worked, in the long term, to reorder the political landscape since "social policies may powerfully affect citizens' relationship to government because they typically provide them with their most personal and significant experiences of government in action" (Mettler 2007: 193; see also Campbell 2003). The administration's confidence in its capacity to implement reform turned out to be misplaced but it is indicative of the mood in Washington DC in the aftermath of the 2004 elections that the White House felt emboldened to venture onto the potentially deadly "third-rail" of American politics. As the Reagan White House unceremoniously discovered, the political consequences of appearing to threaten the United States's public pension scheme were potentially severe. Early in his presidency Reagan briefly put forward plans for cutting Social Security benefits but the administration quickly backtracked when Republicans in Congress warned that the proposal would lose the party votes. That is, as with Medicare, the Social Security programme was traditionally seen as Democratic political and policy turf. Yet, the Bush administration determined that the lessons of the 1980s no longer applied. One obvious, and apparently auspicious, difference from the 1980s was that there was now unified Republican government with Democrats just defeated and apparently roundly dispirited. Social Security reform, therefore, was seen as a plausible policy goal with potentially transformative political effects in the medium to long term; and, unlike the MMA with its ideological compromises, the administration's plan to restructure Social Security was unabashedly conservative.

In 1981 President Reagan's short-lived effort to reform Social Security concentrated on cost control. At the time the worries about fiscal solvency were justified by the impending prospect of a financial shortfall in Social Security's coffers resulting from the economic decline in the late 1970s. In the end, medium-term solvency of the programme was guaranteed by the Social Security amendments of 1983. These constituted a form of retrenchment as the retirement age was gradually raised and the Social Security payroll tax increased. While these changes illustrated that the era of Social Security expansion was over, the 1983 amendments were, as suggested by Jacob Hacker, "On balance . . . a victory for the program's defenders" (Hacker 2002: 159). In contrast to the Reagan administration's approach, the Bush White House proposed a much more far-reaching reform that focused on attacking the collectivist principles underpinning the programme. Partial privatisation of Social Security had been on the agenda of conservative policy entrepreneurs since the 1980s (Beland and Waddan 2000) but it was only with President Bush that a plan to allow people to divert some of the money that they paid into the communal Social Security trust fund into individual retirement accounts was fully articulated.

Bush was a consistent champion of Social Security reform. When formally announcing his candidacy for the presidency in 1999 he identified establishing personal accounts within the Social Security system as one of his main priorities (Barnes 2006: 129) and, once in the White House, he appointed a Commission on Social Security reform. The members of that commission were generally regarded as sympathetic to the president's objectives and presented a report in December 2001 entitled *Strengthening Social Security and Creating Wealth for all Americans* (The President's Commission to Strengthen Social Security 2001). By that time, however, the events of 11 September 2001 had come to dominate the political agenda and no serious legislative plans were developed in the first term. The idea, however, remained on the table as evidenced by Bush's remarks in the 2004 State of the Union address:

> Younger workers should have the opportunity to build-up a nest egg by saving part of their Social Security taxes in a personal retirement account. We should make the Social Security system a source of ownership for the American people.

Throughout the 2004 presidential campaign the two candidates sniped at each other over the future of Social Security. Using the rhetoric of the "ownership society", President Bush proclaimed the advantages of individualising Social Security benefits while John Kerry "adopted the traditional Democratic stance that consists of warning voters against 'Republican plots' to destroy Social Security" (Beland 2005: 183). The extent to which Social Security was a high-profile issue through the campaign should not be exaggerated but the newly re-elected president told a meeting of congressional Republicans in January 2005 that Social Security reform was to be the first major domestic policy goal of the second term. Bush was aware that, even in their moment of triumph, the subject of Social Security would make his audience a little apprehensive but he insisted: "I've got political capital, and now I'm going to spend it" (Draper 2007: 296). In the 2005 State of the Union address Bush reiterated his commitment to reform, while taking care to sound as unthreatening as possible:

> Social Security was a great moral success of the 20th century, and we must honor its great purposes in this new century. The system, however, on its current path, is headed towards bankruptcy. And so we must join together to strengthen and save Social Security

These words masked the reality of a plan that would have radically reorganised the biggest programme of the American welfare state. In hindsight, given the demise of the Bush plan, the ambition set forth all appears rather fanciful. Indeed, Fiona Ross (2007) has argued that the deeply embedded features of the Social Security system had established such an enduring policy legacy that the attempt at reform was politically foolhardy since it was doomed to fail. Yet, it is worth reflecting on how high Social Security reform advocates perceived the stakes to be. Embarking on an effort to rearrange such a huge public policy programme was always going to be politically risky but, according to Fred Barnes, if successful, implementation of the Bush agenda would be "groundbreaking" and "the phrase *ownership society* could someday enter the lexicon of presidential trademarks" along with New Deal and Great Society (Barnes 2006: 126). As George Edwards notes, the administration drew on the experience of the first term when calculating how it would push its aims through. Bush "thought he had a mandate for his Social Security proposals" and "also anticipated unified Republican support in Congress" (Edwards 2007: 264).

The administration's grand strategy was to present reform as a necessary cure for the projected long-term fiscal problems of the Social Security system and also as a means of increasing choice for those currently in the workforce by giving them the opportunity to invest some of their Social Security payroll tax into a personal retirement account. The message was that Social Security reform was both a practical necessity and a virtuous promotion of individual choice. The chosen legislative tactic was to try to build a congressional coalition from the right in – that is, satisfy conservatives first and then attract more centrists. Underpinning this approach was an expectation based on the experience of the first term that at least a small number of Democrats would come on board with the reform plan. This belief proved to be unfounded. At one point Democratic Senator Max Baucus of Montana, who had co-operated with the administration previously, informed Karl Rove that no Democrats would play along with the idea of carving personal accounts out of the existing Social Security payroll tax. Rove replied: "You're wrong. There'll be people who have to come on this" (Draper 2007: 298). But Rove had over-estimated the administration's political capital and underestimated the enduring and robust support for Social Security. Indeed, by the beginning of March 2005, it was clear that resistance to Social Security reform had re-energised the Democrats who were solid in their opposition. Furthermore, many Republicans were uncertain in their support for the administration's plans (Stevenson 2005).

In pursuit of its goals the White House took a twin-track approach. First, it launched a highly visible public relations campaign to persuade the public of the virtues of reform. Indeed, according to Edwards, this was "perhaps the most extensive public relations campaign in the history of the presidency" (Edwards 2007: 252). Second, at the legislative level the administration, repeating tactics it had successfully employed when enacting the No Child Left Behind programme, presented only a skeleton plan in the expectation that Congress would fill in the details (Rosenbaum and Toner 2005). In the end, both tracks backfired. First, ironically, support for reform declined as the president toured the country advocating change. There was some support for the principle of allowing workers to invest in their own accounts but this was not to be done at the expense of draining money from the existing system. Moreover, as people better understood the complexities of reform so opposition to the Bush proposals increased (Jacobson 2007: 210–13). Second, the lack of a detailed plan in Congress meant that even reform advocates remained divided over how best to proceed. As Weiner reflects, "Without a plan, many proposals emerged, fragmenting supporters of reform" (Weiner 2007: 888).

In part this lack of detail reflected a fundamental problem. There was in reality no necessary connection between solving the long-term fiscal problems of the programme and introducing personal accounts. Indeed, in the short term, the opposite was the case. If younger workers were to be allowed to divert some of their Social Security payroll tax into an individual retirement account then that would leave a shortfall in the Social Security trust fund thereby further weakening the capacity of that fund to pay out to current and near-future retirees. The administration never clearly explained how it would deal with these so-called transition costs, especially as it was keen to avoid inflicting any short-term pain on voters by cutting benefits for existing beneficiaries or raising the retirement age. In the end, the parliamentary-style discipline among congressional Republicans witnessed in the first term, particularly in the debate over the MMA, simply failed to materialise. Indeed, the issue galvanised the Democrats and gave them a rallying point after the dejection of the 2004 elections. Hence, Democratic unity contrasted with Republican division. In late 2003, the House Republican leadership had persuaded potentially recalcitrant members of the caucus to give their president an important victory on Medicare. Eighteen months later it proved impossible to pull off the same trick on Social Security as worried Republicans noted that they now had quite different institutional and electoral priorities from the White House (Sinclair 2006: 240–1).

## CONCLUSION

President Bush's Medicare and Social Security initiatives provide a clear illustration of the profound differences between the two terms of his presidency. The first was marked by a series of legislative successes. The tax cuts of 2001 and 2003, the No Child Left Behind programme and, of course, the MMA added up to a significant list of reforms in critical arenas of public policy. The second term saw no such achievement, and the Social Security debacle was the first clear indication that the high expectations of conservatives in the aftermath of the 2004 elections, which left the Republicans controlling the levers of power in Washington, were to be dashed.

Hence, President Bush's record in these domains is a mixed one, particularly since the MMA itself was an ideologically hybrid package. It is certainly ironic that the headline aspect of Bush's legacy with regard to social programmes for the elderly is an expensive new benefit programme. In hindsight, it is apparent that Bush's conservative philosophy and desire to undercut the collectivist principles of the social programmes for the elderly came into conflict with the political reality that Medicare and Social Security, as they currently operate, remain hugely popular not just with the programmes' "army of beneficiaries" but with the wider working-age population as well. Overall, therefore, Bush's capacity to enact conservative reforms to these programmes was seriously constrained. Some, potentially significant, conservative ideas were integrated into the MMA although these passed below the political radar as most attention was focused on the expensive new prescription medicine benefit (Jaenicke and Waddan 2006). On Social Security there was not even a mixed record of success, although Steven Teles (2007: 173) offered some potential consolation to conservatives, arguing that,

> Despite the president's failure to get traction on the issue in 2005, moving the issue from the outer margins of polite discourse to the top of a president's policy agenda is a political victory of the first order [for the conservative movement].

As the Bush presidency drew to a close, however, those words looked less convincing. The dramatic banking collapse and the turmoil on the stock markets made the prospect of investing in stocks and shares rather than in a government-organised, and guaranteed, system seem considerably less attractive.

## BIBLIOGRAPHY


Appleby, Julie (2008), "Drug costs for seniors growing", *USA Today,* 11 November

Aberbach, Joel (2005), "The Political Significance of the George W. Bush Administration", *Social Policy and Administration,* 39 (2), pp. 130–49

Barnes, Fred (2006), *Rebel-in-Chief: Inside the Bold and Controversial Presidency of George W. Bush,* New York: Crown Forum

Bartlett, Bruce (2006), *Impostor: How George W. Bush Bankrupted America and Betrayed the Reagan Legacy,* New York: Doubleday

Béland, Daniel (2005), *Social Security: History and Politics from the New Deal to the Privatization Debate,* Lawrence, KS: University Press of Kansas

Béland, Daniel and Alex Waddan (2000), "From Thatcher (and Pinochet) to Clinton? Conservative Think Tanks, Foreign Models and US Pensions Reform", *Political Quarterly,* 71 (2), pp. 202–10

Campbell, Andrea (2003), *How Policies Make Citizens: Senior Political Activism and the American Welfare State,* Princeton: Princeton University Press

Carey, Mary Agnes (2000), "Bush's Medicare Drug Plan", *Congressional Quarterly Weekly,* 9 September, p. 2084

Carey, M. (2005), "Lott Laments His Medicare Vote", *Congressional Quarterly Weekly,* 27 March, p. 726

Clinton, William J. (1999), State of the Union Address, 19 January, Washington, DC: White House, Office of the Press Secretary

Davies, Gareth (2003), "The Welfare State", in W. Elliot Brownlee and Hugh Davis Graham, eds, *The Reagan Presidency: Pragmatic Conservatism and Its Legacies,* Lawrence, KS: University Press of Kansas

Draper, R. (2007), *Dead Certain: The Presidency of George W. Bush,* New York: Free Press

Dreyfuss, Barbara (2004), "Cheap Trick", *The American Prospect,* (Sept.), 9 (15), pp. 25–8

Edwards, G. C. (2007), *Campaigning by Governing: The Politics of the Bush Presidency,* New York: Pearson Longman

NEP Exit Poll (2000), http://www.cnn.com/ELECTION/2000/epolls/US/P000.html

Hacker, J. S. (2002), *The Divided Welfare State: The Battle Over Public and Private Social Benefits in the United States,* New York: Cambridge University Press

Hacker, Jacob S. (2004), "Privatizing Risk without Privatizing the Welfare State: The Hidden Politics of Social Policy Retrenchment in the United

States", *American Political Science Review*, 98 (2), pp. 243–60

Hacker, Jacob and Paul Pierson (2005), *Off Center: The Republican Revolution and the Erosion of American Democracy*, New Haven: Yale University Press

Jacobson, Gary (2007), *A Divider, Not a Uniter: George W. Bush and the American People*, New York: Pearson Longman

Jaenicke, Douglas and Alex Waddan (2006), "President Bush and Social Policy: The Strange Case of the Medicare Prescription Drug Benefit", *Political Science Quarterly*, 121 (2), pp. 217–40

Light, Paul C. (1995), *Still Artful Work: The Continuing Politics of Social Security Reform*, New York: McGraw-Hill

Mettler, Suzanne (2007), "The Transformed Welfare State and the Redistribution of Political Voice", in P. Pierson and T. Skocpol, eds, *The Transformation of American Politics: Activist Government and the Rise of Conservatism*, Princeton: Princeton University Press

Moore, Stephen (2004), *Bullish on Bush: How George W. Bush's Ownership Society Will Make America Stronger*, Maryland: Madison Books

Oberlander, David (2003), *The Political Life of Medicare*, Chicago: University of Chicago Press

Pear, Robert (2005), "As Deadline Nears, Sorting Out the Medicare Drug Plan", *New York Times*, 11 October

Pear, Robert (2006), "Rules of Medicare Drug Plans Slow Access to Benefits", *New York Times*, 14 February

Pear, Robert (2007), "Medicare Audits Show Problems in Private Plans", *New York Times*, 7 October

Pear, Robert and Robin Toner (2003), "A Final Push in Congress: The Overview; Sharply Split House Passes Broad Medicare Overhaul; Forceful Lobbying by Bush", *New York Times*, 23 November

President's Commission to Strengthen Social Security (2001), *Strengthening Social Security and Creating Personal Wealth for All Americans*, Washington, DC: The Commission

Rosenbaum, D. and R. Toner (2005), "State of the Union: Retirement Plans; Introducing Private Investments to the Safety Net", *New York Times*, 3 February

Ross, F. (2007), "Policy Histories and Partisan Leadership in Presidential Studies: The Case of Social Security", in G. Edwards and D. King, eds, *The Polarized Presidency of George W. Bush*, Oxford: Oxford University Press

Serafini, M. (2002), "An Rx for the Democrats", *National Journal*, 22 June

Sherman, Arloc and Isaac Shapiro (2005), *Social Security Lifts 13 Million Seniors Above the Poverty Line: A State-by-State Analysis*, Washington, DC; Center on Budget and Policy Priorities, http://www.cbpp.org/2-24-05socsec.pdf

Sinclair, B. (2006), *Party Wars: Polarization and the Politics of National Policy*

*Making*, Norman: University of Oklahoma Press

Stevenson R. (2005), "For President's Social Security Proposal, Many Hurdles", *New York Times*, 2 March

Stone, P. (2002), "Peddling Prescription Plans", *National Journal*, 13 July

Teles, Steven (2007), "Conservative Mobilization against Entrenched Liberalism", in P. Pierson and T. Skocpol, eds, *The Transformation of American Politics: Activist Government and the Rise of Conservatism*, Princeton: Princeton University Press

Weiner, T. (2007), "Touching the Third Rail: Explaining the Failure of Bush's Social Security Initiative", *Politics and Policy*, 35 (4), pp. 872–97

*Chapter 12*

# NO CHILD LEFT BEHIND: THE POLITICS AND POLICY OF EDUCATION REFORM

Jonathan Parker

Following his controversial ascendancy to the presidency, George W. Bush promised to be a "uniter, not a divider" (Kagan 2000). In the field of education he fulfilled this promise by successfully shepherding the No Child Left Behind Act of 2001 (NCLB) into law. Despite the highly charged partisanship of that time, he courted and won the support and co-operation of leading Democrats. Even more extraordinarily, President Bush retained the support of his own party in Congress for an education bill that expanded significantly the federal government's influence and involvement in education at the state and local levels. One veteran news commentator wrote at the time that NCLB "may well be the most important piece of federal legislation in thirty-five years" (Broder 2001).

The overall significance of NCLB has been hotly contested. Some scholars dismiss or belittle NCLB as incremental change, noting that the focus on school standards began in the 1980s and evolved into what became NCLB (McDonnell 2005). Others caution that this federal law was the culmination of state reform efforts and was driven more by those state and local successes than by federal leadership (Manna 2006). The NCLB is portrayed, rightly, as the end product of over twenty years of policy evolution and development.

Despite the above qualification, NCLB still represents a dramatic change of the federal role in education. It placed the federal government in the position of approving both the content of curriculums and the testing procedures of the states, things more sweeping than any previous expansion of federal activity in education. The use of strict mandates and regulations signalled a radical departure from previous federal education policy. In achieving these changes, Bush reversed his party's traditional stance and tried to make national leadership in education a Republican issue (McGuinn 2006). The Act also proved important, though more incremental, in its expansion of federal spending.

While the legislation was clearly significant, it met less than universal approval. States, governors, conservatives and teachers' unions united in a loud chorus to criticise NCLB. Conservatives decried the massive expansion of national power over a local area of responsibility. States and governors claimed that it was underfunded. The Bush administration was attacked for failing to implement effectively and enforce the law. Finally, in terms of achieving educational improvements and narrowing the achievement gap between the "haves" and "have-nots", the law seems to have accomplished little for all the effort and resources poured into it.

While NCLB was attacked on a number of grounds as the Obama presidency began, it did not appear under threat of being eliminated or seriously undermined. Strong opposition to the Act did not translate into a unified partisan coalition in either party seeking to abolish or dismantle it. The left split over the benefits of NCLB, with some civil rights groups supporting or accepting the law because it focused attention on traditionally deprived students. No coherent public opposition to the new law developed. Seven years after its initial passage, almost all debate over NCLB revolved not around abolition but around how to amend the bill constructively. Flexibility for states in testing requirements and funding constituted the most prominent proposal in this discussion. The bipartisan strategy Bush adopted to gain passage of the law helped to secure its existence, even with the loss of Republican control of Congress in 2006 and the presidency in 2008. No Child Left Behind represents a cornerstone of Bush's political legacy. It looked poised to survive the initial broad sweep of reforms proposed by the Obama presidency and even showed potential to expand under Democratic control. NCLB's success as public policy is much more ambiguous.

## 1. PREVIOUS FEDERAL EDUCATION POLICY

The first major federal involvement in education came with the Elementary and Secondary Education Act of 1965, which provided aid for disadvantaged children, and was called Title I. Funding was tiny compared to overall education spending by states and local districts but it provided leverage to force states to enact far-reaching federal requirements, or mandates. These mandates cost states and districts far more to implement than Congress provided, and the regulations represent a greater federal intrusion upon state and local governments' authority over education than the relatively low levels of funding suggest.

Concerns over educational standards soared in the 1980s with the publication of the National Commission on Excellence in Education's report (1983), *A Nation At Risk*. State and local districts passed a host of educational reforms during the 1980s and 1990s, developing their testing of students and updating their curriculums and standards. There was, though, no significant federal legislation. The elder President Bush attempted to co-ordinate state efforts at the national level in 1989 but could get little support for any federal action from his own party. President Clinton made a breakthrough with the Goals 2000: Educate America Act of 1994 which sponsored efforts at standards reform while carefully leaving control in state hands. The law required states to test their students but let them design their own academic standards with little federal oversight or enforcement, thus rendering the requirements largely voluntary. The Act helped to encourage the development of ambitious standards, but efforts were patchy across the country.

## 2. THE PASSAGE OF NCLB

As Governor of Texas, Bush had used his record on education reform to undermine the Democrats' traditional advantage on the issue (McGuinn 2006). He increased standardised testing and punished schools for low performance which were popular with the business community and public. He also allowed students in low-performing schools to transfer to different schools.

In the 2000 presidential election, Bush sought to distance himself from traditionally conservative Republican positions on many domestic issues, declaring himself a "compassionate conservative" (Mitchell 2000). Education was a key policy for defining this position. Bush promoted a detailed national reform plan based upon his Texas experience. As a campaign tool, Bush's proposed combination of higher standards and public accountability garnered popular support among the public but his dealings with traditional party constituencies on the issue were more complicated. The conservative Republican right opposed all federal involvement in education policy, and their influence was such that the national party platform routinely called for the abolition of the Department of Education. Bush, however, was trusted by conservatives, particularly the religious right, and could endorse such policies without losing his base of support. Even more ambitiously, Bush portrayed his education reforms as a civil rights issue to create a wedge to attract support from Democrats. Bush adroitly framed the issue by making equality of achievement between minorities and other groups a primary policy goal. He garnered support from traditionally Democratic civil rights groups in a bold attempt to attract minority voters by attacking the "bigotry of low expectations" (Bush 2000).

Upon taking office in 2001, President Bush sent to Congress a blueprint for No Child Left Behind. As was often Bush's legislative strategy, only the basic structures of the plan were included: state testing, corrective action for schools that consistently failed to perform, the right of students to transfer out of failing schools, and government-funded vouchers to help fund transfers to private schools. The details were left for Congress to determine. There were many similarities between Republican and Democratic positions but the Republicans had captured both houses of Congress and could pass partisan bills on slim majorities, as they did later in Bush's term, so a consensual, bipartisan approach was not inevitable. Bush made his bipartisan intentions clear, however, by leaving details unspecified to allow concessions, and he encouraged those compromises. His cultivation of key committee Democrats, such as Massachusetts Senator Edward M. Kennedy and California Representative George Miller, the senior Democrats in the Senate and House education committees, cemented the bipartisan coalition behind the bill (Crabtree 2001). These actions would prove particularly crucial for the future of No Child Left Behind after the Republicans lost control of the Senate in mid-2001 and again after the 2006 mid-term elections.

The plan increased federal spending on education, pleasing Democrats, while the testing requirements were popular among moderates of both parties. The possible significant consequences of the tests for schools, teachers and students, however, made liberals and conservatives uneasy. Liberals suspected that the impact of high-stakes testing would fall most heavily upon poor and minority students, while conservatives distrusted any federal control over the curriculum. School vouchers, which would provide a set amount of public money to any student seeking to transfer out of a failing school into a private one, were among the most controversial aspects of the plan. The Christian right generally supported vouchers as a means of aiding religious schools, and some groups, such as the Family Research Council, claimed they would oppose any bill without vouchers. More liberal organisations, such as teaching unions and civil rights groups, strongly opposed any use of public money to fund private school tuition. Vouchers also attracted opposition from more moderate, centrist Democrats and Republicans in Congress. Senator James Jeffords of Vermont, a moderate Republican and chair of the Health, Education, Labor and Pensions committee, was strongly opposed, and his committee completely eliminated them from the bill. In punishment, the Bush administration excluded him from wider negotiations with Senate Republicans, a snub that, among others, prompted Senator Jeffords to withdraw from the Republican Party and become an independent. Crucially, his defection handed control of the evenly balanced Senate back to the Democrats in May 2001, and Senator Edward Kennedy became the new chair of the committee (McGuinn 2006). Bush's bipartisan approach now became one of necessity rather than choice.

Both parties compromised to get a bipartisan law. Bush conceded on the voucher issue, and Democrats allowed students in failing schools to receive money for special tutoring instead of tuition vouchers. Only a Republican president could have delivered such an education plan given the widespread opposition of conservatives to most of the proposals. Congressional Republicans wanted to support their new president, and Bush secured their votes for legislation they would not have supported otherwise (Nather 2001). The bill passed the House 384 to forty-five and the Senate ninety-one to eight. The 11 September 2001 attacks occurred during negotiations to reconcile the House and Senate versions, further motivating legislators to pass the bill as a symbol of the country's unity in the face of the assault upon it. The final conference report was approved 381 to forty-one in the House and eighty-seven to ten in the Senate, and the bill was signed into law by President Bush on 8 January 2002.

## 3. THE LAW

No Child Left Behind increased federal education funding to states but reduced states' control over how they spent it. In return for extra monies, states accepted highly prescriptive requirements on standards in the core subjects of mathematics, reading or language arts, and science. States had to test annually in grades 3 to 8 and define a clear grade requirement for proficiency, with serious consequences for schools, districts and states that did not meet the new standards.

Holding schools, districts and states accountable for the achievement of all students is the foundation of NCLB. Schools, districts and states must make Adequate Yearly Progress (AYP) towards the goal of 100 per cent academic proficiency for *all* students by the end of the 2013–14 school year (ECS 2007). AYP requires a school's entire student body and all its subgroups to meet state proficiency targets on their test scores. Subgroups include the major racial and ethnic groups, students from economically disadvantaged households, students with disabilities, and those with limited English proficiency. Schools fail to make AYP if the student body in the aggregate *or* a single subgroup fails to meet proficiency targets. Schools also fail if they do not test at least 95 per cent of students. Schools that fail AYP for two consecutive years are labelled "needing improvement", which is interpreted in the public discourse as "failing". States must publish all students' test scores categorised by state, district, school and subgroup. Finally, every public school teacher must be "highly qualified" by holding a qualification in their particular subject.

Schools with large numbers of students from low-income households qualify for extra Title I federal funding. While all public schools must test and report their results, only schools receiving Title I funding are subject to the mandated levels of intervention based upon how many years a school fails to make AYP. After two years the school must develop an improvement plan and allow parents to transfer children to another school. After three years the school must offer extra services, such as tutoring, to students. After four to five years a school can replace staff, replace the curriculum, appoint outside advisers, or change its internal structure. After six years a school can reopen as a charter school, replace all or most of the staff, or be taken over by the state or a private company.

## 4. FUNDING

The Bush administration initially raised federal education spending, mostly for Title I programmes. However, this growth slowed sharply after the first year of NCLB. Between 2004 and 2007 spending barely rose in nominal dollars, and actually decreased when inflation is taken into account. The federal share of total school spending largely remained at its previous level of seven percent, leaving much of the cost of meeting the new federal mandates to states and local districts.

Table 1: Federal appropriations for elementary and secondary education in current dollars and growth in inflation in adjusted dollars, 2000–8

| *Year* | *Appropriation (billions of dollars)* | *Per cent increase (controlling for inflation)* |
|---|---|---|
| 2001 | 27.3 | |
| 2002* | 32.0 | 15 |
| 2003 | 35.1 | 7 |
| 2004 | 36.9 | 3 |
| 2005 | 37.5 | –2 |
| 2006 | 36.4 | –6 |
| 2007 | 36.7 | –3 |
| 2008 | 37.8 | –1 |

*2002 represents the first Bush budget and is also the year NCLB passed
Source: Figures compiled by author from Education Department Budget History

Annual funding for elementary and secondary education rose from $27 billion in 2001 to $38 billion in 2008. Democrats accuse Republicans of reneging on an agreement that the federal government would fully fund NCLB. Its Republican supporters respond that funding has expanded significantly. Though both sides are technically correct, the federal government effectively cut education spending after 2004 and costs to schools far outpaced funding. State and local governments have thus been forced to step in and fund the reforms mandated by Congress. While the federal government has under-funded the NCLB and while spending has become a key political issue, substantively the most important aspect of NCLB is the way states, districts and schools approach education rather than any wrangling over budgetary shortfalls.

## 5. THE IMPLEMENTATION AND FUTURE OF NCLB

Despite its marginal impact on federal spending, NCLB dramatically expanded federal influence. The law's testing and accountability requirements made tremendous demands of state education departments. Many observers predicted the requirements would be relaxed when they became too burdensome to sustain (West and Peterson 2003) but the Bush administration drafted strict regulations on how the law would be implemented and threatened to cut off funding to non-compliant states (Robelen 2003). The expansion of testing was a significant undertaking for which some states were unprepared and lacked the capacity to comply. Designing curriculum standards and creating tests to measure student performance against those standards in every one of the fifty states was itself a monumental task, much less designing a comprehensive approach for dealing with all schools that failed to achieve the required standard. The stakes were high, and failing schools faced serious consequences. Finally, the timetable for implementation of NCLB was very tight. Smooth implementation of the law was all but impossible.

Most states did not have the expertise to design and administer student tests, particularly on such short notice. The private testing industry largely filled that gap, though it had to expand exponentially over a short period to meet demand. By 2005, twenty-three states had not fully implemented the law's testing requirements (Olson 2005). By 2006, approximately twenty-six million students had to be tested annually (Sternberg 2006). The only comparable annual high-stakes tests are the college entrance examinations, the SAT and the ACT. These established tests are taken by about 2.6 million students each year, yet they have experienced recent public scandals over failures in their administration. Ten times this number had to be assessed in 2006 under No Child Left Behind (Sternberg 2004, 2006). Such an undertaking requires careful development and testing of the exams to work successfully, and it is not surprising that scoring errors and reporting delays, among other daunting challenges confronting the testing industry and states, have undermined NCLB (Toch 2006).

NCLB's strict regulations and the funding shortfall encouraged many states to resist the law. The requirements hit states with the most rigorous testing hardest, forcing them to abandon systems that did not fit NCLB. States such as Connecticut abandoned their established and rigorous writing tests for cheaper, computer-scored multiple-choice exams (Sternberg 2006). Connecticut sued in federal court but lost because NCLB's regulations are technically a condition of aid rather than a mandate. States are not required to enact NCLB but must forego all the funding attached to it which would be impractical and unaffordable.

Other states protested over the lack of adequate resources. Utah's legislature passed legislation to prohibit state and local districts from implementing NCLB without adequate federal funding (Sack 2005). These protests subsided but then re-emerged and intensified as testing got underway and schools began to fail in large numbers in the face of increasing proficiency requirements. All schools must test students annually and meet state targets for AYP, which rise to 100 per cent by 2014. As the number of schools failing to make AYP rose, the Bush administration resisted pressure to show more flexibility over testing. Civil rights advocates generally supported Bush's approach because it focused attention on their constituencies: minority subgroups. The necessity of meeting proficiency targets for the poor, racial and ethnic groups, non-English speakers and the disabled forced schools to consider carefully the attainment of these student groups or risk failing AYP (Wong and Sunderman 2007).

Despite protests, the states failed to resist the federal government's implementation of NCLB. The states retained control over certain technical aspects of how AYP is calculated, however, which allowed them to influence pass rates. These aspects included determining the cut-off size for subgroups in each school, taking account of confidence intervals for test scores, and defining proficiency levels more leniently. Because NCLB requires all student subgroups to reach 100 per cent proficiency by 2014 and because failure by any group to make AYP means the entire school fails, statistically it is more likely a particular school will fail to make AYP the more subgroups it has. States can establish the minimum number of students required to identify a subgroup. If there are fewer students than the minimum in a school, the subgroup does not officially exist. For example, Texas does not report separate scores for any of the state's 65,000 Asian students and several thousand Native American students because no school has a large enough population to count as a subgroup (Bass and Dizon 2006). Over twenty states raised the minimum sizes for subgroups by 2006 in order to improve pass rates.

Confidence intervals refer to the natural fluctuations in test scores due to errors and natural differences in student cohorts. Scores within a confidence interval may be high or low because of random factors, so schools that fail to make AYP within this interval are still counted as passing. By 2006 confidence intervals had been approved and used by forty-one states, which prevented schools that narrowly missed AYP from being labelled as failing (Fulton 2006).

Finally, while NCLB requires all students to reach 100 per cent proficiency by 2014, individual states determine how well students must perform on the tests to reach proficiency. As more schools fail AYP, the pressure to relax standards increases. Ironically, states with the highest standards are most penalised by NCLB because rigorous standards cause more schools to fail AYP. For example, Minnesota had the top eighth-grade scores in the country for mathematics and was at a similar level to the top countries in the world in standardised test scores, yet 80 per cent of its schools were on track to be labelled failing according to NCLB rules (Darling-Hammond 2007). Mississippi, by comparison, had the second lowest passing rate in the country for fourth graders on the National Assessment of Educational Progress (NAEP), a single national benchmarking test administered across every state, yet its students have the highest pass rate in the country on the state-administered NCLB test. Academic studies (Cronin et al. 2007; Hamilton et al. 2007) found that official gains in student achievement could be largely explained by the adoption of easier standards.

State calls for leniency became more urgent as the number of failing schools facing the highest level of sanctions continued to climb. After the 2004 election, Secretary of Education Rod Paige was replaced by Margaret Spellings who began making more conciliatory gestures towards states on a case-by-case basis to head off opposition (Sunderman 2006). States were allowed more leeway to exclude test scores from students with disabilities and language barriers. Also, the deadlines by which states had to meet the qualified teacher requirements were extended (Keller 2005).

## 6. THE IMPACT OF SANCTIONS ON SCHOOLS

While the Bush administration maintained a relatively tough line over testing requirements, supporters of NCLB were frustrated over the reluctance of states, local districts and schools to employ the more sweeping sanctions allowed in the law, including restructuring schools, removing teachers and administrators, contracting out to private providers, or reconstituting as charter schools. Forty per cent of failing schools took none of the five restructuring actions stipulated by NCLB, and about 42 per cent received no help from their local districts, though most received some help from the state government (Government Accountability Office 2007). Parents also declined to use school choice and tutoring assistance options (Hess and Finn 2007). Nationwide, less than 1 per cent of students opted to transfer out of failing schools and only 17 per cent of eligible students took advantage of free tutoring (Zimmer et al. 2007).

States, local districts and schools all face a looming crisis as the target for NCLB approaches 100 per cent proficiency for students in 2014. More and more schools will consistently fail AYP and be subject to the most severe sanctions, yet many states lack the capacity to intervene (Sunderman and Orfield 2006). Schools most likely to be labelled failing are concentrated within high-poverty, urban areas where struggling districts do not have the staff or resources to take over or restructure so many schools. State departments of education have never carried out these sorts of activities, either. There appears to be no system capable of running or managing large numbers of failing schools, and it is unclear that the NCLB sanctions are enforceable. Instead, state and local districts have relied on more familiar, though less drastic, approaches than restructuring, making NCLB's impact less than revolutionary.

## 7. REAUTHORISATION

NCLB was scheduled for reauthorisation in 2008, though the law would continue as originally passed if Congress took no further action. The 2006 elections had elevated the Democrats to the majority party in Congress. The chorus of complaints from state and local governments, teachers and their unions, and education researchers provided impetus to amend the law. Although Bush's chief allies in the passage of NCLB, Representative George Miller and Senator Edward Kennedy, took over the chairs of the relevant committees in the House and Senate respectively, both were highly critical of Bush's handling of NCLB's implementation. Bush called for reauthorisation of the Act in his 2007 State of the Union address knowing that the act's future was precarious.

While the [illegible] coalition that passed NCLB in 2001 was strained, it pro[illegible] two factors contributed to its survival. First, President Bush[illegible] reaching out to Democrats like Kennedy and Miller suc[illegible]cted one of his most significant domestic achievements [illegible]ral politics sidelined reform during the 2008 presiden[illegible] election campaigns prompted much criticism of N[illegible]. The two mainstream presidential candidates, though [illegible]pressed few serious differences over the law itself. For example, Barack Obama supported many aspects of NCLB and his criticisms focused primarily upon funding. Despite the high level of consensus in the issue positions of the presidential candidates, the pressure on the campaigns and congressional candidates to stake out distinctive positions made it difficult, if not impossible, to obtain the necessary legislative compromises on both sides to win bipartisan agreement on reauthorisation. With neither side willing to compromise, the task was put off until after the elections.

Despite the inability to pass the reauthorisation during an election campaign, Obama's victory does not seriously threaten the law's future. Criticisms of NCLB focused primarily upon its underfunding. The framing of the debate in terms of whether the federal government provided enough money demonstrated the inherent resilience of NCLB. The easy response to such criticisms was to provide more money, leaving the basic provisions of the law intact. The debate was not framed in terms of whether the law should be overturned or its enforcement provisions reduced. The policy framework of NCLB, with its focus upon widespread annual testing and accountability through public identification of school, district, and state results against ambitious targets, seemed likely to continue in its original form and even expand in some areas.

## CONCLUSION

Bush's tenure witnessed a considerable change, if not revolution, in the field of education. His major legislative accomplishment, NCLB, set the agenda and shifted power decisively over the curriculum and testing to the national level, despite a host of political obstacles that most commentators thought insurmountable. As Paul

Peterson and Martin West (2003) declared soon after the passage of the law,

> NCLB . . . stands alongside the pioneering compensatory and special education laws enacted in 1965 and 1974 . . . The crucial aspect of all three pieces of legislation is not so much the money authorized as the policy framework imposed . . . No, it is not the federal dollar contribution but the direction given to all school spending – whether federal, state, or local – that is key.

NCLB framed education policy as a debate over standards and accountability, and this framework will continue to shape future developments in education over the next decade at the least. State and local governments still formally control education policy, but their attention and efforts are now focused, and are likely to continue to be focused, upon testing and accountability, courtesy of NCLB. The need to improve test scores will become even more fraught as the financial crisis and deepening recession from 2008 savage the budgets of state and local governments, although Obama's stimulus packages may provide some resources to help states soften their budgetary crises. Nevertheless, every state, district and school is concentrating upon improving test scores and reducing the achievement gap for underperforming subgroups, consuming the attention and resources of teachers and education officials at every level. Indeed, it is now difficult to see how any other major reform efforts could be brought forward except in the context of influencing test scores – a major legacy of Bush and his NCLB Act.

Despite its successful passage and its successful expansion of federal influence, NCLB has run into massive difficulties in implementation. The main goal of the law, that all children in the United States will be proficient in reading and mathematics by 2014, is simply unattainable (Ravitch 2007). Two prominent commentators on, and scholars of, education policy, Chester Finn and Frederick Hess (2007) note:

> While there is no doubt that the number of proficient students can and should increase significantly from the 30 or so per cent (using the National Assessment definition of proficiency) when Bush left office, and while the achievement of children below the proficient level also can and should rise closer to proficiency,

> no educator in America believes that universal proficiency will be attained by 2014, as required by NCLB, at least not by any reasonable definition of proficiency. Only politicians promise such things. The inevitable result is cynicism and frustration among educators and a compliance mentality among state and local officials.

The United States, ever a country of optimism, has proposed a utopian goal for its education system, echoing the famous line from Garrison Keillor's *Prairie Home Companion* where "all the children are above average". The problems identified above highlight why the federal government struggles to impose sweeping policy change on states and communities without their consent and co-operation. NCLB represents an attempt to "overreach" by the federal government (Petrelli 2007). Data from the National Assessment of Educational Progress (NAEP) suggest that state assessments overstate the proportion of students reaching proficiency and the rate of improvement (Fuller et al. 2006; Lee 2006). More ominously, a systematic analysis of NAEP national and state-level achievement results shows that test scores have remained steady, despite significant improvements in the NCLB's favoured metrics. It is too early to judge the eventual impact of NCLB but scores on reliable national tests should not be so strongly out of line with state assessments. Despite a substantial and concerted nationwide effort by every state, school district and school, NCLB failed to show a significant impact on student achievement or to narrow the achievement gap between underprivileged students and others (Lee 2006). While NCLB was a major political and legislative achievement of the Bush presidency, and also further strengthened the federal government at the expense of state autonomy, it has not demonstrated benefits in terms of educational outcomes.

## BIBLIOGRAPHY

Bass, Frank and Nicole Ziegler Dizon (2006), "States Help Schools Dodge No Child: Accused of 'Gaming the System'", *Chicago Sun Times*, 18 April

Broder, David (2001), "Long Road to Reform: Negotiators Forge Education Legislation," *Washington Post*, 17 December

Bush, George W. (2000), Speech to Republican National Convention, 3 August

Crabtree, S. (2001), "Changing His Tune, Kennedy Starts Work with Bush on Education Bill", *Roll Call*

Cronin, J., Michael Dahlin, Deborah Adkins and Gage Kingsbury (2007), "The Proficiency Illusion", Washington, DC: Thomas B. Fordham Institute

Fuller, Bruce, Kathryn Gesicki, Erin Kang and Joseph Wright (2006), "Is the No Child Left Behind Act Working? The Reliability of How States Track Achievement", Berkeley, CA: Policy Analysis for California, University of California, Berkeley

Fulton, Mary (2006), "Minimum Subgroup Size for Adequate Yearly Progress (AYP)", Denver, CO: Education Commission of the States

Gallup Organization (2000), "Phi Delta Kappan's Thirty-Second Annual Survey of the Public's Attitude Toward the Public Schools", 169

Government Accountability Office (2007), "No Child Left Behind Act: Education Should Clarify Guidance and Address Potential Compliance Issues for Schools in Corrective Action and Restructuring Status", Washington, DC: United States Government Accountability Office

Hamilton, Laura S., Brian M. Stecher, Julie A. Marsh, Jennifer Sloan McCombs, Abby Robyn, Jennifer Lin Russell, Scott Naftel and Heather Barney (2007), "Standards-Based Accountability Under No Child Left Behind: Experiences of Teachers and Administrators in Three States", Santa Monica, CA: RAND

Hess, Frederick and Chester E. Finn, Jr (2007), *No Remedy Left Behind: Lessons from a Half-Decade of NCLB*, Washington, DC: American Enterprise Institute

Kagan D. (2000), "Gov. Bush: 'I'm a Uniter, Not a Divider'", Cleveland, OH: CNN, 29 February 29, Transcript at: http://transcripts.cnn.com/

Keller, B. (2005), "States Given Extra Year on Teachers", *Education Week*, 2 November

Lee, Jaekyung (2006), "Tracking Achievement Gaps and Assessing the Impact of NCLB on the Gaps: An In-depth Look into National and State Reading and Math Outcome Trends", Cambridge, MA: The Civil Rights Project at Harvard University

McDonnell, Lorraine M. (2005), "No Child Left Behind and the Federal Role in Education: Evolution or Revolution?", *Peabody Journal of Education* 80 (2), pp. 19–38

McGuinn, Patrick J. (2006), *No Child Left Behind And the Transformation of Federal Education Policy, 1965–2005*, Lawrence, KS: University Press of Kansas

Manna, Paul (2006), *School's in: Federalism And the National Education Agenda*, Washington, DC: Georgetown University Press

Mitchell, Alison, (2000), "Bush Draws Campaign Theme From More Than 'the Heart'", *New York Times*, 11 June

Nather, D. (2001), "Compromises on ESEA Bills May Imperil Republican Strategy", *CQ Weekly*, Vol. 59, No. 18 (5 May 2001), pp. 1009–11

Nather, D. (2001), "Democrats Leave Their Stamp on Bush's Education Bill", *CQ Weekly*, 1079

National Commission on Excellence in Education (1983), *A Nation at Risk: The Imperative for Educational Reform*, Washington, DC: USGPO

Olson, L. (2005), "State Test Programs Mushroom as NCLB Mandate Kicks In", *Education Week*, 30 November

Olson, L. (2007), "Get Congress Out of the Classroom", *New York Times*, 3 October

Petrelli, Michael J. (2007), "The Problem with Implementation Is the Problem", in Frederick M. Hess and Chester E. Finn Jr, eds, *No Remedy Left Behind: Lessons from a Half-Decade of NCLB*, Washington, DC: American Enterprise Institute

Posner, Paul (1998), *The Politics of Unfunded Mandates: Whither Federalism*, Washington, DC: Georgetown University Press

Posner, Paul (2007), "The Politics of Coercive Federalism in the Bush Era", *Publius*, 37 (3), pp. 390–412

Ravitch, Diane (1987), *The Troubled Crusade: American Education 1945–1980*, New York: Basic Books, Inc.

Ravitch, Diane (2007), "Get Congress Out of the Classroom", *New York Times*, 3 October

Robelen, E. (2003), "Department Levies $783,000 Title I Penalty On GA", *Education Week*, 28 May

Sack, J. L. (2005), "Utah Passes Bill to Trump 'No Child' Law", *Education Week*, 27 April

Sternberg, Betty J. (2004), "When Less Is More", *Education Week*, 16 June

Sternberg, Betty J. (2006), "Testimony before the Commission on No Child Left Behind", Paper presented at The Commission on No Child Left Behind

Sunderman, Gail L. (2006), *The Unraveling of No Child Left Behind: How Negotiated Changes Transform the Law*, Cambridge, MA: The Civil Rights Project at Harvard University

Sunderman, Gail L. and Gary Orfield (2006), "Domesticating a Revolution: No Child Left Behind Reforms and State Administrative Response", *Harvard Educational Review* 76 (4), pp. 526–56

Toch, Thomas (2006), *Margins of Error: The Education Testing Industry in the No Child Left Behind Era*, Washington, DC: Education Sector

West, Martin R. and Paul E. Peterson (2007), "The Politics and Practice of Accountability", in Paul E. Peterson and Martin R. West, eds, *No Child Left Behind? The Politics and Practice of School Accountability*, Washington, DC: Brookings Institution Press

Wong, Kenneth and Gail L. Sunderman (2007), "Education Accountability as a Presidential Priority: No Child Left Behind and the Bush Presidency", *Publius* 37, pp. 333–50

Zimmer, Ron, Brian Gill, Paula Razquin, Kevin Booker, J. R. Lockwood III, Georges Vernez, Beatrice Birman, Michael Garet, and Jennifer O'Day (2007), "State and Local Implementation of the No Child Left Behind Act: Vol. I", Santa Monica, CA: RAND

## *Chapter 13*

# THE BUSH ADMINISTRATION AND THE POLITICS OF SEXUAL MORALITY

Edward Ashbee

Much has been said about George W. Bush's associations with the organisations and individuals comprising the Christian right and white evangelical Protestantism.[1] Countless biographical portraits recount his struggles with alcohol in the mid-1980s and the born-again character of his faith. Commentaries on his presidency record the part played by evangelicals in contributing to his re-election and in turn note his support for the Christian right's political agenda, speaking in forceful terms about building a "culture of life", using an executive order to prohibit the use of federal funds for embryonic stem-cell research, boosting federal government funding for abstinence-only sex education, and opposing same-sex marriage, for example. Others record the appointment to the federal courts of judicial conservatives committed to strict constructionist or originalist readings of the Constitution and with little sympathy for the "right to privacy" that served as the basis for rulings such as *Roe* v. *Wade* and *Doe* v. *Bolton* (1973) which extended abortion provision across the country. Still others make reference to the formal and informal issue networks that brought together the White House and activists from the Christian right, and the ways in which the administration, perhaps mindful of how the conservative movement fractured during George H. W. Bush's presidency (1989–93), assiduously courted the Christian right and continuously liaised with the movement's leading figures.

This chapter suggests, however, that these representations should be qualified and placed in context. The relationship between Bush and the Christian right was not as close as, and had considerably less solidity than, many accounts assert. While the longer-term impact of changes in the character of the federal judiciary should not be underestimated, the gains secured by the Christian right during Bush's terms of office, and his second term in particular, were often ephemeral and largely symbolic if set against the movement's overall ambitions and goals.

## 1. ELECTORAL POLITICS

### *a. The 2000 Republican Primaries*

When George W. Bush first appeared in pundits' lists of potential presidential contenders ahead of the 2000 election, there were doubts about the extent to which the Christian right and other core Republican constituencies would back him. There were memories of his father's pragmatism and what some evangelicals saw as Episcopalian aloofness. George W. Bush had liaised between his father's 1988 presidential campaign and some of those most closely associated with the Christian right, but the relationship had not been sustained during the 1990s. As Texas governor (1995–2000), Bush did not actively or overtly court the movement but instead sought co-operation with Democratic lawmakers and reached out towards Latino voters.

Faced, however, by the competitive realities of the Republican presidential primaries, Governor Bush and the Christian right found each other and established a relationship. Senator John McCain, Bush's most credible rival for the party's nomination, had long been distrusted by leading figures within the movement and, as the 2000 election approached, structured his campaign around a bid to secure moderate and independent votes in some of the key primary states. His earlier opposition to *Roe* was qualified and, in an address delivered in Virginia in February 2000, McCain criticised the Christian right's leading figures, warning against "pandering to the outer reaches of American politics and the agents of intolerance, whether they be Louis Farrakhan or Al Sharpton on the left, or Pat Robertson or Jerry Falwell on the right" (CNN.com 2000).

Set against this, Bush increasingly directed his efforts towards core Republican constituencies, and Christian conservatives in particular. He constructed a personal narrative structured around a born-again experience – while almost always shrinking from using the phrase itself – after winning his battles with alcohol and dissolute forms of living. Although a Methodist and before that a worshipper in Presbyterian and Episcopalian churches, Bush had an almost instinctive grasp of the evangelical denominations' cultural forms, and frequently used their terminology, citing resonant Biblical passages and talking, in the wake of the Lewinsky scandal, of restoring honour and dignity to the Oval Office. Bush's discourse enabled him to win many evangelical hearts and the backing of some influential figures within the Christian right. Although Gary Bauer of the Family Research Council initially stood as a presidential primary candidate and subsequently offered his backing to McCain, and James Dobson of Focus on the Family held back from endorsing anyone, most of the movement's leaders threw their weight behind the Bush campaign. Their support proved decisive in the South Carolina primary where defeat halted McCain's momentum and victory helped Bush secure the Republican nomination.

Nonetheless, Bush's words and phrases imposed few, if any, specific policy commitments on himself. Whereas President Ronald Reagan had specifically referred to the "tragedy" of *Roe*, Bush instead echoed Pope John Paul II's phrase and talked more vaguely of a "culture of life". Furthermore, his attitude to gay and lesbian relationships remained uncertain and, while he emphasised the importance of marriage, talk of moral concern was not generally matched by policy specifics.

### *b. The 2000 Presidential Election*

Although Bush secured the backing of many in the Christian right during the primary contests, turnout among grass-roots evangelicals in the November 2000 battle with Al Gore was rather lower than some had forecast. Indeed, Karl Rove, Bush's principal election strategist and senior adviser to the president, argued that the reluctance of some evangelicals to vote explained the very close character of the result:

> We probably failed to marshal support of the base as well as we should have . . . There should have been 19 million of them, and instead there were 15 million of them. So four million of them did not turn out to vote. (quoted in Berke 2001)

Rove did not offer reasons but, according to the *New York Times*, Bush aides suggested that evangelicals were alienated by revelations, which became public just before election day, that Bush had been arrested in 1976 for drunken driving (Berke 2001). Rove's assertion about the missing millions was subsequently challenged and the empirical basis for it remains uncertain but the claim provided a rationale for future White House efforts to reduce equivocation within the Christian right and among voters aligned with the movement.

### *c. The 2004 Presidential Election*

While the Bush–Cheney ticket's margin of victory in November 2004 was narrow, it won majorities in both the popular vote and the electoral college vote, and the Republicans extended their advantage in both chambers of Congress. The president's and his party's victories helped him secure the legitimacy and political capital that he had been denied by the confused outcome four years earlier when he narrowly won in the electoral college but lost the popular vote to Al Gore by half-a-million votes.

Bush's victory owed much to the campaigning zeal of activists and volunteers, many of whom were drawn from the churches and the organisations associated with the Christian right. Their canvassing efforts with neighbours and friends may have been pivotal. The significance of the evangelical vote is, however, open to question. Exit polls showed that the Bush–Cheney ticket secured the votes of 78 per cent of those describing themselves as born again or evangelical, 4 per cent more than in 2000 (Green et al. 2005: 8). Furthermore, according to the Pew Research Center, the move towards Bush was backed by a shift in partisan identification which is generally a longer-term and more stable form of attachment than voting loyalties, with the proportion of evangelicals identifying as Republicans rising from 39 per cent in 1999 to 49 per cent in 2004 (Keeter 2006). Despite the assertions frequently made in the immediate aftermath of the election, however, which suggested that a dramatic rise in turnout among evangelicals handed victory to Bush, the rise in evangelicals' participation rates from 2000 to 2004 was about the same as that of most groups; more evangelicals turned out to vote but so did more non-evangelicals. Evangelicals therefore remained unchanged as a proportion of the electorate (Green et al. 2005: 8).

## 2. REWARDS

### *a. Judicial Rewards*

It is tempting to conclude that the Christian right secured significant gains in return for its perceived electoral efforts. Certainly, the Christian right took succour from many of Bush's appointments to the federal courts. The courts occupied a pivotal place in the strategies employed by the movement because the judicial branch had, through concepts such as the living constitution, extended constitutional rights to encompass abortion and homosexuality. The 1965 *Griswold* ruling established an implied right to privacy that, in following years, much to the chagrin of those committed to strict constructionist or originalist readings of the Constitution, was progressively extended and expanded to provide the basis for a constitutional right to abortion. Then, in 2003, the majority opinion in *Lawrence* v. *Texas* not only struck down state laws criminalising sodomy but went beyond privacy and spoke in wide-ranging terms of a "right to liberty" in matters of private conduct, based on its reading of the Fourteenth Amendment's due process clause.

The assertion of these rights by the Court in so expansive a form sent shudders through the Christian right. Although few associated with the movement's peak organisations had sought the proactive criminal prosecution of gay couples, they worried about the extension of privacy rights and were concerned that *Lawrence* would, through its insistence on parity between different forms of relationships, open the way for same-sex marriage. In its amicus curiae brief to the Court, the Family Research Council (FRC) sought to limit the scope of constitutional rights, arguing that existing constitutional law rightly drew distinctions between different forms of sexual relationship on the basis of moral and social considerations, with incest and polygamy prohibited, and that states could still if they so chose constitutionally forbid fornication: "the sexual intimacies of married couples are constitutionally protected; non- and extra-marital sexual acts are not" (Family Research Council 2004).

The fear that activist judges would write yet further rights into the Constitution led the FRC and others to maintain a close watch on appointments to all three tiers of the federal court structure. Although there was no opportunity to nominate a member of the United States Supreme Court bench in Bush's first term, the administration reshaped the federal judiciary at a lower level through appointments to the district courts and circuit courts of appeal. The importance of the lower courts should not be underestimated. Although constrained by Supreme Court precedent, the circuit courts of appeal considered 63,000 cases in 2007 which, as Russell Wheeler (2008) notes, made them "the courts of last resort except for those federal litigants granted review on the Supreme Court's annual docket of less than 100 cases". Bush himself noted that he had appointed more than a third of all sitting federal judges (Savage 2008), and David M. McIntosh, a co-founder and vice chairman of the Federalist Society, the foremost conservative legal organisation, told the *New York Times* towards the end of Bush's period of office that "the nation's appeals courts [are] now more in line with a conservative judicial ideology than at any other time in memory" (Savage 2008).

Despite comments such as these, the Christian right and other sections of the conservative movement had continuing anxieties which grew as speculation intensified about an impending opportunity to make an appointment to the United States Supreme Court. They worried that the administration might waver and put forward more moderate nominees or that the Democrats would, though the minority party, exploit the Senate's rules and filibuster the nominees. There were some grounds for these anxieties. During the 108th Congress (2003–5), Senate Democrats filibustered Miguel Estrada and nine other courts of appeal nominees. Tensions rose and, at the beginning of 2005 in the wake of Bush's re-election and Republican gains in the congressional elections, Dr James Dobson promised "a battle of enormous proportions from sea to shining sea" if the president failed to nominate strict constructionist judges or if the nomination process was blocked in the Senate (Leaming 2005). Focus on the Family and the FRC organised a series of nationally televised rallies (dubbed Justice Sundays) demanding an end to the threatened filibusters and affirming the place of faith-based values in the public square. Against this background and urged on by the Christian right, Senate Republicans threatened the Democrats with deployment of the so-called nuclear option which would have removed the provision in the chamber's rules that permitted filibusters on nominations. In the event, the nuclear option was averted but only through the adoption of a compromise formula that had been negotiated by fourteen moderate senators drawn from both parties.

An opportunity finally arose to reshape the United States Supreme Court in 2005. Samuel Alito replaced the retired Justice Sandra Day O'Connor, and John Roberts, who had originally been proposed to replace O'Connor, was elevated to the post of chief justice after the death of William Rehnquist. While Roberts was similar in ideological terms to Rehnquist, both the right and left agreed that Alito's appointment marked a significant shift in the overall ideological balance on the bench. Whereas O'Connor had often cast a swing vote to decide the outcome of cases and would at times side with the more liberal members of the Court, Alito quickly aligned himself with figures such as Antonin Scalia and Clarence Thomas, customarily regarded as the most unyielding of the conservatives on the bench. Furthermore, the conservative bloc's relative youth suggests that they will serve for many years to come.

While Alito's impact, and that of Bush's appointees to the lower federal courts, should not be underestimated, it is an exaggeration to think, as some have done, in terms of a "judicial revolution". Russell Wheeler of the Brookings Institution has pointed out that over the course of eight years President Bush was able to increase the number of Republican appointees, as a proportion of the total number of judges serving in the federal courts, by only 14 percentage points. In contrast, President Clinton (1993–2001) reduced the proportion of Republicans by 22 points. The election of Barack Obama as president will moreover offer an opportunity to reverse the shift that took place in the circuit courts of appeal and the district courts during the Bush years. Indeed, Wheeler (2008) has forecast that Obama could by 2013 "reduce the proportion of Republican appointees from 56% to 42%" (Wheeler 2008).

Furthermore, despite the appointment of Samuel Alito, conservatives have not fully captured the Supreme Court, and the outcome of cases, particularly so far as privacy rights and moral issues are concerned, is often uncertain beforehand. The evidence suggests that there is still a majority, albeit resting on a single vote, to uphold *Roe*. While the Court upheld in *Gonzales* v. *Carhart* (2007) the constitutionality of Congress's ban on partial-birth abortion, even though it lacked an exemption where the health of the mother was concerned, Justice Anthony Kennedy asserted in the majority opinion that abortion provision was constitutionally protected.

Indeed, Bush's commitment to the judicial revolution sought by many within the conservative movement is open to question. Before nominating Alito to replace O'Connor, Bush put forward Harriet Miers, then White House Counsel. Her anti-abortion credentials were uncertain and Bush might have nominated Miers instead of potential candidates more opposed to *Roe* because he felt that overturning the landmark abortion decision presented significant political dangers for Republicans (Ashbee 2007: 236). In the event, her candidacy foundered, in part because some thought that she lacked experience, was not in command of key judicial issues and had been nominated simply because she was a Bush loyalist and Texas insider. There were also fears among the Christian right and conservatives, however, that she might be another David Souter, the judge appointed to the Court by President George H. W. Bush who, more often than not, joined forces with the more liberal members of the Court.

### *b. Public Policy*

Alongside President Bush's appointments to the courts, the Christian right also influenced and was reassured by several policy changes. In August 2001 Bush ended federal government funding for research on embryonic stem-cell lines not then in existence. No further embryos, he said, would be destroyed for research purposes. There were other policy shifts. The tax reforms pursued by the administration and passed by Congress ended (at least until 2010) the marriage tax penalty incurred by couples who jointly filed their tax returns and had, because of the progressive character of the tax structure, been required to pay more in taxes than two single people. Funding for abstinence-only sex education, through which young people were instructed about the dangers of premarital sexual activity and firmly encouraged to remain celibate until married, was increased dramatically. The decline in rates of teenage pregnancy and birth seemed to offer confirmation that such programmes were effective. The Born-Alive Infants Protection Act (2002) sought to introduce notions of personhood to the foetus by extending legal protection to a child born alive as a consequence of an abortion, and the ban on partial-birth abortion, twice vetoed by President Clinton, was signed into law by President Bush in November 2003. Two years later, in 2005, the administration and congressional Republicans fought to extend the life of Terri Schiavo, the Florida woman who had from 1990 onwards been in a persistent vegetative state. After long battles, the state courts sanctioned the removal of her feeding tube. Congress in turn hurriedly passed legislation transferring jurisdiction over the case to the federal courts. In a dramatic move, which the Christian right applauded, the president flew from Texas to Washington DC to sign the bill. Nonetheless, the United States Supreme Court would not hear the case and Schiavo died some days later.

These issues were, however, overshadowed by same-sex marriage. The issue did not come to the fore because of policy decisions by the White House, congressional Republicans, the Christian right or, for that matter, gay and lesbian activists. Instead, both the course of events and its pace were largely determined by state courts. In November 2003 the Massachusetts Supreme Judicial Court, the state's highest court, declared that the denial of marriage rights to same-sex couples violated the state constitution (Friedman 2006). The judgment inevitably provoked consternation within the ranks of the Christian right. Despite the existence of the Defense of Marriage Act (DOMA), a federal law signed by President Clinton in September 1996 which expressly empowered states to deny recognition to same-sex marriages conducted in other jurisdictions, the Christian right feared that other state courts would make similar rulings to that in Massachusetts or that other states would, under the provisions of the US Constitution's full faith and credit clause, be compelled to recognise same-sex marriages performed in Massachusetts. DOMA, the Christian right feared, could be struck down.

Pressure built on Congress and the states to pass a constitutional amendment prohibiting same-sex marriage across the United States. Although a president has no formal role in the passage of an amendment, his ability to draw public attention to, and advocate for, a proposal is regarded as pivotal. The Christian right and its allies in the counter-mobilisation against same-sex marriage sought an unequivocal statement of support for their arguments from President Bush. The president endorsed the proposed amendment in public statements and in the January 2004 State of the Union address:

> On an issue of such great consequence, the people's voice must be heard. If judges insist on forcing their arbitrary will upon the people, the only alternative left to the people would be the

> constitutional process. Our nation must defend the sanctity of marriage.

They also hoped that lobbying by the White House, together with a threat that the issue would be used against members of Congress when they sought re-election, would ensure that the amendment gained the required two-thirds majorities in the House and in the Senate before the issue could be put before the states. The amendment did not succeed, however. It not only failed to secure the necessary congressional supermajorities in 2004 and 2006 but its supporters were in a minority in the Senate when votes were taken on cloture motions to bring debate to a close.

Nonetheless, although the White House had supported the amendment, reined in abortion rights and funded abstinence-only sex education, Christian right campaigners were frustrated. While some organisations, most notably the FRC, operated as insider pressure groups and held back from open criticism of the White House, others were less restrained. Bush's affirmations of support for the amendment were seen as far too guarded in character. From their perspective, his statements concentrated rather too much on the perils of judicial activism rather than on stressing the importance of traditional marriage itself. The president had also tied his remarks to a plea for restraint and respect – "The outcome of this debate is important – and so is the way we conduct it. The same moral tradition that defines marriage also teaches that each individual has dignity and value in God's sight" (2004 State of the Union address) – that few campaigners against same-sex marriage relished. There was particular disappointment after Bush's re-election victory in November 2004. The president had boasted of the political capital that he had secured and yet little, it seemed, would be spent on moral issues. In January 2005, the Arlington Group, which brought together the individuals and organisations spearheading the campaign to secure passage of the same-sex marriage amendment, sent a private letter to Karl Rove indirectly threatening to derail the administration's efforts to privatise Social Security if the amendment was not assigned greater importance:

> We couldn't help but notice the contrast between how the president is approaching the difficult issue of Social Security

> privatization where the public is deeply divided and the marriage issue where public opinion is overwhelmingly on his side . . . Is he prepared to spend significant political capital on privatization but reluctant to devote the same energy to preserving traditional marriage? . . . When the administration adopts a defeatist attitude on an issue that is at the top of our agenda, it becomes impossible for us to unite our movement on an issue such as Social Security privatization where there are already deep misgivings. (Kirkpatrick and Stolberg 2005)

Bush's statements on abortion were also more restrained than many pro-life activists wished. Although there were exceptions, his statements were generally framed in terms of opposition to abortion on demand rather than backing calls to end all terminations, and his August 2001 statement on embryonic stem-cell research was, in essence, a compromise. Federal funding of research using existing stem-cell lines was not withdrawn, and the administration's revised rules were set out in an executive order rather than via legislative action, making it relatively straightforward for a future president to reverse – as, indeed, President Obama did in March 2009. Similarly, the president's backing for abstinence-only sex education was based not on moral judgements or the principle that sexual activity should remain within the confines of marriage but, instead, was framed in consequentialist terms. His statements asserted that an abstinence-only approach deterred young people from engaging in sex and therefore reduced the incidence of sexually transmitted disease.

## 3. EXPLAINING BUSH'S FAILURE TO DELIVER THE CHRISTIAN RIGHT'S AGENDA

All in all, the Bush administration delivered relatively little when set against the trust that the Christian right and many white Protestant evangelicals had placed in the president. There were five principal reasons for this.

First, there is evidence that many in the administration were personally and politically dismissive of those associated with the Christian right. Although observers and some participants have highlighted and stressed the ties between many staffers and the Christian right and the commitment to faith that many personally shared, the collective culture of the Bush White House was structured around loyalty to the president rather than to particular forms of ideology. David Kuo, who served as special assistant to the president between 2001 and 2003, described it in bitter terms:

> I watched as George W. Bush's "compassionate conservatism" that promised to "restore hope for all Americans" was repeatedly stiff-armed by his own White House staff, and then preened to look good for the religiously inclined . . . I heard the mocking of religious conservative leaders by that staff. I learned that votes were "god" even if getting them meant blaspheming God. (Kuo 2006: xiii)

Second, the Christian right was divided and, at times, naive politically. It is an unstructured movement, and the organisations involved do not have formal membership structures which permits particular individuals, through either personal charisma or the effective command and application of organisational resources, to acquire positions of influence within its ranks. Although some leaders have political experience – Tony Perkins of the Family Research Council was a Louisiana state legislator, for example – not all do. Many have a background in theology and faith which leaves them unprepared for Washington realpolitik. Indeed, the rise of Dr James Dobson as the foremost public representative of the Christian right was, in some respects, a step backwards in terms of the politicisation of Christian conservatives. During the 1990s, Ralph Reed, executive director of the Christian Coalition, pulled the movement towards an incrementalist political strategy resting upon relatively small-scale changes and closer co-operation with other conservatives and Republicans around, for example, tax policy or anti-crime measures. Whereas the Reverend Jerry Falwell and Pat Robertson often talked in apocalyptic terms drawn from biblical prophecy, Reed insisted that Christians merely sought "a place at the table", meaning they just wanted to be heard and have their views considered alongside those of others. His arguments around family decline or gay lifestyles drew not upon fundamentalist theology but consequentialist claims about the socially dysfunctional character of moral relativism. In contrast, Dobson stressed personal transformation through Christ, with formal politics and calls for legislative reform often subordinate to other approaches.

In the absence of the kind of political strategy that Reed had envisaged a decade earlier, Dobson embraced personal connections and relationships based upon mutual trust. If judged by policy results, Dobson's personalised brand of politics looks to have been ineffective.

Third, despite misgivings, the Christian right remained loyal to the Republican Party, which inevitably curtailed its influence. There had been earlier suggestions of a shift away from the Republicans and from the abrasive forms of politics with which the Christian right had often been associated. The suggestions took different forms. Some had said that younger evangelicals were becoming more pragmatic and tolerant.[2] Others noted that figures with a more open and inclusive style and less of a commitment to political advancement, such as Pastor Rick Warren of the Saddleback Church, came to the fore. The Democrats were, it was said, finding opportunities that would allow them to make inroads into evangelical constituencies. Nonetheless, there was little substance to all of this and no serious partisan competition for the evangelical vote. When Obama came to debate with Senator John McCain at the Saddleback Church during the prelude to the 2008 conventions, there was a backlash against Obama because of what were seen as his equivocations when answering questions about abortion. In the November election, Senator McCain won the white evangelical/born-again Protestant vote by a margin of 74 to 25 per cent, 4 percentage points less than Bush secured in 2004 but 6 points more than in 2000. Despite attempts by the Obama campaign to make inroads into the white evangelical vote, his 25 per cent share was 5 points less than Al Gore's in 2000 (Linker 2008).

Fourth, as the Bush years unfolded, an undeclared ceasefire on the courts developed between progressives and traditionalists. There were concerns among some in the pro-life movement and Christian right that a head-on challenge to *Roe* would be dismissed by the Supreme Court, therefore re-establishing abortion rights for another generation. On the other side of the spectrum, some in the pro-choice movement feared that the Court might rein in abortion provision still further. At the same time, many gay rights campaigners believed that, if the Court struck down the Defense of Marriage Act, the backlash would increase the chances that a constitutional amendment outlawing same-sex marriage would pass. Such concerns ensured that moral issues lacked the traction and salience that they had in earlier years.

Fifth, Republican electoral strategists had to accommodate social, cultural and economic conservatives and national security hawks while also trying to appeal to more moderate voters and the increasingly large and influential Latino electorate. Rove considered that all were essential to the construction of a permanent Republican majority but each required different messages and policy inducements. Bush could not have implemented or pursued without restraint the Christian right's agenda because it would have alienated other core constituencies. The electoral mathematics of appealing simultaneously to different constituencies was made more difficult by data suggesting that Americans generally were becoming more liberal on some issues, most notably same-sex relationships. In this light, the Bush administration was perhaps right to distance itself from the excesses of the Christian right. It rushed to condemn remarks made by the Reverend Jerry Falwell who, to much opprobrium from middle America, blamed 9/11 on "the pagans, and the abortionists, and the feminists, and the gays and the lesbians who are actively trying to make that an alternative lifestyle, the ACLU, People For the American Way – all of them who have tried to secularize America – I point the finger in their face and say 'you helped this happen'". Nonetheless, there were misjudgements. The moves to prolong the life of Terri Schiavo provoked a backlash and highlighted the extent to which much of the public had anxieties about what was seen as government intrusion into a private matter. In a March 2005 *Time* poll, 70 per cent of respondents said that it was wrong for President Bush to have intervened in the matter (PollingReport.com 2005).

## CONCLUSION

The Christian right was, arguably, weaker at the end of George W. Bush's years in the White House than it had been at their onset, and its impact on the 2008 Republican nominating process was therefore limited. The movement was fragmented. Some rallied behind former Arkansas governor Mike Huckabee although there was concern that his campaign was a lost cause and that his economic populism might alienate the wider conservative movement. While there were deep suspicions of his Mormon faith, others embraced former Massachusetts governor Mitt Romney. There was even some support for former New York mayor Rudy Giuliani, despite his social liberalism. In the event, the Republican primaries reached a relatively swift conclusion and the Christian right had, like other conservatives, to rally behind Senator John McCain although many continued to recall the way in which he had equivocated on core issues, most notably abortion, as the 2000 election had approached, his failure to back the same-sex marriage amendment (on the grounds that marriage was a state rather than a federal issue) and his advocacy of campaign finance reform which the Christian right and other conservatives asserted curtailed their First Amendment rights of expression.

The selection of Alaska Governor Sarah Palin as the Republicans' vice presidential nominee energised temporarily both the Christian right and some other core Republican constituencies. Palin's popularity and the movement's anxieties about the prospect of a Democratic victory helped McCain win the overwhelming support of Christian conservatives.[3] Nonetheless, despite victories of constitutional amendments prohibiting same-sex marriage in California, Arizona and Florida, the issues that defined the Christian right played more or less no role in the 2008 contest. Even before the depths of the financial crisis became evident, only 6 per cent of those asked by a 10–11 September *Newsweek* poll identified abortion, guns or marriage as the most important issues determining their presidential vote (PollingReport.com 2009). At the end of the Bush years, the movement had not only lost its allies in the White House and on Capitol Hill but was markedly less relevant to political debate than it had been for many years.

## NOTES

1. The Christian right refers to the loose network of individuals and organisations that promote cultural conservatism and traditional values. It incorporates peak organisations such as the Family Research Council and Focus on the Family, as well as outsider groupings, such as the Traditional Values Coalition. Although some Roman Catholics and Episcopalians are active in the movement's ranks, or support its positions, the Christian right largely draws upon white evangelical and "charismatic" Protestants.
2. Polls suggest, however, that, although a significant proportion of younger evangelicals turned away from President Bush during his second term and became more accepting than their older counterparts of same-sex unions, they are often more hard line on abortion (Cox 2007).
3. Andrew Kohut, President of the Pew Research Center, noted after the election that Sarah Palin was "the only vice presidential candidate in my

recollection whose image has had a measurable effect on voting preference" (Kohut 2008).

## BIBLIOGRAPHY


Alliance for Justice (2008), *Judicial Selection During the Bush Administration: An Alliance for Justice Report*, Alliance for Justice, http://www.afj.org/

Ashbee, Edward (2007), *The Bush Administration, Sex and the Moral Agenda*, Manchester: Manchester University Press

Berke Richard L. (2001), "Aide Says Bush Will Do More to Marshal Religious Base", *New York Times*, 12 December

Blumenthal, Max (2004), "The Christian Right's Humble Servant", *AlterNet*, 15 November, http://www.alternet.org/

CNN.com (2000), "Transcripts: Special Event – Sen. John McCain Attacks Pat Robertson, Jerry Falwell, Republican Establishment as Harming GOP Ideals," 28 February, http://transcripts.cnn.com/

CNN.com (2001), "Bush to allow limited stem cell funding", *CNN.com – Inside Politics*, 10 August, http://edition.cnn.com/

CNN.com (2004), *US President/National/Exit Poll*, http://edition.cnn.com/

CNN Election Center 2008 (2008), *President – National Exit Poll*, http://edition.cnn.com/

CNN Law Center (2007), "Justices uphold ban on abortion procedure", 18 April, http://edition.cnn.com/

Cooperman, Alan and Thomas B. Edsall (2004), "Evangelicals Say They Led Charge For the GOP", *Washington Post*, 8 November

Cox, Dan (2007), "Young White Evangelicals: Less Republican, Still Conservative", *The Pew Forum on Religion and Public Life*, 28 September, http://pewforum.org/Family Research

Family Research Council (2004), "Amicus Brief: Lawrence & Garner v. Texas", http://www.frc.org/

Friedman, Lawrence M. (2006), "Ordinary and enhanced rational basis review in the Massachusetts Supreme Judicial Court: a preliminary investigation", *Albany Law Review*, Spring

Fund, John (2005), "Judgment Call: Did Christian conservatives receive assurances that Miers would oppose Roe v. Wade?", *Wall Street Journal*, 17 October

Green, John C., Corwin E. Smidt, James L. Guth and Lyman A. Kellstedt (2004), *Religion and the 2004 Election: A Post-Election Analysis*, Pew Research Center for the People and the Press

Keeter, Scott (2006), "Evangelicals and the GOP: An Update – Strongly Republican Group Not Immune to Party's Troubles", Pew Research Center for the People and the Press, 18 October, http://pewresearch.org/

Kirkpatrick David D. and Sheryl Gay Stolberg (2005), "Backers of Gay Marriage Ban Use Social Security as Cudgel", *New York Times,* 25 January

Kohut, Andrew (2008), "Post-Election Perspectives", Pew Research Center for the People and the Press, 13 November, http://pewresearch.org/

Kuo, David (2006), *Tempting Faith: An Inside Story of Political Seduction,* New York: Free Press

Leaming, Jeremy (2005), "James Dobson: The Religious Right's 800-Pound Gorilla", February, Americans United for Separation of Church and State, http://www.au.org/

Linker, Damon (2008), "Sticking With the Devil They Know", *The New Republic,* 7 November

PBS – Frontline (2005), "Chronology: Karl Rove's Life and Political Career", http://www.pbs.org/

Pew Forum on Religion and Public Life (2008a), "Voting Religiously", 5 November, http://pewresearch.org/

Pew Forum on Religion and Public Life (2008b), "How the Faithful Voted", 10 November, http://pewresearch.org/

PollingReport (2005), "Miscellany – Terri Schiavo", http://www.pollingreport.com/

PollingReport.com (2009), "Problems and Priorities", http://www.pollingreport.com/

Savage, Charlie (2008), "Appeals Courts Pushed to Right by Bush Choices", *New York Times,* 29 October

Stein, Rob (2009), "Obama to loosen stem cell funding: move will repeal limits on embryonic research", *Washington Post,* 7 March

Wheeler, Russell (2008), "What Will the Presidential Election Mean for the U.S. Courts of Appeals?", The Brookings Institution, 21 October, http://www.brookings.edu/

*Chapter 14*

# COMMUNICATIONS STRATEGIES IN THE BUSH WHITE HOUSE

John Anthony Maltese

Like most recent presidents, George W. Bush embraced an approach to governing that is sometimes referred to as "the permanent campaign". Sidney Blumenthal helped to popularise that phrase in a 1982 book of the same name. But it was the Democratic consultant Pat Caddell who is often said to have originated the concept of an ongoing campaign in a December 1976 memo to President-elect Jimmy Carter titled "Initial Working Paper on Political Strategy". In that memo, Caddell wrote: "Essentially it is my thesis that governing with public approval requires a continuing political campaign" (Caddell 1976; see also Klein 2005).

The goal of the permanent campaign is to rally public support that can then be used to pressure members of Congress to implement presidential policy. Instead of a deliberative bargaining process in which Congress and the White House work together to create policy, "governing with public approval" assumes a more adversarial relationship in which presidents try to coerce members of Congress to follow their lead by using the force of public opinion and the threat of electoral retaliation as their primary weapons. Presidents try to build that support by "going public" – issuing campaign-like appeals to the public through speeches and other forms of direct communication (Kernell 2006).

The creation of the White House Office of Communications in 1969 helped to institutionalise this practice (Maltese 1992). Its embrace, though, has led to a breakdown of the traditional distinction between campaigning and governing. Campaigning, by its very nature, is adversarial, while governing is – or at least should be –

largely collaborative. As Hugh Heclo (2000: 11) puts it, "campaigning is self-centered, and governing is group-centered". The permanent campaign, by definition, makes collaboration difficult and has helped to remake government "into an instrument designed to sustain an elected official's popularity" (Blumenthal 1982: 7).

George Edwards (2000: 33) identified the presidency of Bill Clinton as a quintessential example of the permanent campaign in action, and Charles O. Jones suggested that he remained in full campaign mode even in his final year in office. As Jones put it, the Clinton presidency "was a prime example of the campaigning style of governing, practiced by a virtuoso" (2000: 185). More recently, Scott McClellan, who served as George W. Bush's White House press secretary, criticised the Bush administration for embracing the same approach:

> The permanent campaign approach we [the Bush team] publicly denounced and distanced ourselves from in the 2000 campaign was vigorously embraced [by the Bush administration] after Election Day. The massive Bush campaign machine was integrally woven into his White House governance, without adequate controls or corresponding checks and balances . . . [I]f President Bush and his team had recognized and understood the many pitfalls of the permanent campaign approach to governance, the administration as well as the nation would have been better served. (McClellan 2008: 311–12)

McClellan argues that the Bush administration's "excessive embrace of the permanent campaign" was most consequential in terms of policy with regard to the war in Iraq. From the outset, the administration chose to sell the idea of invading Iraq "through a political marketing campaign" (McClellan 2008: 312; see also Schulman 2006). In retrospect, critics charged that the administration used selective evidence to make the threat posed by Iraq "seem more serious than it really was and thereby create a sense of urgency and gain necessary public backing [for an invasion]" (McClellan 2008: 8). Then, when confronted with these allegations that it had misled the nation into war, the Bush administration seemed to ratchet up the campaign. "When candor could have helped minimize the political fallout from the unraveling of the chief rationale for war, spin and evasion were instead what we employed" (McClellan 2008: 229).

Before turning specifically to the Bush administration's campaign to sell the invasion of Iraq, both the administration's approach to the permanent campaign and to the White House staff units designed to implement it should be examined. All modern presidents recognise both the need to co-ordinate the flow of information from the executive branch and the benefits of using symbolism to promote presidential policy. As Dick Cheney (1989) once noted, the most powerful tool that a president has "is the ability to use the symbolic aspects of the presidency to promote [the administration's] goals and objectives". But symbolism alone is not enough. The president must also control the flow of information and, with it, the agenda. "You don't let the press set the agenda," Cheney insisted. "The press is going to object to that. They like to set the agenda. They like to decide what's important and what isn't important. But if you let them do that, they're going to trash your presidency."

Controlling the agenda and using symbolism to promote that agenda are core elements of the permanent campaign. So, too, is going public. The shift towards the permanent campaign is reflected in the dramatic increase in the number of speeches given by presidents. Major speeches, such as the annual State of the Union address and other prime-time televised addresses to the American people, have always been used sparingly. But presidents also give minor speeches that are delivered to specific constituencies, often on trips around the country. It is the number of these minor speeches that has increased dramatically in recent years. Samuel Kernell (2006: 122–3) tallied the average number of minor speeches given by presidents since Hoover during their first three years in office. He noted that Nixon, Carter and Reagan gave five times as many minor speeches as Hoover, Roosevelt and Truman; that George H. W. Bush doubled that already high number and averaged a minor address every three days; and that both Clinton and George W. Bush averaged a minor address almost every other day. This tendency to give frequent minor speeches to narrowly targeted constituencies increases the likelihood that presidential messages will be more extreme in their tone. While major speeches to a national audience need to appeal to a broad constituency, and therefore tend to be moderate in tone, narrowly targeted minor speeches are often designed to appeal to a narrow interest or to the party base, and therefore tend to be more strident (Cohen 2008: 189–95).

The increased number of presidential speeches has also led to a corresponding increase in the number of days presidents spend travelling. Kernell (2006: 129) notes that George W. Bush engaged in more domestic travel during his first three years in office than his predecessors: an average of almost eighty-five days a year on the road (and an average of an additional thirty days a year of foreign travel). In comparison, Hoover, Roosevelt and Truman averaged less than fifteen days of domestic travel a year. Hoover spent only three days outside the country during his entire four years in office, and Roosevelt devoted only nine days to foreign travel during his first four years in office. In contrast, "going international" is now commonplace. Richard Rose (1991: 38) notes that Nixon spent fifty-nine days outside the country during his first term and Carter fifty-six. According to Mark Knoller (2003, 2008), a reporter for CBS News who gathers presidential statistics, George W. Bush surpassed those numbers during his first two-and-a-half years in office (sixty-five days of foreign travel to thirty-two nations by August 2003). By October 2008, Bush had visited seventy-five countries – several more than once.

The permanent campaign was on display from the earliest days of the Bush administration. First, following the example of Ronald Reagan, it settled on a clear, simple agenda that focused primarily on four issues: education reform, faith-based initiatives, tax cuts and military preparedness (including the need for a missile defence system). Then it unveiled those issues by devoting a week of public events to each, starting with education reform during its first week in office. According to White House Chief of Staff Andrew Card, Bush was mindful of his father's failure to "market and sell" an agenda, so the younger Bush plunged head first into a campaign to promote his. During his first two months in office, Bush spent thirty days visiting twenty-five states to campaign for his agenda while his father visited seventeen states during the same period and Bill Clinton twelve (Burke 2004: 123).

Bush unveiled his full agenda in a televised speech before a joint session of Congress on 27 February 2001, and then immediately followed it up with speaking tours to promote the centrepiece of his agenda – a proposed $1.6 trillion tax cut – to targeted audiences. In just two days following his address to Congress, Bush gave speeches touting his tax cut in Pennsylvania, Nebraska, Iowa, Arkansas and Georgia. This tactic represented the purest form of going public. In speech after speech, he urged his audiences to pressure Congress into passing his initiative. When the House of Representatives voted to approve the tax cut on 8 March, the president was still on the road, targeting states where Democratic senators who opposed the tax cut would be facing close re-election battles in 2002. In Fargo, North Dakota, Bush urged a cheering, flag-waving crowd to contact their senators: "If you like what you hear today, maybe e-mail some of the good folks from the United States Senate from your state. If you like what you hear, why don't you just give'em a call and write'em a letter" (ABC 2001).

Not only did the president mobilise public support to pressurise members of Congress, he seemed unwilling to compromise. As Richard Stevenson (2001) of the *New York Times* put it on 7 April: "On tax cuts, President Bush has had a single, relentless message for months: It is my way or the highway." In the end, the Senate voted on 23 May to approve a $1.3 trillion tax cut – slightly less than the $1.6 trillion the president had originally sought but with twelve Democratic senators crossing the aisle to vote with all fifty Republicans.

A key original architect of Bush's communications operation was his long-time confidante, Karen Hughes. She had performed a similar role when Bush was governor of Texas. Hughes became known for instilling strict discipline in the administration's efforts to control the agenda and to avoid information leaks and in-fighting among staff. She helped to prioritise issues and then market them through carefully co-ordinated events. At the same time, Karl Rove served as senior adviser to the president, offering advice on political affairs. He maintained close ties with the conservative base of the Republican Party and also devised the strategic plan for introducing Bush's policy agenda in a way that would achieve the greatest political benefit (Burke 2004: 80–1). Martha Joynt Kumar (2007: 75) has written that the team of Rove and Hughes served as a professional "marriage of communications and politics" that "made Bush's style of governing an extension of his style of campaigning, and vice versa". Scott McClellan agrees:

> The most obvious evidence that the Bush White House embraced the permanent campaign is the expansive political operation that was put in place from day one. Chief political strategist Karl Rove was given an enormous center of influence within the White

> House from the outset. This was only strengthened by Rove's force of personality and closeness to the president. He would be one of three key players – along with Karen Hughes and Andy Card – beyond the president himself who most defined the way the Bush White House operated. (McClellan 2008: 73)

The Bush administration's emphasis on the permanent campaign led it to reorganise its communications staff. It cut the size of the White House Press Office by more than half while actually increasing slightly the overall number of staff devoted to other aspects of communications, including long-term planning and speech-writing. The Office of Media Affairs was moved out of the Press Office and made a separate department (Burke 2004: 79). Arguably these adjustments reflected the administration's desire to plan and execute a public relations campaign while, at the same time, playing down the importance of the White House press corps.

The idea of using targeted communications to bypass the critical filter of the establishment media was not new – nor was the desire of presidential administrations to avoid leaks – but the Bush administration seemed particularly adept at implementing both strategies. As Bush's first press secretary, Ari Fleischer (2005: 40), later wrote, "Unlike in most White Houses, the top staff of the Bush White House showed little interest in talking with the press, making reporters' jobs more difficult. Andy Card and [deputy chief of staff] Josh Bolten didn't think it was their job to answer reporters' phone calls. They preferred to focus on their governing responsibilities."

The president himself expressed little interest in what the mainstream media wrote. In an interview with Brit Hume (2003) on Fox News, President Bush said that he rarely read newspapers. He said that he glanced at the headlines to get a flavour of what issues were moving, but that he rarely read the stories, because "a lot of times there's opinions mixed in with the news". He added, apparently without irony, that he preferred to get the news from "objective sources . . . and the most objective sources I have are people on my staff who tell me what's happening in the world". He also held few solo press conferences – only seventeen in his first term, the lowest number for any president in recent memory. In comparison, his father held eighty-four during the same period (Kumar 2007: 266–7). The number rose slightly in Bush's second term: by October 2008 he had given an additional twenty-six solo press conferences (Knoller 2008).

At the end of 2001, Ryan Lizza bemoaned in the *New York Times* magazine that Bush had ushered in the era of the "pressless presidency". "It's a simple idea", Lizza wrote, "the press (more specifically, the national press) does not matter to the administration's success". Or, as Martha Kumar told Lizza, "'The Bush people want to develop a message and stay on it. They use the Press Office to deliver the message and not answer a lot of questions about it'". Kumar has since written that the Bush communications operation excelled in areas where that of Clinton had been weak: long-term planning and discipline. It was weak where the Clinton administration had excelled, however: providing rapid response to critics and seizing opportunities to turn unexpected events to its advantage. In short, the Bush communications apparatus was set up as "an advocacy operation" designed "to make news on the president's terms and spend little time responding to the agenda of others, including that of reporters" (Kumar 2007: 71–3).

Part of that advocacy operation included co-ordinating rhetoric with stagecraft. Again, the Bush administration took a page from Ronald Reagan's book. Both Reagan and Bush recognised that, in conveying messages, visual images can be more powerful than words. White House aide Michael Deaver perfected the technique of stagecraft during the Reagan administration. As Reagan's Chief of Staff, Donald Regan, later wrote, Deaver

> saw – designed – each presidential action as a one-minute or two-minute spot on the evening network news, or a picture on page one of the Washington Post or the New York Times, and conceived every presidential appearance in terms of camera angles . . . Every moment of every appearance was scheduled, every word was scripted, and every place where Reagan was expected to stand was chalked with toe marks. (1988: 248)

It came as no small praise, then, when Deaver said in 2003 that the Bush administration understood stagecraft "as well as anybody ever has" (quoted in Bumiller 2003).

The man who was responsible during most of the Bush administration for setting the stage and making the president look good on television was Scott Sforza, a former ABC News television producer who served as deputy communications director for Bush until the summer of 2007. Sforza's most infamous example of stagecraft – one that ultimately hurt the president – was Bush's May 2003 "tail-hook" landing aboard the USS *Abraham Lincoln* in a S-3B Viking Navy jet. Developments in fibre-optics technology allowed a clear, stable, live transmission from almost anywhere – including from a ship at sea (Kumar 2007: 103). As the cameras rolled, the president emerged from the jet in full "top gun" gear: wearing a green flight suit and holding a white helmet. The image reinforced the message of a strong, courageous leader in control. "Yes, I flew it", the president shouted with a big smile as he strode among the crew of the ship, slapping backs and shaking hands (CNN.com 2003). Bush became the first sitting president to wear a military uniform – not even Dwight D. Eisenhower (1953–61), a five-star general, had done so while in office (Basen 2007). Hours later, now dressed in a suit and tie, the president, surrounded by sailors, gave a speech aboard the ship announcing the end of major combat operations in Iraq. Behind him, a huge banner declared Mission Accomplished.

Originally, the White House told reporters that the president had to fly by jet to the aircraft carrier because it was too far out to sea for him to come by helicopter. As it turned out, the ship was within easy helicopter range – only 30 miles from the coast of California – and cameras were carefully poised on the ship to avoid seeing the shoreline (Milbank 2003). Press Secretary Fleisher insisted that the ship made faster progress than expected but the impression lingered that the event was staged to mislead the public. As the war in Iraq dragged on for months and then years after that event, the Mission Accomplished sign also became a symbol of miscalculation on the part of the Bush administration.

The White House later insisted that the crew of the USS *Abraham Lincoln* had requested the Mission Accomplished sign to signify the end of their ten-month tour of duty but Sforza routinely placed catch-phrases behind the president when he spoke to reinforce the essence of the presidential message. Sometimes those phrases were on large signs or banners but often they appeared as "wallpaper" – panels behind the president that displayed multiple images of the phrase repeated in small print. Wherever the president spoke, the catch-phrases followed: Foundation for Growth when he spoke about the economy; Protecting the Homeland when he spoke about homeland security; No Child Left Behind when he spoke about education reform (Jackson 2005). Sforza described the tactic as communicating the president's message by snapshot: any photograph of the event should communicate what the president was talking about (Kumar 2007: 100–1). Mission Accomplished on the day that the president declared the end of major combat operations in Iraq fitted that pattern.

Careful attention to the backdrop on the USS *Abraham Lincoln* was thus part of a familiar pattern. For example, when Bush spoke at Mount Rushmore in 2002, the *New York Times* (Bumiller 2003) noted that his aides positioned the platform for television crews "off to one side, not head on as other White Houses have done, so that the cameras caught Mr. Bush in profile, his face perfectly aligned with the four presidents carved in stone". And, when the president spoke to thousands of Marines and families at the Marine Corps Air Station in Miramar, California, in August 2003, Air Force One landed next to two rows of fighter jets lining the tarmac. The *Los Angeles Times* (Chen 2003) reported the scene: "From Air Force One, Bush strode between the AV-8B Harrier IIs and F/A-18 Hornets, wearing a lightweight, military jacket despite the warm temperatures." Once again, the image was picture perfect.

Sometimes the backdrop for a presidential speech was designed to convey a more subtle message. Thus, when President Bush went on television a few weeks after the 11 September 2001 terrorist attacks to announce military strikes in Afghanistan, Sforza chose the Treaty Room because the president could deliver the speech in front of a window through which viewers could see midday traffic on Constitution Avenue. That image of the traffic, Sforza said, sent a "message to the world that we're still in business here" (Kumar 2007: 100–1).

At the outset of the Bush administration, Karen Hughes oversaw four primary communications units in the White House: the Press Office, the Office of Communications, Speechwriting and the Office of Media Affairs. The Press Office was responsible for daily interactions with the White House press corps, the Office of Communications with long-term planning and stagecraft, and the Office of Media Affairs for reaching out to local media where messages could be targeted to particular constituencies.

In the aftermath of 9/11, a fifth unit was added. Originally called the Coalition Information Center (CIC), it was designed as an around-the-clock communications operation to build public support abroad, especially among Muslims in the Middle East, for the war on terror. The CIC co-ordinated daily press briefings around the world, including Washington, London, Islamabad and Kabul. Jim Wilkinson, who ran the CIC, said that a primary aim was to set the agenda for foreign reporters. Echoing Cheney's assertion that you can't let the press set the agenda, Wilkinson said: "We've learned that you either start the news wave or you're swamped by it" (Keen 2001). The CIC was also designed to provide rapid response to events overseas, and to book pro-American guests on foreign television and radio programmes. In January 2003, in the days leading up to the invasion of Iraq, the White House expanded the CIC and turned it into the Office of Global Communications but that office was disbanded in 2005 and its functions transferred to Karen Hughes when she became Undersecretary of State for Public Diplomacy. Together, these units played to the Bush administration's strengths: controlling the agenda-setting priorities, planning ahead and co-ordinating the flow of information (Kumar 2007: 109–10, 118).

In addition to decreasing the size of the press office, the Bush administration abolished in 2008 the informal morning "gaggle" between the press secretary and reporters (Abramowitz 2008). The gaggle was a fifteen-minute, off-camera interaction that became firmly established during the Clinton administration when the practice of televising the daily press briefing began. Television made the briefings more confrontational. Reporters played to the cameras, and the press secretary was forced to be more guarded since every minute of the briefing was filmed. In comparison, the off-screen gaggle provided an opportunity for the sort of informal exchange that used to characterise the relationship between reporters and the press secretary. As Martha Kumar noted, it "served to reinforce camaraderie rather than antagonism", and it also helped both sides to gauge what issues would be important that day (2007: 223, 233). Bush Press Secretary Dana Perino replaced the gaggle with a new on-camera briefing in the morning. Perino argued that this additional briefing was necessary because of foreign deadlines and the emergence of the twenty-four-hour news cycle but the change did away with the only regularly scheduled off-camera opportunity for reporters as a group to meet the press secretary (Abramowitz 2008).

In the early days of the Bush administration, some pundits predicted that Bush would follow Bill Clinton's tactic of "triangulation":

moving to the centre and co-opting the opposition party's issues. Bush had won the White House but had lost the popular vote in the 2000 election, so a centrist approach seemed to make sense. He had also campaigned as a compassionate conservative and on the mantra of being a "uniter, not a divider". Instead, once elected, Bush largely played to his base and proceeded to act as if he had a mandate for his agenda. In the beginning that seemed to be a risky strategy. After all, he entered office with a *dis*approval rating of 25 per cent, the highest of any new president since polling began, and an approval rating of 57 per cent. Disapproval increased to 39 per cent by early September 2001 and approval declined to just 51 per cent. Then, overnight, the terrorist attacks propelled his approval rating to 90 per cent and cut his disapproval rating to 6 per cent. His approval ratings stayed above 80 per cent for almost six months, according to Gallup's polling.

Bush's high ratings gave him political capital to push his agenda, and he embarked upon an intensive effort to regain Republican control of the Senate in the 2002 mid-term elections. His decision to campaign aggressively for Republican candidates was a risky one. The party of the president typically loses seats in mid-term elections. Indeed, the president's party had gained seats in the House of Representatives only twice between the Civil War (1861–5) and Bush's inauguration (Fortier and Ornstein 2003: 166). Had the Republicans followed form and lost seats, the election could have been perceived as a direct repudiation of Bush. Instead, the Republicans regained control of the Senate and extended their majority in the House.

The president campaigned furiously for sixteen Republican Senate candidates in the 2002 mid-term elections, and the Republican Senatorial Campaign Committee launched an aggressive series of advertisements attacking Democratic incumbents for their supposed failure to support homeland security. The most notorious was an advert against Senator Max Cleland of Georgia, run by his Republican opponent Saxby Chambliss. It portrayed Cleland – a decorated war hero who lost both his legs and his right arm in a grenade explosion in Vietnam – as unpatriotic for supposedly voting against the Department of Homeland Security, and it juxtaposed images of Cleland with Osama bin Laden. In fact, Cleland had supported the creation of a Department of Homeland Security before President Bush had, and his votes against specific amendments to the bill creating the department were on procedural grounds designed to strengthen the bill. The advertisement helped to propel Chambliss to victory and secure a Republican majority in the Senate, but it infuriated Democrats and ultimately helped to unify them against the president (Fortier and Ornstein 2003: 171). In the aftermath of 9/11, Bush chose to use his new-found popularity not to reach across the aisle and build a new consensus in Washington but, rather, as a tool to build a partisan coalition. In so doing, he ratcheted up the permanent campaign and fuelled the hyperpartisan atmosphere of Washington.

As the president campaigned for Senate candidates in the 2002 mid-term elections, the Bush administration also began another campaign: to convince Congress and the American people of the need to invade Iraq. This brings us back to Scott McClellan's (2008: 120) charge that the Bush administration sold the idea of going to war through a political marketing campaign that the administration called "educating the public about the threat". As McClellan later wrote:

> In the fall of 2002, Bush and his White House were engaged in a carefully orchestrated campaign to shape and manipulate sources of public approval to our advantage. We'd done much the same on other issues – tax cuts and education – to great success. But war with Iraq was different. Beyond the irreversible human costs and the substantial financial price, the decision to go to war and the way we went about selling it would ultimately lead to increased polarization and intensified partisan warfare. Our lack of candor and honesty in making the case for war would later provoke a partisan response from our opponents that, in its own way, further distorted and obscured a more nuanced reality. (2008: 125)

The campaign to sell the war centred on the allegation that Iraq possessed weapons of mass destruction that posed an imminent threat to the United States. These were said to include stockpiles of chemical and biological weapons, and an active pursuit of uranium for a nuclear weapons programme. The administration also claimed that Iraq had links with al-Qaeda. The administration was ready to start the campaign in August 2002 but, as White House Chief of Staff Card told the *New York Times*, "From a marketing point of view you don't introduce new products in August" (Bumiller 2002). Therefore they decided to use the first anniversary of the 9/11 attacks to launch the campaign. The president gave a carefully choreographed speech from

Ellis Island in New York with the Statue of Liberty in the background. Sforza arranged for the White House to rent three barges of spotlights to place around the base of the Statue of Liberty so that it would be perfectly illuminated behind the president (Bumiller 2003).

The campaign actually began a few days before the president's 11 September speech from Ellis Island. A former United Nations weapons inspector in Baghdad had claimed that the administration was overstating its case about Iraq's weapons of mass destruction, so White House speech-writer Michael Gerson came up with a retort designed to scare Congress and the American people: "We don't want the smoking gun to be a mushroom cloud." Originally meant to be unveiled by Bush, the line was deemed so effective that it was used first by an unnamed White House source and then by National Security Advisor Condoleezza Rice (Isikoff and Corn 2006: 35). The *New York Times* conveniently ran a story on 8 September – based in part on unnamed administration sources – suggesting that Saddam Hussein was intensifying efforts to secure parts to manufacture nuclear weapons. The story noted that administration officials were "alarmed that American intelligence underestimated the pace and scale of Iraq's nuclear program" and added: "The first sign of a 'smoking gun,' they argue, may be a mushroom cloud" (Gordon and Miller 2002).

The same morning that the story appeared in the *New York Times*, Vice President Dick Cheney went on NBC's Meet the Press. He said that he did not want to cite intelligence sources but, since "it's now public" as a result of the *Times* article, Cheney talked about Iraq's efforts to obtain aluminium tubes for use in the manufacture of nuclear bombs. Cheney added that it was important "not to focus just on the nuclear threat". One of the real concerns about Saddam Hussein, he said, "is his biological weapons capability; the fact that he may, at some point, try to use smallpox, anthrax, plague, some other kind of biological agent against other nations, possibly including even the United States" (Cheney 2002).

A couple of hours later Condoleezza Rice appeared on CNN's Late Edition with Wolf Blitzer. "There is no doubt that Saddam Hussein's regime is a danger to the United States", she said. Asked about former chief UN weapons inspector Scott Ritter's assertion that Iraq posed no serious threat to the United States, Rice also made the claim that aluminium tubes "that are only really suited for nuclear weapons programs" had been shipped to Iraq, and then added: "The problem here is that there will always be some uncertainty about how quickly he can acquire nuclear weapons. But we don't want the smoking gun to be a mushroom cloud" (Rice 2002).

The first anniversary of 9/11 also reinforced the fear of terrorist threats. The White House announced on 10 September that Vice President Cheney had been sent to a secure, undisclosed location while the terror alert was raised to orange (Isikoff and Corn 2006: 42). In his address to the nation from Ellis Island the next day, the president asserted that "we will not allow any terrorist or tyrant to threaten civilization with weapons of mass murder" (Bush 2002a). Then, on 12 September, the president condemned Iraq in a speech before the United Nations, and he followed up more specifically about the threat of Saddam Hussein in a speech on 7 October. After continually linking Iraq and al-Qaeda, noting that Saddam's regime had produced "thousands of tons of chemical agents" and arguing that Iraq was led by a "homicidal dictator who is addicted to weapons of mass destruction", the president concluded: "Facing clear evidence of peril, we cannot wait for the final proof – the smoking gun – that could come in the form of a mushroom cloud" (Bush 2002b). Four days later, Congress passed a joint resolution authorising the president to use military force against Iraq, which the president signed into law on 16 October.

The invasion of Iraq did not come until March 2003, and the administration continued its campaign to build public support for war. In doing so, it used questionable intelligence claims that Iraq had recently attempted to obtain uranium from Niger. White House speech-writers had considered including the claim in the president's 12 September 2002 speech to the United Nations, but the CIA did not want Bush to use the allegation so it was excluded from the speech. Despite continued doubts about the accuracy of the allegation, Bush included it in his 2003 State of the Union address on 28 January: "The British government has learned that Saddam Hussein recently sought significant quantities of uranium from Africa." As Scott McClellan (2008: 5) wrote, "Those sixteen words would become the nexus of the controversy that delivered a near-fatal blow to the credibility of the president and his administration."

By March, the Director General of the International Atomic Energy Agency, responsible for nuclear inspection and verification, denounced the uranium claim as not credible. Later that month, the *New Yorker* published an article by Seymour Hersh (2003) that claimed the documents that served as the basis for the uranium claim were forgeries. Then, in May 2003 – five days after the president's Mission Accomplished speech on the USS *Abraham Lincoln* – the Pulitzer Prize-winning journalist Nicolas Kristof (2003) published a column in the *New York Times* claiming that the vice president's office had, more than a year earlier, "asked for an investigation of the uranium deal". That led to a "former U.S. ambassador to Africa" being dispatched to Niger to look into the claim. Kristof said that the envoy reported to the CIA and the State Department that the claim was "unequivocally wrong and that the documents [supporting the claim] had been forged". If true, that meant that the administration had deliberately used false information to mislead the country into war.

Furious at the story, the vice president's office sought and found the identity of Kristof's unnamed source: the former United States ambassador Joseph Wilson. The vice president and his aides then engaged in a series of leaks meant to discredit Wilson. Those leaks revealed that Wilson's wife, Valerie Plame, was a CIA agent. They were designed to show that she, not the vice president's office, had arranged Wilson's trip to Niger. In so doing, they publicly exposed Plame's covert identity as a CIA agent – a federal crime, if a government official knowingly "outs" an undercover agent. The leak led to criminal investigations that culminated in the conviction of Cheney's Chief of Staff Lewis "Scooter" Libby for perjury, obstruction of justice and making false statements to federal investigators.

The allegation that the Bush administration misled the nation into war was further buttressed by the failure to find weapons of mass destruction in Iraq after the US-led invasion in March 2003. A CIA report, released on 6 October 2004, concluded that most of Saddam Hussein's weapons of mass destruction had been destroyed in 1991 and that no stockpiles of such weapons remained at the time of the 2003 invasion. In December 2004 the United States government quietly called a halt to its search for biological, chemical and nuclear weapons in Iraq (Linzer 2005). Nonetheless, the administration's pre-war rhetoric was so effective that polls in January 2005 showed that about 40 per cent of Americans still believed that there were weapons of mass destruction in Iraq when the United States invaded (*USA Today* 2005).

In retrospect, many observers have suggested that the press did not live up to its responsibility to serve as a "watchdog" as the administration made the case for invading Iraq in 2002 and 2003 (McClellan 2008: 125; Boehlert 2006). A study conducted by the University of Maryland's Center for International and Security Studies noted that, after 11 September 2001, "the Bush administration [was] . . . especially successful at getting the American media to confirm its political and diplomatic agenda". The report added that the media tended to repeat the administration's blanket assertions about weapons of mass destruction without question or analysis, and that they failed to make important distinctions between things like a nuclear energy programme and a nuclear weapons programme, or to parse distinctions between nuclear, chemical and biological threats. All were lumped together under the broad heading of weapons of mass destruction. As the report noted, "The media's failure to recognize these and other distinctions distorted reporting on the cost-benefit calculations to manage those risks." At the same time, the report noted that the Bush administration used "cute" terms like "mini-nuke" and "bunker-busters" to refer to American nuclear weapons because it did not want them to be portrayed as weapons of mass destruction, and concluded that the "dramatic tightening of information flow from the White House to reporters" also aided the administration in its manipulation of media coverage of its case for war (Moeller 2004: 6–12).

Attempts to control the media even led the Bush administration to pay for favourable media coverage. In early 2005, the *Washington Post* revealed that the Education Department paid conservative commentator Armstrong Williams $241,000 to promote the No Child Left Behind education bill (Kutz 2005). Soon media stories revealed that others, including syndicated columnists, Maggie Gallagher and Michael McManus, were paid by the Department of Health and Human Services to promote marriage. The president quickly ordered cabinet secretaries to stop hiring columnists to promote administration policy (*CBS News* 2005) but, later in that year, it was revealed that similar tactics continued to be used abroad. The Pentagon had hired a Washington-based public relations firm called the Lincoln Group to plant pro-American articles in Iraqi newspapers. The articles appeared to be written by Iraqis but were actually written by the Pentagon, and Iraqi newspapers were paid to publish them (Gerth and Shane 2005). It was also revealed that the Pentagon's US Special

Operations Command had awarded contracts worth $300 million to the Lincoln Group and to two other organisations "to develop slogans, advertisements, newspaper articles, radio spots and television programs to build support for US policies overseas" (Kelley 2005). At the direction of the Pentagon, the Lincoln Group even hired Iraqi religious leaders to participate in the propaganda efforts (Cloud and Gerth 2006). In March 2006, a Pentagon study concluded that the military paying Iraqi newspapers to print positive stories did not violate military policy and could continue unless the Pentagon chose to change its policy (Shanker 2005).

A final aspect of the permanent campaign that deserves mention is the use of polling data to formulate presidential appeals. Every president since Nixon has retained his own paid polling consultants, and earlier presidents, such as Franklin Roosevelt, secretly sought polling data from unpaid, unofficial advisers (Heath 2000: 382; Eisinger 2003: 3). These pollsters go far beyond simple tracking of presidential approval. Highly specific polling data on everyone from homeowners to born-again Christians allow administrations to gauge the views of particular constituencies and then fashion messages that appeal to them (Heath 2000: 384). The rise of new media technologies has made highly targeted public appeals much easier.

Presidents also use polling and focus groups to test the language that they plan to use in speeches. Reagan did this extensively, especially towards the end of his administration, and Clinton made wide use of polls in formulating his agenda. In contrast, George W. Bush publicly scoffed at those who tailored policy to fit the latest poll results. He praised people "who are willing to stand on principle; people not driven by polls or focus groups", and, throughout the 2000 presidential campaign, he pledged not to govern by public opinion polls (Bush 2007). Nonetheless, political scientist Kathryn Dunn Tenpas (2003: 32–5) noted that the Bush administration used polls much as other recent presidents have while, at the same time, "shrouding his polling apparatus" and denying its impact. "What is unusual about the Bush team's political operation is the chasm between its words and actions", she wrote. "Never before has a White House engaged in such anti-polling rhetoric." She also noted that pollsters were distanced from the president himself, the first time that a modern president had "built up such a buffer between the pollsters and the president".

Despite its enthusiastic embrace of the permanent campaign, Bush's presidency ended in failure. By April 2008 he had the highest disapproval rating of any president in the history of Gallup polling: 69 per cent. In October 2008, his approval rating hit the lowest point of his presidency, 25 per cent, only three points higher than Harry S. Truman's all-time low of 22 per cent in 1952 (Newport 2008). Exogenous events such as the financial crisis contributed to the low rating, as did the unpopularity of the war in Iraq and perceptions that Bush had mishandled it. But arguably some of the more strident aspects of the permanent campaign may have made it worse for the president. For example, his decision to stake out an adversarial approach with Congress left little goodwill to fall back on in bad times. Senator Chuck Hagel, a Nebraskan Republican, told the *New Yorker* magazine that the Bush administration "viewed Congress as an appendage, a nuisance. Clinton was just the opposite. Reagan was the opposite. Bush's father was the opposite. They understood the value of making Congress their ally" (Bruck 2008).

The fact that the president appeared intentionally to mislead the country into war also undermined his trustworthiness on other issues. A *USA Today/Gallup* poll conducted 28–30 April 2006 found that only 41 per cent of respondents felt that President Bush was "honest and trustworthy", while 56 per cent did not (PollingReport.com). And, while many reporters liked the president personally, the administration made little secret of the fact that it viewed the press to be irrelevant. As Ken Auletta (2004) wrote,

> What seems new with the Bush White House is the unusual skill that it has shown in keeping much of the press at a distance while controlling the news agenda. And perhaps for the first time the White House has come to see reporters as special pleaders – pleaders for more access and better headlines – as if the press were just another interest group.

Arguably, Bush's approach contributed to the escalation of polarised politics that had been building for some years. The period since 1969 has been marked by long periods of divided government and a pronounced increase in partisanship. Parties in Congress became more polarised, with a dramatic increase in partisan voting in both houses (Fleisher and Bond 2000: 3–4). At the same time, partisanship rose among the electorate: party loyalty increased, split-ticket voting decreased and the ideological gap between the two parties widened. Polarised politics – exacerbated by the controversial outcome of the 2000 election – led to a dramatic "partisan wedge", illustrated in public support for President Bush. An analysis by Gary Jacobson (2003: 199–201) of twenty-eight opinion polls conducted between Bush's inauguration in January 2001 and the terrorist attacks in September showed that 88 per cent of self-identified Republicans approved of Bush's performance compared with only 31 per cent of self-identified Democrats. The 11 September attacks narrowed that 57-point gap and, had Bush then made more of an effort to reach across the aisle, he possibly could have helped to bridge the partisan divide. Instead, he chose to accentuate partisanship and increase pressure on opponents in Congress through the use of the permanent campaign. As a result, the partisan gap again widened, measuring 54 points by the time of the November 2002 mid-term elections.

No modern president can afford to operate without a carefully orchestrated communications agenda. Style is part of enacting substance. But it must be coupled with deliberation and co-operative relationships with other power centres. A permanent campaign that ignores that reality is doomed to failure. Barack Obama may have a unique opportunity to use his extraordinary skills as a communicator to sell his policies while, at the same time, easing the polarisation and partisanship spawned by an excessive reliance on the permanent campaign. In Gallup polls taken in early November 2008, Bush and Obama were almost mirror images in terms of popularity: Obama had a 70 per cent favourability rating and 25 per cent unfavourable while Bush had a 27 per cent job-approval rating and 66 per cent disapproval. Even more significantly, 65 per cent was confident of Obama's ability to be a good president (Saad 2008). That alone should help Obama as he takes on the daunting challenges that await him.

Those around Obama also suggest that he will represent something new. Asked by Steve Inskeep (2008) on National Public Radio's Morning Edition whether the Obama presidency will embrace a Clinton-style permanent campaign, Obama's Deputy Campaign Manager Steve Hildebrand replied that, if Washington "continues to be just as polarized as it is today, we're just not going to get enough done". Time will tell if Obama is willing or able to bridge the partisan divide but it would be naive to expect other aspects of the permanent campaign to disappear. Ever-expanding opportunities provided by new technology for blogging, posting videos and targeting specific constituencies make the logistics of running a permanent campaign easier than ever. The Obama administration took advantage of these opportunities in its early days in office, and it will surely continue to do so. In short, the rougher edges of the permanent campaign may be in for an overhaul but the basic strategy seems destined to endure.

## BIBLIOGRAPHY


ABC Television (2001), "Bush Tax Cuts Clear First Hurdle", *World News Tonight*, 8 March

Abramowitz, Michael (2008), "Goodbye, Gaggle", *Washington Post*, 8 September

Auletta, Ken (2004), "Fortress Bush: How the White House Keeps the Press Under Control", *The New Yorker*, 19 January

Basen, Ira (2007), "Spinning War: Episode 5 – 'The best presidential picture in years'", CBC News, 15 February, www.cbc.ca/news

Blumenthal, Sidney (1982), *The Permanent Campaign*, New York: Simon and Schuster

Boehlert, Eric (2006), *Lapdogs: How the Press Rolled Over for Bush*, New York: Free Press

Bruck, Connie (2008), "Odd Man Out", *The New Yorker*, 3 November

Bumiller, Elisabeth (2002), "Bush Aides Set Strategy to Sell Policy in Iraq", *New York Times*, 6 September

Bumiller, Elisabeth (2003), "Keepers of Bush Image Lift Stagecraft to New Heights", *New York Times*, 16 May

Burke, John P. (2004), *Becoming President: The Bush Transition, 2000–2003*, Boulder, CO: Lynne Rienner

Bush, George W. (2002a), "President's Remarks to the Nation", Ellis Island, 11 September

Bush, George W. (2002b), "President's Remarks on Iraq", Cincinnati, 7 October

Bush, George W. (2007), Remarks at the National Republican Congressional Committee Dinner, 15 March

Caddell, Pat (1976), "Initial Working Paper on Political Strategy", 10 December, quoted in Karlyn Bowman, "Polling to Campaign and to Govern", in Ornstein and Mann, *The Permanent Campaign and Its Future*

*CBS News* (2005), "Third Columnist on Bush Payroll", 28 January

Chen, Edwin (2003), "President Rallies Marines but Warns of Risks in Iraq", *Los Angeles Times*, 15 August

Cheney, Dick (2002), "Meet the Press", NBC, 8 September

Cheney, Dick (1989), Author Interview, Washington, DC, 10 March

Cloud, David S. and Jeff Gerth (2006), "Iraqi Clerics Found on Pentagon Payroll", *International Herald Tribune*, 2 January

CNN (2003), "Commander in Chief Lands on USS Lincoln", 2 May, www.cnn.com

Cohen, Jeffrey E. (2008), *The Presidency in the Era of 24-Hour News*, Princeton: Princeton University Press

Edwards, George C. (2000), "Campaigning is Not Governing: Bill Clinton's Rhetorical Presidency", in Colin Campbell and Bert A. Rockman, eds, *The Clinton Legacy*, New York: Chatham House

Eisinger, Robert M. (2003), *The Evolution of Presidential Polling*, New York: Cambridge University Press

Fleischer, Ari (2005), *Taking Heat: The President, the Press, and My Years in the White House*, New York: William Morrow

Fleisher, Richard and Jon R. Bond (2000), "Congress and the President in a Partisan Era", in Jon R. Bond and Richard Fleisher, eds, *Polarized Politics: Congress and the President in a Partisan Era*, Washington, DC: CQ Press

Fortier, John C. and Norman J. Ornstein (2003), "President Bush: Legislative Strategist", in Fred I. Greenstein, ed., *The George W. Bush Presidency: An Early Assessment*, Baltimore: The Johns Hopkins University Press

Gerth, Jeff and Scott Shane (2005), "U.S. Said to Pay to Plant Articles in Iraq Papers", *New York Times*, 1 December

Gordon, Michael R. and Judith Miller (2002), "Threats and Responses: The Iraqis; U.S. Says Hussein Intensifies Quest for A-Bomb Parts", *New York Times*, 8 September

Heath, Diane J. (2000), "Presidential Polling and the Potential for Leadership", in Robert Y. Shapiro, Martha Joynt Kumar and Lawrence R. Jacobs, eds, *Presidential Power: Forging the Presidency for the Twenty-first Century*, New York: Columbia University Press

Heclo, Hugh (2000), "Campaigning and Governing: A Conspectus", in Norman J. Ornstein and Thomas E. Mann, eds, *The Permanent Campaign and Its Future*

Hersh, Seymour M. (2003), "Who Lied to Whom? Why did the Administration Endorse a Forgery About Iraq's Nuclear Weapons Program?", *New Yorker*, 31 March

Hume, Brit (2003), "An Exclusive Interview with President Bush", *Fox News*, 23 September, www.foxnews.com

Inskeep, Steve (2008), "Keys to Obama's Victory", *National Public Radio, Morning Edition*, 5 November

Isikoff, Michael and David Corn (2006), *Hubris: The Inside Story of Spin, Scandal, and the Selling of the Iraq War*, New York: Crown Publishers

Jackson, David (2005), "Bush team puts it pithily to capture the nation's attention", *USA Today*, 4 December

Jacobson, Gary C. (2003), "The Bush Presidency and the American Electorate", in Fred I. Greenstein, ed., *The George W. Bush Presidency: An Early Assessment*, Baltimore: The Johns Hopkins University Press

Jones, Charles O. (2000), "Preparing to Govern in 2001: Lessons from the Clinton Presidency", in Ornstein and Mann, *The Permanent Campaign and Its Future*

Keen, Judy (2001), "Information Center Deploys Its Own Troops", *USA Today*, 19 December

Kelley, Mat (2005), "Three Groups Have Contracts for Pro-U.S. Propaganda; Deals for Work in Iraq and Elsewhere Worth up to $300M", *USA Today*, 14 December

Kernell, Samuel (2006), *Going Public: New Strategies of Presidential Leadership*, 4th edition, Washington, DC: CQ Press

Klein, Joe (2005), "The Perils of the Permanent Campaign", *Time*, 30 October

Knoller, Mark (2003), e-mail to author, 13 September

Knoller, Mark (2008), e-mail to author, 11 October

Kristof, Nicholas D. (2003), "Missing in Action: Truth", *New York Times*, 6 May

Kumar, Martha Joynt (2007), *Managing the President's Message: The White House Communications Operation*, Baltimore: The Johns Hopkins University Press

Kurtz, Howard (2005), "Administration Paid Commentator", *Washington Post*, 5 January

Linzer, Dafna (2005), "Search for Banned Arms in Iraq Ended Last Month", *Washington Post*, 12 January

Lizza, Ryan (2001), "The White House Doesn't Need the Press", *New York Times Magazine*, 9 December

McClellan, Scott (2008), *What Happened: Inside the Bush White House and Washington's Culture of Deception*, New York: PublicAffairs

Maltese, John Anthony (1992), *Spin Control: The White House Office of Communications and the Management of Presidential News*, Chapel Hill: The University of North Carolina Press

Milbank, Dana (2003), "Explanation for Bush's Carrier Landing Altered", *Washington Post*, 7 May

Moeller, Susan D. (2004), "Media Coverage of Weapons of Mass Destruction", Study for Center for International and Security Studies at Maryland, University of Maryland, 9 March

Newport, Frank (2008), "Bush Approval at 25%, His Lowest Yet", Gallup.com, 6 October

Ornstein, Norman J. and Thomas E. Mann, eds (2000), *The Permanent Campaign and Its Future*, Washington, DC: Brookings Institution Press

Regan, Donald T. (1988), *For the Record,* New York: Harcourt Brace Jovanovich

Rice, Condoleezza (2002), "Late Edition with Wolf Blitzer", CNN, 8 September

Rose, Richard (1991), *The Postmodern President,* 2nd edition, Chatham, NJ: Chatham House

Saad, Lydia (2008), "Obama and Bush: A Contrast in Popularity", Gallup.com, 10 November

Schulman, Daniel (2006), "Mind Games", *Columbia Journalism Review,* May/June

Shanker, Thom (2005), "No Breach Is Seen in Planting U.S. Propaganda in Iraq Media", *New York Times,* 1 December

Stevenson, Richard W. (2001), "An Instructive Vote", *New York Times,* 7 April

Tenpas, Kathryn Dunn (2003), "Words vs. Deeds: President George W. Bush and Polling", *The Brookings Review* 21 (Summer)

*USA Today* (2005), "End to Search for WMD Seals Doubt About Pre-emption", 14 January

*Chapter 15*

# A LASTING REPUBLICAN MAJORITY? GEORGE W. BUSH'S ELECTORAL STRATEGY

Kevin Fullam and Alan R. Gitelson

George W. Bush could hardly be accused of failing to have lofty goals. After winning the White House, he set his sights on no less than the Republican realignment of the national electorate and a new era of Republican congressional dominance. By the close of his administration, however, his presidency had failed to engineer this transformation, at least as measured by the success of the Democratic Party in the 2008 presidential and congressional elections. Barack Obama captured the White House while Democrats increased the size of their majorities in both chambers of Congress. This chapter examines the nature of Bush's electoral legacy and, particularly, Republican designs to cement a lasting electoral majority. It explains how, by the end of his administration, Bush actually damaged the party's standing. In many respects, these failures can be tied to the ever-increasing blurring of the lines between campaigning and governing.

## 1. PLANNING A REPUBLICAN REALIGNMENT

Bush envisioned himself as the vanguard of a Republican dynasty. He believed he could engineer an electoral realignment as significant as that of the Democrats in 1932. Republicans might have seized control of Congress in 1994 after a forty-year exile but the party's margins were slim. Bush wanted to fortify that advantage and turn Congress into impregnable Republican territory.

The figure most entrusted with designing this realignment was Bush's long-term associate Karl Rove. Rove was Bush's chief strategist for his successful campaign in 1994 for the governorship of Texas, steered his presidential campaign in 2000 and, upon Bush's inauguration in 2001, served as a senior adviser to the president. Rove operated within Bush's innermost circle of White House policymakers. While there would be other actors in the Bush administration who would play significant roles – for example, Vice President Dick Cheney in the realm of foreign policy – none would play as sizeable a role as Rove in joining the political and campaign interests of the administration with the policymaking process. In effect, Bush tapped Rove to serve as the chief architect of a permanent realignment.

Bush and Rove appear to have shared a vision for achieving realignment. Both saw many similarities between the political landscape in 2000 and President William McKinley's victory in 1896. Rove identified the similarities thus: "Politics were changing. The economy was changing. We're at the same point now: weak allegiances to parties, a rising new economy" (Green 2007). These circumstances were perceived as an opportunity that Bush and Rove believed could reshape the partisan commitments of the electorate. Their strategy to exploit this opportunity consisted initially of two distinct elements: the new ideological initiative of "compassionate conservatism" and a whole-hearted embrace of the permanent campaign.

Bush was not driven by traditional conservative ideology, such as that underpinning the Contract with America movement that catapulted the Republican Party to power in the 1994 congressional elections. Instead, compassionate conservatism would be his chief weapon. While dismissed by some as mere posturing driven by electoral expedience, it involved a Republican appeal on a series of issues that had been viewed historically as Democratic strengths, including education, social security, health care and immigration. The strategy called for using the White House to co-opt these issues through a series of centrist policy stances. Great emphasis would be put on community involvement, and particularly faith-based initiatives, to address enduring social problems.

> They felt that the "compassionate conservative" notion provided an umbrella that let them not only speak to the base, but to speak to others who might be swing voters, others who might be a little more moderate in the party . . . [The] issues always fit in, but it was always a sense of those issues as a way of stitching together

> the strongest Republican base you could have and build out from there. (*Washington Post* reporter Dan Balz 2005)

In compassionate conservatism, the Bush team saw the chance to cut Democrats off from moderates in the American electorate, as well as co-opting the support of a growing Latino electorate. Latinos had been especially targeted because of their growing numbers and voter participation. Economic conservatives would approve of the government's use of private organisations to dispense charity, while social conservatives would appreciate the government's resources being directed toward their churches' programmes and, subsequently, their bank accounts.

Compassionate conservatism would be wedded to an aggressive pursuit of the permanent campaign. The framework of election campaigning has changed significantly over recent decades. This evolution has had a marked, some think corrosive, effect on the governance process. Norman J. Ornstein and Thomas E. Mann, editors of the collection of essays, *The Permanent Campaign and Its Future* (2000), painted a bleak picture of the political environment, one in which technology had made it possible for elected officials to monitor and, theoretically, cater to the most minute shifts in public opinion on any issue. Paradoxically, Ornstein and Mann also noted that Americans were more dissatisfied with government than they had ever been. Whereas American political seasons formerly had strict delineations between campaign and governing cycles, Ornstein and Mann theorised that the advent of polling technology and twenty-four hour news stations, among other factors, meant that the two were now continually intertwined, and that policy positions were formulated with one eye towards their potential impact at the ballot box. Ornstein and Mann's book, published towards the end of the Clinton presidency, echoed much criticism of Clinton's conduct as president. The outgoing administration was accused by some of taking a "finger in the wind" approach to decision-making with its reliance on polling data. Indeed, the entire style of the administration was taken to task for its over-reliance on campaign techniques. Early in Clinton's term, Charles O. Jones described his style as "campaigning to govern", arguing that "Clinton vigorously employed the traveling salesman approach to building support for his proposals" (Jones 1996).

Ornstein, Mann and Jones, however, could not predict the extraordinary attention that would be paid to political concerns within the Bush White House. Bush's intertwining of political strategy and policy was unprecedented. His compassionate conservative approach was to be publicised through a series of aggressive public campaigns designed to build his public image, create support for his policies, and demand subservience from Congress (Edwards 2007). Staffing would reflect this blurring of the line between campaigning and governing, best exemplified by the later decision to have Karl Rove assume dual responsibilities as both chief political strategist and Deputy Chief of Staff in 2005. In the latter position, Rove co-ordinated the policies of the National Security Council, the Domestic Policy Council, the National Economic Council and the Homeland Security Council.

By marketing compassionate conservatism through an extensive public relations campaign, Bush could portray himself as the "uniter, not a divider" he had promised to be throughout his 2000 campaign. By these means, he hoped to generate the permanent Republican majority.

## 2. THE REPUBLICAN PARTY IN TROUBLE: THE 2006 AND 2008 ELECTIONS

If, in 2006, Bush still had any hopes of cementing a Republican majority, the congressional elections of that year served to disabuse him of that notion. Democrats seized control of both the House and the Senate for the first time since 1994, unseating a number of incumbents who had helped usher in the Republican revolution that year, notably Senators Rick Santorum and Mike DeWine. In addition, the Republicans suffered significant defeats in state governorships and legislatures around the country, losing more than 300 state legislative seats. Two years later, the Republican Party surrendered the White House to Democratic Senator Barack Obama. Both parties saw increased electoral participation during their primary elections but Democratic primary turnout rose sharply over the preceding two campaign cycles. In the general election, Bush's unpopularity was largely seen as an albatross around the neck of the 2008 Republican presidential candidate, Senator John McCain.

The 2006 and 2008 election cycles offered much evidence of Republican difficulty beyond the simple defeats. Whether party identification, fund-raising or perceptions of the Republican brand are examined, the news was bad for the Republican Party.

Republican identification suffered a precipitous decline during the Bush era. In particular, a significant movement of young voters to the Democratic Party took place. While many observers consider youth and liberal leanings to be inextricably linked, historically this has not always been the case. According to the Pew Research Center, in 1992 the youngest segment of the electorate was one of the most Republican. Pew analysts theorised that this was because these voters had come of age during a time when Ronald Reagan and conservative ideology drew many young people to the Republican Party (Keeter et al. 2008). By 2004, however, the one age group among which Democrat John Kerry won majorities in his presidential battle against Bush was the under thirties. As the 2008 election approached, Republican political consultant Ed Rollins summed up the grim prognosis for the party:

> I think, at the end of this, the party will be weaker in numbers in the Congress, numbers of governors, numbers of state legislatures, and numbers of Republicans . . . Anybody who's a Republican today became a Republican during the Reagan era. Nobody who's come of age during the Bush era will stand up and say, "I'm a Bush Republican. I'm going to spend the rest of my life being a Bush Republican". (Horton 2008)

The electoral evidence seemed to support Rollins's assertion: in the 2008 elections, voters aged eighteen to twenty-nine preferred the Democratic Party by a significant 34-point margin (Pew Research Center 2008).

Even the Republicans' traditional fund-raising advantage, which began to disappear during the 2004 election cycle, was eliminated by the Democratic Party in 2008. While the Republican National Committee raised more than its Democratic equivalent in 2007–08, it raised less money than during the two previous election cycles, and the Democratic congressional fund-raising committees raised significantly more funds than their Republican counterparts. The depleted Republican congressional party coffers may have indicated low party morale. The coffers also served as a factor in a further blow to the party, the near-record number of congressional Republicans who chose to retire, thus creating open seats that were vulnerable to the

2008 nationwide Democratic surge. Over two dozen Republican congressional incumbents announced that they would not be defending their seats.

The world of twenty-first-century marketing is one geared frequently around the concept of branding, or a "collection of perceptions in the mind of the consumer" (BuildingBrands.com 2008). The application of branding to the political world assumes that political issues, ideologies and party tenets are essentially marketable entities. Voters who pull a lever for a party's candidate do not have to know in detail that party's platform; political campaigns and behaviour over many years, filtered through various media entities, enable voters to evaluate the parties in the absence of extensive information. All accounts of the Republican Party brand noted that, by 2008, it was very weak. In a leaked twenty-page memorandum, seven-term Republican House Representative Tom Davis brazenly remarked that "the Republican brand is in the trash can . . . if we were a dog food, they would take us off the shelf" (Barr 2008). Democratic registration and turnout in the spring's presidential primaries dwarfed that of the Republican Party and, while the strength of the Democratic brand is debatable, it is certainly clear that the Republican brand was an unwelcome anchor for any candidate carrying the party's flag in the 2008 elections. Representative Tom Cole, chair of the National Republican Congressional Committee, the organisation responsible for raising funds and electing Republicans to Congress, even suggested to Republican candidates that they might want to distance themselves from their party. "Don't be afraid to say you are disappointed in fellow Republicans . . . don't hesitate to be anti-Washington, D.C." (Kucinich 2008). Taking his advice to heart, many Republican candidates in highly contested races found that alleged scheduling conflicts prevented them from attending the 2008 Republican National Convention (Drogin 2008). The Republican brand was clearly in deep trouble and there was little evidence of a permanent Republican majority.

## 3. FROM COMPASSIONATE CONSERVATISM TO PARTISANSHIP

The plan to unite the United States under the Republican Party's banner seemed to have failed seven years after Bush's inauguration.

The mismatch between Bush and Rove's initial aspiration and the eventual outcome can be explained, to a large extent, through an examination of the administration's actions. Primarily, the administration's initial strategy would not survive intact for as long as a year, being replaced by an approach to both governing and campaigning based upon blunt partisanship. A White House that initially seemed to model its reach for the political centre after Clinton's Third Way ultimately exacerbated the partisan polarisation in Washington and in the nation at large.

Even the first months of Bush's first term were not devoid of partisan manoeuvring. When the 2000 presidential election turned into a month-long battle for control of the White House, any impetus for a sweeping Bush legislative agenda dissipated amid a hardening of political battle lines in Congress. What had been a relatively polite pre-election climate devolved into hard-edged partisan warfare. While a slight majority of Americans in 2001 was willing to recognise Bush as the presidential victor and wished to move on, a large number of Democrats did not, and never would, accept Bush's claim to the White House. Furthermore, Bush did not endear himself to congressional moderates during the first year of his presidency. His No Child Left Behind education bill proved to be one of the few times when he forged common ground with Democrats in Congress. After successfully pushing through tax cuts, withdrawing from the Kyoto Treaty negotiations, and limiting stem-cell research, however, Bush was labelled by many as a Republican partisan who had betrayed his campaign message. Most notably, the administration faced a crisis in May 2001 when Vermont's moderate Republican Senator James Jeffords left the party, declaring himself an independent and caucusing with the Democrats. His departure shifted control of the Senate to the Democrats by a margin of one.

It was, though, the September 2001 terrorist attacks that would have a dramatic and long-term impact on the Bush administration's campaign and governing strategies. After the events of 9/11, the American public rallied around its leaders. Bush's immediate promise of retribution served to cement his up-to-then shaky claim to legitimacy, and his approval ratings rocketed to around 90 per cent, the strongest show of support any American president has received since Gallup and Roper polling began in the 1930s. Displays of national pride and solidarity were ubiquitous. Congress famously gathered on the steps of the Capitol to sing "God Bless America", and the song emerged as a patriotic rallying cry at sporting events across the country.

Where national unity reigned, the Bush administration recognised an opportunity. The 9/11 disaster was the catalyst Bush felt could propel his dream of instituting an era of Republican realignment, both among the electorate and in the institutions of Washington. With the nation's attention focused on the investigations surrounding the identities of the 9/11 attackers and the plans to invade Afghanistan, the administration planned to take advantage of the revised political climate. Bush's response to 9/11 was to become more partisan in his approach to policymaking, Congress and the electorate. His administration moved towards a fifty-plus-one goal of energising enough base voters, both in the Congress and the electorate, so that fighting for moderates would not be necessary. This strategy was shaped around the administration's new foreign policy. Under the guidance of neoconservative thinkers in Bush's team, the concept of a war on terror emerged, as did the administration's focus upon Saddam Hussein's regime in Iraq. In these changes, the administration saw partisan opportunities that they would use the permanent campaign to exploit. The war on terror was quickly adopted as a tool for partisan advantage.

In Congress, the new Bush strategy would revolve around mobilising the slim Republican majorities to achieve party-line victories on legislation. This approach to Congress was the first element of the fifty–plus-one strategy, where 50 per cent of congressional votes plus the 1 required for a majority would suffice. Bush sought and quickly obtained approval for the formation of the Department of Homeland Security, the passage of the Patriot Act, and congressional authorisation to invade Afghanistan soon after 9/11. The war on terror provided a vehicle to reduce Democratic opposition, given the political vulnerability invited by appearing to oppose measures designed to stop terrorism. The administration went further, apparently engineering difficult choices for Democratic legislators. As the Iraq issue developed, the president was eager to use such a crisis for political gain in the 2002 mid-term elections, and the White House pushed for pre-election congressional votes on whether to grant the president the authorisation to depose Saddam's regime. While the *Washington Post* would later report that the administration did not want to rush the vote on Iraq for fear of politicising the issue, there is every reason to question this assertion, given that holding the vote prior to the election could only benefit Bush, as lawmakers on both sides of the aisle essentially stated afterwards.

The electoral corollary of this approach was clearly described in a PowerPoint presentation written by Karl Rove, which was found in June 2002 in Lafayette Park directly across from the White House. The presentation emphasised using the newly coined war on terror to attack Democratic congressional candidates, even those who supported the president during the preceding months. The partisanship was unambiguous. With the prospect of war in Iraq looming over the months preceding the election, any Democratic resistance to granting the administration the authority to invade would be painted as weakness on national defence. Bush made sure to capitalise on America's long-standing leanings towards the Republican Party on matters of national security by using the terror issue as a major campaign plank in 2002 and 2004. The techniques of the permanent campaign were now employed as an integral part of partisan warfare.

The partisan use of the war on terror was part of a broader shift in the administration's approach to the electorate. The second plank of the fifty-plus-one strategy was the decision to try to win elections by concentrating on activating Republican voters and sympathisers, particularly those in the evangelical voting bloc. The administration calculated that mobilising its natural vote effectively would ensure electoral triumph – a decision that flew in the face of conventional political wisdom which argues that, in a general election, a candidate should always battle for the middle of the ideological spectrum rather than cater to a partisan core.

The strategy for governing and campaigning also had an executive power dimension. Bush used the presidency to maximise partisan advantage. His political campaigns were often marked by negative campaigning and smear tactics, both covert and overt. Negative campaigns and smear attacks may be a part of life in the campaign trenches but, in the era of the permanent campaign, President Bush mobilised the executive branch to order attacks on political rivals. One such case involved the US attorney's office which punished Bush-appointed federal prosecutors who refused to pursue aggressively Democratic political candidates for often unsubstantiated and ill-founded campaign improprieties.

In sum, the administration continued to use the permanent campaign but compassionate conservatism was usurped by the use, for partisan advantage, of the newly established war on terror. The new strategy depended on raw partisanship, with its fifty-plus-one approach to Congress and the electorate. This change would have electoral repercussions in the short term and significant repercussions for the future of Bush's ability to govern, his party and their legacy.

## 4. ELECTORAL SUCCESSES: 2002 AND 2004

Rove and Bush oversaw a dramatic shift in policy priorities and in political strategy as they approached the 2002 mid-term elections. In the short term, the tactics were successful, contributing to the Republican Party's success and challenging the historical trend of the president's party losing ground in mid-term elections. The Republicans picked up seats in both the House and the Senate and retook control of the latter. The White House insisted that the party's success was a clear signal that Republican Party realignment was taking place despite the fact that the party's advantage in Congress remained narrow.

The Bush White House carried the same tactics forward into the 2004 presidential election but the 2004 electoral environment presented one major challenge to the administration that demanded adjustments to electoral strategy: American voters were increasingly turning against the war in Iraq. With the military immersed in an Iraqi civil war since Bush's Mission Accomplished photo opportunity on the aircraft carrier USS *Abraham Lincoln,* and with no weapons of mass destruction in sight, the president looked vulnerable on the primary issue of the 2004 campaign. Not only had the invasion drawn worldwide condemnation from nearly every major United States ally except Britain but a growing number of Americans believed that the operation was a mistake, too.

In this environment, the selection of Massachusetts Senator John Kerry as the Democratic presidential nominee seemed designed to threaten Bush's tenure. Kerry's status as a Vietnam veteran brought attention to Bush's patchy military record. It had been alleged that Bush, who enlisted in the National Guard in lieu of service in Vietnam, had his application expedited through family connections. Both campaigns recognised that Kerry might be portrayed as more capable of managing the struggling war on terror than the incumbent president, given their relative and contrasting records of service.

Kerry was not allowed to capitalise on the American public's discontent, however. During the 2004 campaign, Kerry stated "I voted for it [the war in Iraq] before I voted against it." These nine words, spoken in reference to an $87 billion war appropriations bill, serve as exhibit A for why senators with documented congressional votes and policy positions often have difficulty winning the top job. The Bush team hammered Kerry with his own words throughout the campaign, ignoring the nuances of the relevant bill, to reinforce its preferred image of Kerry as a "flip-flopper". The public may not have approved of Bush overwhelmingly but voters appreciate a decisive leader. Fair or otherwise, Kerry was painted as someone who could not be counted on to be resolute in times of crisis. Additionally, Kerry's military service was tarnished by high-profile allegations by the Swift Boat Veterans for Truth, an independent group that some believed was connected to the Republican Party. The group suggested that Kerry had misrepresented his service and questioned the validity of his combat medals, including his Purple Heart. Whatever the truth, the attacks devalued his military experience, one of his major electoral assets, and allowed the Bush campaign to exploit the Republican Party's traditional advantage on national security issues.

The Bush team also had to rally the Republican base in line with the fifty-plus-one strategy. Focusing on the issue of gay marriage, the president hoped to mobilise evangelicals by calling in February 2004 for a constitutional amendment to ban same-sex marriage. While the constitutional effort was unsuccessful, Republicans managed to place the issue on eleven state ballot initiatives that autumn. All eleven passed. While a Pew Research Center study argued that the measures had no across-the-board impact on the presidential race, the analysis suggested that the gay marriage ban might have helped Bush win Ohio which turned out to be the election's pivotal battleground. Bush captured the state with only 51 per cent of the vote, his smallest margin of victory in any major state (Taylor 2006). The campaign had committed a great deal of its resources to organisational activities involving black and evangelical churches in the area, receiving substantially more support from these groups than Bush had obtained four years earlier.

Between 2000 and 2004, the administration shifted from compassionate conservatism to a new focus upon foreign policy, particularly terror. The switch was accompanied by a move to the fifty-plus-one strategy and increasing partisanship while the administration retained its aggressive conduct of the permanent campaign.

## 5. THE SECOND TERM

As Bush began his second term, he announced that reforming one of the oldest and most complicated domestic programmes, Social Security, would be his first priority. Making reform a key part of his 2005 State of the Union address, Bush offered a proposal for partial privatisation of the programme. The proposal allowed for the establishment of Social Security savings accounts held by individuals, as a diversion of funds from the programme's traditional trust fund. Bush embarked upon a national tour to drum up support for the measure.

Despite concerted efforts to gain support, the president's attempts at partial privatisation were met with strong opposition from members of Congress and a sceptical public. Democratic legislators would not support Bush's initiative, and Republicans had little interest in spending their own political capital on promoting reforms opposed by their constituents.

Bush's second-term honeymoon was markedly short. Developments in Iraq clearly contributed to his difficulties. The absence of weapons of mass destruction, coupled with increasing sectarian violence, contributed to a growing public sense that the post-war occupation was a failure. Unpopular positions regarding high-profile incidents such as the Terri Schiavo case and Hurricane Katrina only accentuated his slide. Schiavo, a woman who had suffered massive brain damage and had spent fourteen years in a vegetative state, was the subject of an ugly court battle regarding the removal of her feeding tubes, with the president and other pro-life groups in opposition to such action. By the time Hurricane Katrina hit New Orleans in August 2005, most observers thought Bush's Social Security reform long lost. Any doubt on this front was erased, however, as Katrina spelled disaster for Bush's presidency. In stark contrast to his personal investigation of the World Trade Center wreckage after 9/11, Bush was nowhere to be found on the ground in Louisiana; his aeroplane flew over the area days after the hurricane struck but did not land. This public relations gaffe, together with the overwhelming blame the federal government received for its slow response to the catastrophe – Federal Emergency Management Agency (FEMA) head Michael Brown was viewed as an incompetent Bush crony, unqualified to head the major federal disaster response organisation – effectively destroyed the post-9/11 image of Bush as a strong and capable leader. Any political capital the White House had garnered after the 2004 elections was lost. Effectively, the disaster also removed Social Security reform from the national agenda, condemning Bush's already ailing effort to failure.

Bush shifted his focus to immigration reform but this, too, failed. Bush proposed a "grand bargain", intended to allow existing illegal immigrants a difficult route to citizenship, and a series of measures to prevent future illegal immigrants from entering and staying in the country. By 2006, hostility to Bush's policy and minimal support for the president from the Republican congressional caucus on the issue condemned to failure both his proposed immigration reform and any attempt to attract Latino voters to the Republican Party.

Indeed, despite the fact that Bush won two terms and the Republicans held control of Congress until 2006, relatively few of the administration's goals were met. Three major tax cuts, the No Child Left Behind education bill, and the Medicare prescription medicine benefit were major policy victories during the early years of the administration but, subsequently, the White House experienced one legislative failure after another. While a long historical perspective is needed to evaluate fully the Bush legacy, it appears possible, even likely, that his presidency will be judged as one of the nation's most ignoble. Most of Bush's second-term legislative vision never made it out of congressional committees, and even his early accomplishments have attracted less-than-overwhelming approbation. The only foreign policy initiative that has drawn bipartisan praise has been Bush's effort to address the growing medical ills of Africa (Becker 2003).

## 6. THE COSTS OF BUSH'S PARTISAN STRATEGY

Many of the administration's disappointments can be explained by the partisan fifty-plus-one strategy and its repercussions. The strategy may have assisted Bush's electoral success in both 2002 and 2004 but it also imposed serious costs when the Bush administration tried to govern. The administration's approach alienated Democrats. The use of terror as a partisan weapon, for example, hurt Democrats willing to support Bush's war. The administration recognised the enormous goodwill towards it as it confronted the challenges of the post-9/11 world, but spurned it.

> What Bush went out and did in 2002 . . . with an eye toward the permanent Republican majority, was very aggressively attack those Democrats who voted with him and were for him. There's no question that the president helped pick up seats. But all of that goodwill was squandered. (Unnamed former Bush administration official quoted in Green 2007)

The goodwill was replaced by deep partisan rancour. The fifty-plus-one strategy demanded that Bush use the White House machinery to publicise positions to activate loyal Republican supporters, necessarily antagonising Democrats in the process. The administration denied itself the opportunity to finesse policy positions because of the need to trigger its own supporters' allegiances, making it easy for Democrats to demonise Bush as leader of the Republicans. His partisan tactics energised Democratic opposition to the extent that, by 2004, he would not enjoy the same financial advantage he held over Al Gore in 2000. Against Kerry, campaign fund-raising was fairly even on both sides, with "527" groups (organisations free to politic for each side but not restricted by spending limits) leaning in favour of the challenger. Equally, Bush's failure to appeal to moderate Democrats among the public during the 2004 election cycle may have made it harder for him to win those Democrats' support when he attempted to return to his permanent campaign techniques in support of his policy reforms.

The administration's focused agenda of destroying the opposition served to reduce Bush's credibility with leaders across the aisle. In turn, the loss of this credibility would, eventually, reduce his effectiveness as a policy leader as he became less capable of winning support from the opposition party in Congress.

The partisan strategy might have been expected to hurt Bush's ability to persuade Democrats but the use of the permanent campaign also served to make the administration's dealings with Republicans more difficult in at least two ways. The administration's emphasis on unrestrained executive power was reflected in the use of the permanent campaign. As explained by Kernell (1997), the process of presidents garnering public support for policy proposals effectively entails bullying Congress and, arguably, denying its legislative prerogative. Even congressional Republicans chafed at the White House's aggressiveness, especially Bush's senior political adviser, Rove, who, it was felt, wielded too much power in the realm of policy. The Republicans' House majority whip, Tom DeLay, held a personal antipathy to Rove, having been on the receiving end of his mudslinging campaign style years earlier when DeLay first ran for Congress in Texas against a candidate managed by Rove. DeLay's unease with the political strategist turned policymaker was shared by many of his colleagues. The tensions were evident in the observations of one Republican congressional aide.

> Every once in a while Rove would come to leadership meetings, and he definitely considered himself at least an equal with the leaders in the room. But you have to understand that Congress is a place where certain decorum is expected. Even in private, staff is still staff. Rove would come and chime in as if he were equal to the speaker. Cheney sometimes came, too, and was far more deferential than Rove – and he was the vice president. (quoted in Green 2007)

Among the many other assertions of executive power made by the Bush administration, Rove and Bush's expectation that policy should be driven by the Oval Office was not well received on the Hill.

Furthermore, the fifty-plus-one strategy of activating loyalists became problematic when the White House did not want to take on board those loyalists' policy positions. The strategy of the 2002 and 2004 elections meant that many representatives from Republican Party districts catered disproportionately to red state voters, such as evangelicals. While tax cuts were certainly acceptable, talk of an "amnesty" or "legalisation" for illegal immigrants was anathema. During Bush's first campaign for president, immigration reform had been envisioned as a crucial weapon to garner Latino voters from the Democratic camp. In the second term, it became an embarrassment as Bush's own party turned on him and blocked reform. The partisan strategy drove away Republican moderates, as reflected in Jeffords's defection, reinforced the position of those on the party's conservative right and heightened congressional partisanship further.

By the start of his second term, Bush had few, if any, true allies in Congress. The administration had made a fundamental miscalculation concerning the relationship between campaigning and governing. Arguably, Bush never understood that it was necessary not only to conceptualise good public policy and sell it to the public but also both to comprehend and to appreciate the legislative process in both chambers of Congress. Indeed, as Ornstein and Mann recognise, "The more campaigning absorbs governing, the more difficult it becomes to facilitate coalition building and the more strained are intraparty relations" (Ornstein and Mann 2000: 255).

The administration compounded its errors through its interpretation of the 2004 result and its consequent choice of issues. Bush believed, inaccurately, that the 2004 elections represented a clear mandate for his administration's policies. Having just spent the previous year making the 2004 presidential election a referendum on the war effort, Bush then attempted to convince lawmakers to enact wholesale changes to Social Security and the immigration laws. Whether one blames the hubris derived from winning a presidential election or the administration's adoption of the unitary executive principle, Bush misinterpreted his mandate by focusing on major, difficult and unpopular domestic reforms. Having generated a partisan strategy that would make it very hard to win over moderate votes in Congress, such reforms required these very votes. The fifty-plus-one strategy that succeeded in the electoral environment rebounded badly in the governing environment. Enacting controversial reforms without bipartisan support is often a losing cause. Ronald Reagan attempted to enact Social Security overhauls after entering the White House in 1981 but an initial Republican-only push contributed to heavy Republican Party losses in the Senate in 1982. Reagan learned his lesson, however, and a compromise with Democrats was achieved in the following session; the opposition provided political cover, and Republican legislators emerged unscathed. Bush, in contrast, did not learn from Reagan's experience, and ploughed on with his fifty-plus-one strategy even though it could not deliver legislative successes on controversial domestic policy measures. In targeting Social Security and immigration reform, Bush chose issues that required Republicans to take a leap of faith, and numerous Democrats to follow. They did not and Bush's proposals were defeated.

The permanent campaign failed the administration during the

second term. It trades upon presidential popularity and image. An unpopular or distrusted president is less likely to win public support for his policies or to cow wavering legislators into submission. Bush's popularity ratings were remarkable: no modern-day president has accumulated as long a string of poor poll numbers. His standing had not been high on re-election, with only 49 per cent approval in December 2004 – ten to twenty points lower than every re-elected president at similar points in time since Gallup began tracking such data in 1948 (Wallsten 2004). The Iraq conflict appeared an important cause of this low standing, given that the same poll also found that, just weeks after voters had re-elected the invasion's chief proponent, a majority of Americans felt that the war, the number one issue in the 2004 campaign, was a major foreign policy mistake. Schiavo and Katrina added to the downward momentum. Support for Bush was scarce: only the most stalwart Republicans continued to support the president. It is ironic that an administration that, holding to the tenets of the permanent campaign, paid more attention to polling data than any other was one of the most unpopular since World War II. In the week following the 2008 election, Bush's unpopularity surpassed even that of scandal-plagued Richard Nixon.

In the face of such ratings, the Bush team struggled to persuade the public to support the administration's policies. Efforts were still made to use the permanent campaign but Bush could not gain any serious traction for reforms among the public and, in many instances, seemed peripheral to the discussions of reforms going on in Washington. The permanent campaign could not help the lame-duck president, and the permanent campaign also hurt his capacity to employ alternative bargaining routes with Congress.

Unsurprisingly, legislative failures, the president's unpopularity and policy blunders translated into bad news for Republicans at the polls. The Bush administration appeared to have damaged the Republican brand very badly. The 2006 elections in particular, in which Republicans lost their majorities in the House and Senate, appeared to be a repudiation of the party's behaviour rather than an indicator of any deep support for Democratic policies. Many of the Democrats who gained seats in the normally strong southern Republican territory shared the social views of the officials they were replacing. Of course, while the White House can be blamed for a host of failures leading up to 2006, there was a number of congressional representatives who curtailed their own careers and damaged the party without help from Bush. The corruption allegations regarding Republican lobbyist Jack Abramoff cast a dark cloud over the entire Republican Party, and played a direct role in the resignation of Republican House Majority Leader Tom DeLay. In addition, sexual misconduct cases, such as those involving Republican Representatives Mark Foley and Don Sherwood, helped suppress Republican turnout, especially among social conservatives. The 2008 result suggested, however, that the problems ran far deeper than a few scandals. Bush's partisan approach to campaigning and governing played a key role in driving the party on to the rocks.

## CONCLUSION

The efforts of the Bush administration were largely directed towards linking public policy triumphs and electoral dominance. While this single-minded focus resulted in two presidential terms, it sacrificed nearly everything else the president hoped to accomplish, from sweeping legislative reforms to the legacy of a lasting Republican majority.

The administration began with a plan to employ compassionate conservatism and the permanent campaign to generate a full-scale realignment. Within a year of taking office, the administration changed its approach. The permanent campaign technique was retained but used to project more partisan messages post 9/11, especially regarding the war on terror. The Bush team failed to understand the repercussions that this approach would have. It appeared that, for the administration, there was no difference between running an election and running a nation, no divergence between campaigning and governing. Yet, the approach adopted served to antagonise the Democratic opposition, make Republican allies in Congress harder to manage and, when combined with an over-interpretation of the 2004 mandate and poor issue choices, led to legislative failure and to electoral defeats for the Republican Party.

## BIBLIOGRAPHY

Balz, Dan (2005), "Interview with Dan Balz", *Frontline: Karl Rove, The Architect,* http://www.pbs.org

Barr, Andy (2008), "Rep. Davis Paints Bleak Picture for G.O.P.", *The Hill's Blog Briefing Room,* http://briefingroom.thehill.com/

Becker, Elizabeth (2003), "With Record Rise in Foreign Aid Comes Change In How It Is Monitored", *New York Times*, 7 December

Building Brands.com (2008), "Marketing Definitions: Brand", BuildingBrands.com, http://www.buildingbrands.com

Drogin, Bob (2008), "Lots of No-Shows Expected at Republican National Convention", *Los Angeles Times*, 31 August

Edwards, George C. (2007), *Governing By Campaigning: The Politics of the Bush Presidency*, New York: Pearson Longman

Green, Joshua (2007), "The Rove Presidency", *The Atlantic*, September

Horton, Scott (2008), "Six Questions for Paul Alexander, Author of *Machiavelli's Shadow*", *Harper's Magazine Online*, 1 July 2008, http://www.harpers.org

Jones, Charles O. (1996), "Campaigning to Govern: The Clinton Style", in Colin Campbell and Bert A. Rockman, eds, *The Clinton Presidency: First Appraisals*, Chatham, NJ: Chatham House Publishers

Keeter, Scott, Juliana Horowitz and Alec Tyson (2008), "Gen Dems: The Party's Advantage Among Young Voters Widens", Pew Research Center for the People and the Press, http://pewresearch.org

Kernell, Samuel (1997), *Going Public: New Strategies of Presidential Leadership*, Washington, DC: CQ Press

Kucinich, Jackie (2008), "Run against the GOP, Cole tells hopefuls", The Hill.com, http://thehill.com

Ornstein, Norman J. and Thomas E. Mann, eds (2000), *The Permanent Campaign and Its Future*, Washington, DC: AEI Press

Pew Research Center (2008), "Inside Obama's Sweeping Victory", Pew Research Center for the People and the Press, http://pewresearch.org

Taylor, Paul (2006), "Wedge Issues on the Ballot: Can State Initiatives on Gay Marriage, Minimum Wage Affect Candidate Races?", Pew Research Center for the People and the Press, http://pewresearch.org

Wallsten, Peter (2004), "Bush Approval Rating at Historic Low: Unpopular Iraq War Dampens Effect Of Re-Election Win", *Los Angeles Times*, 29 December

*Chapter 16*

# CONCLUSON: THE LEGACY OF GEORGE W. BUSH

Jon Herbert and Andrew Wroe

> We will write, not footnotes, but chapters in the American story.
> (George W. Bush accepting the 2000 Republican Party nomination for the presidency, Philadelphia, 3 August 2000)

Before Bush was elected, he projected a presidency of extraordinary ambition. He, and the administration he headed, subsequently seemed driven by a desire for the momentous and the dramatic to the degree that it might be considered an administration mentality. Bush hated the "small ball" and his advisers consistently labelled him a "transformative president" (*Economist* 2009). The ambitious rhetoric was backed by aspirations to institute major policy reforms. In foreign policy, Bush attempted a spectacular redirection of United States priorities and of its methods. In economic policy, he pursued an agenda of substantial tax cuts and extensive deregulation. In social policy, he launched radical reforms under the "compassionate conservative" label, trying to co-opt traditionally Democratic Party policy areas such as Medicare, education and Social Security. These reforms, Bush hoped, would change his Republican Party's direction and image, trigger a realignment of the American electorate and create a permanent Republican majority. At the completion of Bush's second term, it became legitimate to ask to what degree Bush had achieved these high goals and to identify the inheritance he passed on to his successor.

As Ralph (Chapter 6) explains, the assessment of Bush's legacy will depend on the perspective of those writing the history. Assessments of the Clinton presidency, for example, rarely focused on the administration's handling of the al-Qaeda threat until late in 2001. There will undoubtedly be changes in perspective. Some of the Bush administration's actions will look more significant in the context of future events, others less so. At the moment, we cannot be sure which will be which. The Bush legacy is likely to change from generation to generation. This conditionality applies no more than to the two headlines of the Bush legacy: the state of the American economy and the wars in Iraq and Afghanistan. In each case, outcomes are uncertain. While it seems unlikely that Iraqi nationalism will ever tolerate the erecting of a George W. Bush statue in Baghdad's Firdos Square, his administration might one day be credited with triggering the development of democracy in the Middle East. In the same way as Truman left the United States apparently trapped in a war in Korea but his historical reputation recovered, some argue that Bush may come to be seen as founding father of a new American foreign policy. The Bush economic legacy will depend upon the depth of the recession that unfolded as he left office. A speedy recovery will present Bush's tenure in a more positive light than will an economic catastrophe. Nevertheless, it is a legitimate time to assess Bush's two terms, before the self-righting quality of American democracy imposes itself: the worst blunders usually generate the greatest attempts by a presidential successor to address them. If President Obama addresses a crisis in one particularly dire area successfully, Bush's contribution to generating that crisis will appear less significant.

For all this qualification, however, the basic shape of the Bush legacy seems to be in place, and to reflect badly upon his presidency. Indeed, it is difficult to imagine the series of events that would portray the Bush administration as a triumphal success.

## 1. FOREIGN POLICY

The Bush foreign policy project began with a promise to reject the Clinton style and, within a year, generated a radical rethinking of the American approach to the world. As Ralph and Houghton detail (Chapters 6 and 8), the administration's unilateralism was apparent before 9/11. The pledge to focus on American interests rather than on nation-building underpinned a different approach to the post-Cold War era. United States primacy would be defended and bolstered. However, 9/11 refocused the administration upon the threat of terrorism. The wars in Afghanistan and Iraq, and the conceptual framework of the "war on terror", the right to pre-emption and the desire for regime change, marked a radical shift. This approach, however, was allied to the early move to unilateralism and the pursuit of American interests. Bush chose to invade Iraq, and his unilateral approach allowed him to dismiss international concerns over American adventurism lightly. As Ralph details, he launched a "war" that was new in political, military and legal terms.

Even given the malleable foreign policy environment induced by 9/11, Bush's achievements in winning domestic support for the war were significant. With minimal political conflict, he won congressional resolutions supporting his adventurism. Even more remarkably, when he decided to launch the so-called surge in Iraq, he did so despite the domestic forces lined up in opposition. The prosecution of the wars, however, was not a triumph and must be considered to be a significant part of the Bush legacy. The extraordinary expenditure of blood and money was notable in its own right but the mixed results derived from these sacrifices make the wars worthy of even more attention. As Bush left office, he passed the two unresolved conflicts on to his successor with uncertainty remaining over their final outcome. Many argued that the wars had been bungled, at the cost of thousands of lives, largely due to poor planning for the aftermath of initial hostilities. Donald Rumsfeld's vision of a new United States military is often blamed for this failure although Ralph also blames the failure to examine neo-conservative assumptions about the Middle East population's receptiveness to democratic revolution. While the administration argued that it deserved credit for the absence of further terrorist attacks upon the American homeland during Bush's time in office, many claimed that Bush's approach had actually antagonised and radicalised many elements in the Middle East, and made resisting terrorism far more difficult. The administration could argue, though it largely remains an untold story, that it had done much to decapitate the al-Qaeda network and wreck its funding networks. Hurst (Chapter 7) examines the administration's efforts to develop its homeland security policy, and is cautiously positive. Others noted instead that al-Qaeda might be considered more dangerous as a more numerous series of loosely affiliated cells that could recruit easily from among the newly radicalised.

Considering the potential for terrorists to strike the United States is to judge the Bush administration by its own chosen measure. Halting terror was its declared goal. A more standard analysis of Bush's legacy considers the status of American power in the world. America's military power, soft power and economic power have all changed for the worse during Bush's two terms.

America's actual military capability remains great. The speed at which both the Taliban government in Kabul and the Saddam regime in Baghdad were toppled defied many expert military predictions and seemed to warrant the label "shock and awe". The Bush presidency still undermined the United States military's status, however. First, the military proved good at winning standard battles but poor at dealing with those battles' aftermath. The military could not police and rebuild the battlefield and therefore remake nations as the Bush administration required. The neo-conservative vision was dashed, although neo-conservatives contended that Rumsfeld's poor planning and dreams of lower troop commitments were to blame. Second, at the end of Bush's term, military resources, particularly personnel, were clearly stretched. Demanding more tours of duty from enlistees and recruiting aggressively, the United States military's capacity was nonetheless restricted by its presence in Iraq and Afghanistan, and arguably found its capacity limited even in those locations. Furthermore, the unwillingness of the United States polity to sustain such drawn-out actions undermined the utility of military power. The "Vietnam syndrome", allegedly kicked by Bush's father, seemed to have returned, bringing the nation's ability to commit the military to extended conflict into doubt.

Bush's legacy also includes a serious denuding of America's soft power. Joseph Nye argues that American power is drawn partly from the American capacity to "attract others by the legitimacy of U.S. policies and the values that underlie them" (Nye 2004). To a degree, American leadership depends upon the moral argument implicit in a rhetoric of liberty, democracy and justice. United States politicians present the nation as the upholder of these values. The Bush administration's willingness to abandon them damaged American's standing internationally.

Most obviously, events at Guantánamo and Abu Ghraib squandered the United States's claim to moral leadership as it became clear that it was willing to torture and abuse prisoners rather than respect human rights. As the Abu Ghraib story broke, Bill Graham, Canada's foreign minister at the time, had a meeting with Bush. He described Bush's reaction to hearing about the abuse thus: "This is un-American. Americans don't do this. People will realize Americans don't do this." Graham argues, however, that

> the problem for the United States, and indeed for the free world, is that because of this – Guantanamo, and the "torture memos" from the White House . . . – people around the world don't believe that anymore. They say, No, Americans are capable of doing such things and have done them, all the while hypocritically criticizing the human-rights records of others. (Murphy and Purdum 2009)

Quite apart from bequeathing the problem of how to handle the unconvicted enemy combatants held at Guantánamo Bay, Bush passed on to his successor a much tarnished image of the United States and, with it, weakened American persuasiveness in the world.

This weakened persuasiveness was compounded by the administration's international application of media spin. As most dramatically demonstrated by Colin Powell's presentation to the United Nations of the case for war against Iraq, the administration frequently manipulated information for political effect. The subsequent absence of weapons of mass destruction in Iraq did much to fritter away America's intelligence advantage in the world. If trusted, the United States can claim that their technological capabilities allow them unique access to intelligence. In contrast, Florida's Democratic Senator Bob Graham argued:

> One of our difficulties now is getting the rest of the world to accept our assessment of the seriousness of an issue, because they say, You screwed it up so badly with Iraq, why would we believe that you're any better today? And it's a damn hard question to answer. (Murphy and Purdum 2009)

Diminished American soft power was reflected in public attitudes to the United States across the world. The loss of moral authority also provided an opportunity for other leaders to trumpet their anti-Americanism. Iraq and Guantánamo were a boon to Venezuela's Hugo Chavez, for example.

After its first term, the administration acknowledged the need to change approach. A conscious attempt was made to recover soft power, most notably through Secretary of State Rice's peripatetic charm offensive. Ralph argues that this change reflected a shift towards realism at the expense of the neo-conservative vision. North Korea and Iran would be drawn into diplomatic talks over their development of nuclear weapons, rather than being isolated. The administration began to recognise more fully the significance of China's rise and the increased hostility of Russia under Putin. Ironically, Bush's second-term activities seemed to echo more faithfully his original campaign pledges of 2000 to promote American interests in an unfriendly world of great powers. The legacy of these efforts was limited. Both Houghton and Ralph argue that this revised approach generated some recovery of American credibility abroad. Houghton argues, however, that structural tensions between Europe and the United States remained over issues such as torture, terror and global warming, and that, despite the rise of Atlanticist leaders in Europe, the Bush administration was still very much part of the problem.

The inheritance passed on to President Obama, therefore, looked dire. Two ongoing wars and diminished American power are a very poor legacy. The end of the Bush administration was even marked by a new wave of declinist thinking based on diminishing American power. Scholars observed that the United States might lose its pre-eminent status in the world. Perhaps as importantly, fundamental questions remained on the future direction of American foreign policy. The question posed by 9/11 remained: how would the United States address the terrorist threat to prevent more attacks? Bush made terror his central focus and attempted to attack existing terrorist networks, to eliminate terrorist havens through an aggressive strategy to bring rogue states under control, and to prevent the spread of weapons of mass destruction. The war on extremist Muslim fundamentalism was unambiguously the first priority. Lynch and Singh argue a case for continuity based on this approach and see, therefore, the Bush doctrine as the key constituent of his legacy (Lynch and Singh 2008).

Others argue that the Bush approach was discredited. Obama inherited a foreign policy in great disrepute. At home, Americans felt that war in Iraq, particularly, was a mistake, and domestic support for the war on terror was low. Policymakers recognised the costs implicit in the Bush approach, noting diminished American moral suasion and international standing. The ability to co-opt the support of multilateral institutions, on the rare occasions the Bush administration chose this route, declined accordingly. Additionally, not all policy problems fitted comfortably within the war on terror's frame of reference. For example, how could the Bush doctrine inform conduct of United States–Chinese relations? The identification of terror as the overriding concern guiding American foreign policy involved costs that even the Bush administration, in its second term, became unwilling to bear, as demonstrated by the shift back towards realism. It seems likely that Bush's foreign policy will come to be seen as another experiment among American attempts to find a coherent post-Cold War policy. Bush rejected the previous experiment, Clinton's "engagement and enlargement", and pursued instead a neo-conservative alternative. That approach seems largely discredited, involving costs that the United States could not bear.

The discrediting of the Bush experiment bequeathed an opportunity to the incoming Obama administration. Despite two ongoing wars, Obama was given the chance to develop a fresh experiment in American foreign policymaking. He could define what the prime concerns would be, particularly whether the pursuit of terrorists would play a definitive role. He could reshape this pursuit, and re-examine the interaction between this priority and other American interests. The very interpretation of terror as a policy problem could be reassessed, begging questions about its status as a foreign and military challenge rather than a criminal one. The impacts of Abu Ghraib, Guantánamo and torture memorandums allowed Obama to address the balance between civil liberties and resisting terror. Indeed, Bush's failings may allow Obama the opportunity to change direction radically again, perhaps returning to Jimmy Carter's emphasis on human rights or reinventing Clinton's democratic enlargement. The opprobrium attached to Bush's foreign policy is an integral part of his legacy but it also gave his successor substantial leeway to reinvent American foreign policy.

Bush's foreign policy after 9/11 was intended to reshape the world and maintain American primacy. Even if the conflict in Iraq succeeds and triggers a wave of Middle East democratisation, Bush oversaw a decline in American power and left his successor a series of unresolved policy problems at the expense of many lives. As many of

Bush's ideas were discredited, Bush effectively issued President Obama with a warrant for leadership. Whether Obama will have the opportunity to concentrate on these potential reinventions is unclear, however, since his first priority proved to be the well-being of the American economy.

## 2. ECONOMIC POLICY

The Bush legacy in economic policy was transformed by the events late in his second term but the administration had already had a significant impact. This impact suggested unquestioning support for many tenets of "Reaganomics": the Bush administration advocated low taxes, restrictive monetary policy and deregulation.

On entering office, Bush declared tax cuts to be his first major priority, as achieved through the Economic Growth and Tax Relief Reconciliation Act of 2001 and, later, the Jobs and Growth Tax Relief Reconciliation Act of 2003. The former, which included a tax rebate and cuts in income tax, capital gains tax and estate tax, was a particularly notable achievement, given the inauspicious circumstances under which Bush was elected and his limited political capital. As Wilson details (Chapter 10), the administration embarked upon an extensive campaign of deregulation.

Where Bush seemed to diverge from the Reagan orthodoxy was in federal spending. Under Bush, the federal government greatly increased its overall spending. Bush was labelled a "big government conservative" as the budget surplus he inherited was replaced by a record annual deficit and the United States national debt soared (Barnes 2003, 2006). These changes rendered the United States more dependent upon those prepared to lend to it to sustain its deficits, notably the Chinese government, which bought high volumes of treasury bonds.

The deficit and debt are clearly central parts of the Bush legacy. In themselves, they would have demanded attention from Bush's successor. Most of the economic headlines from Bush's tenure date from his last year, however. Bush oversaw the development of a major recession. Gross domestic product fell and unemployment rose. The precipitous decline in the Dow Jones index represented trillions of dollars in lost investments. Federal funds were further drained as tax revenues dropped. The financial crisis induced the Bush administration to propose a $700 billion bank bail-out plan while the Fed spent reserves fighting the collapse. Bush left federal finances and the American economy in a parlous state.

Wilson suggests that responsibility for the recession beginning in 2008 can be distributed widely; bankers' reckless risk-taking, flawed regulatory systems, capital carelessly or even ignorantly invested, consumers taking the wrong attitude to the bubble, low interest rates, bankers' overcompensating after the crisis broke and denying the economy liquidity, house owners gambling on rising prices. Many are implicated. There is strong reason, however, to consider the recession part of Bush's legacy. The administration held a unique vantage point from which to observe and address many of the mistakes listed above but failed to do so. This failure, Wilson explains, was rooted in the administration's ideological commitment to free markets as well as in poor policymaking processes that prevented it from examining assumptions and alternatives properly.

This criticism is tempered by the administration's pragmatism in response to the financial crisis. The administration did not deliver a coherent or immediately effective answer but its response was not bound rigidly by neo-liberal ideology. Taking Fannie Mae, Freddie Mac, AIG and numerous banks into federal ownership, even if only partially, hardly sat comfortably with the mantra of "let the market decide". Admittedly, the decision to allow Lehman Brothers to go bankrupt may have triggered the worst of the crisis but Wilson credits the administration with ideological flexibility in the face of disaster. The Bush administration's response may be remembered as averting complete financial collapse in 2008, even if it may also be remembered as contributing significantly to the cause of the crash. Nonetheless, Bush's legacy included passing on to his successor a range of serious economic problems, including, amid the recession, a developing avalanche of foreclosures, a corresponding collapse in the housing market and the continuing presence of so-called toxic assets poisoning banks' balance sheets and restricting liquidity.

Just as significantly, the administration's policies in response to the crisis posed a challenge to the Reagan economic orthodoxy. Emphasising the widespread support in Washington for re-regulation of financial markets, and noting much greater federal involvement in the economy, some commentators saw the crisis as the end of the small-government, market-driven, low-tax era. Faith in markets as allocatory tools was shaken considerably. The economic failures were seen not just as Bush's failure but represented the decline of an entire series of economic values. In the simplest interpretations, Bush was cast as the modern-day Herbert Hoover, the poster-boy for the end of the Reagan era, helplessly bound by the collapsing regime's ideology. While this narrative would be a particularly harsh judgement, given the administration's abandonment of the orthodoxy during the financial crisis, Bush's legacy may include the start of a substantial shift in ideology away from an ultra-free-market American economy. At the least, the free-market agenda suffered a public relations disaster of proportions last exceeded in the 1920s and 1930s. Recession, mass foreclosures, public resentment of bankers and the collapse in value of individuals' 401k retirement accounts (tax-privileged savings invested in the stock market) all suggested that the Reagan orthodoxy had been discredited in the American public's eyes.

As did the recession, this discrediting of the free-market orthodoxy spread more widely than United States domestic politics, having profound repercussions for American power. Over a sixty-year period, the United States had constructed a limited international consensus over a particular value system in international economics. The series of economic values embodied in the "Washington consensus" of free markets, limited public sectors, low inflation and low taxes looked less convincing in early 2009 than in early 2008. Advocates of alternative approaches were quick to articulate this fall, some even suggesting that they detected the rise of a competing Beijing consensus. The persuasiveness of American economic values had been compromised.

Further sources of American power were jeopardised by the financial collapse and recession. The increased federal debt made the United States more vulnerable to those holding that debt, as demonstrated by stateside concerns when the Chinese expressed worry over the size of their United States treasury bond holdings (Wines 2009). The status of the dollar as the world's reserve currency was called into question, suggesting that the United States might lose the benefits associated with the dollar's special standing. Neither did the administration capture the credibility to be gained as primary advocates of free trade. As Chorev describes (Chapter 9), failures at the World Trade Organization drove the Bush administration to a strategy of competitive liberalisation through bilateral agreements that seemed subordinated to foreign policy concerns. While blame for WTO disagreements should not fall directly on Bush, he still passed the stalled development round of negotiations to the new administration with little immediate potential for resolution. Just as Bush's term was marked by a decline in America's military and soft power, his final months also involved a distinct weakening in American economic power.

In many senses, Bush's economic bequest to Obama looked like a liability. An ongoing recession with major problems unresolved and a weakening of American international economic power presented an extraordinary challenge for the new president. The enormous and growing federal debt seemed likely to constrain the new administration's policy options. Furthermore, the new administration faced the problem of what to do with newly nationalised corporations; federal part-ownership was unlikely to be a permanent arrangement so the Obama administration would have both to manage these assets in the short term and dispose of them in the longer run. Nevertheless, the Bush administration's failures and the discrediting of the values associated with the Reagan regime did offer Obama a further leadership opportunity. It fell to the new president to propose a new level of federal intervention in the economy, to interpret the nature of the ongoing crisis and the measures needed to alleviate it at a time when the nation required action. Arguably, Bush presented Obama with not just the presidency but with an environment in which he could propose radical changes in federal economic policy.

## 3. SOCIAL POLICIES

Bush had ambitious plans to reform American social policy. His vision was not the traditional conservative one of cutting federal programmes. Instead, he advocated a compassionate conservatism designed to win the Republican Party long-term electoral dominance and to change the American welfare state radically. Expectations, then, were high but his legacy here was distinctly mixed.

Bush certainly piloted radical reforms in education and Medicare. As Parker details in Chapter 12, Bush's No Child Left Behind Act (NCLB) installed a framework of accountability and testing in public schools that seemed set to endure as its primary advocate left office. It represented a step change in federal influence over public schools' conduct. The legislation attracted widespread criticism from diverse viewpoints. One of the most serious was that the Act had little effect on children's learning. Given the importance attached to education in a globalised economy, there was little sense that Bush had solved America's educational problems, or even improved matters much. Whatever the criticisms of the programme, NCLB represented a significant political victory for Bush.

In Chapter 11 Waddan describes the significance of the massive new Medicare benefit for prescription medicines established under the Medicare Modernization Act of 2003 (MMA). The new benefit provided many elderly people with relief from oppressive medical costs, but at great cost to the federal government and therefore to the American taxpayer. For this reason, Bush was criticised by many Republicans for further expanding the size of government but the MMA was significantly conservative in some respects, as Waddan shows. By cranking up the cost of Medicare and challenging the basic presumptions of the original programme, Bush may, ironically, have brought a future radical, and perhaps conservative, reform of Medicare closer.

To balance these achievements, there is a substantial list of legislative failures in social policy. Bush's proposals for faith-based initiatives did not gain any legislative traction. His Social Security proposal's demise reinforced the reputation of the issue as the untouchable "third rail" of American politics, and dissipated the momentum derived from Bush's 2004 victory. His liberal immigration proposal failed to command the bipartisan coalition needed, and collapsed amid the acrimony of election season. Bush particularly struggled under the conditions of divided government after the 2006 mid-terms, a shortcoming Fullam and Gitelson (Chapter 15) blame upon the administration's attempt to combine partisanship with the permanent campaign between 2001 and 2005.

In the areas of immigration and Social Security, Bush passed on developing crises to his successor. The immigration system was widely recognised as in crisis, with over ten million undocumented persons living in the United States and a seemingly porous border, although definitions of that crisis varied according to political perspective. The problem can be presented in cultural, budgetary, labour-market, administrative, humanitarian and security terms. Given Bush's failure, Obama would need to find policy solutions as well as political consensus to resolve these problems. The Social Security failure contributed to an even greater problem. Having increased the federal government's liabilities through the MMA, Bush left the United States facing an entitlements crisis. The crisis cannot be blamed on Bush alone as it pre-dated his time in office but he failed to resolve it, allowing a full business cycle to pass without addressing the fiscal problems implicit in the ageing of the baby-boom generation. Indeed, Bush left an enormous deficit, starving the federal government of resources to target the entitlements crisis. More jaundiced observers saw these outcomes not as chance circumstance but as a conscious ideological effort to "starve the beast", the federal government, by denying it the money needed to sustain its commitments. Whether an intentional product of a starve-the-beast strategy, a more benevolently motivated product of compassionate and big-government conservatism, or simple misjudgement, Bush passed a serious social policy problem to his successor. America's environmental problems and broad health-care problems beyond Medicare could be added to the list of concerns passed to President Obama.

The Bush legacy could also include the damage done to the reputation of his unsuccessful policy ideas. Compassionate conservatism and the ownership society were both concepts offered to underpin the administration's approach to social policy. While the phrase compassionate conservatism is unlikely to be revived in the United States, the ideas that underpinned it were substantive. Under compassionate conservatism, the Republicans offered centrist policy positions in policy areas normally associated with the Democratic Party – for example, recognising the disadvantaged's plight and presenting policies designed to improve social justice, often through local-community institutions and empowerment (Gerson 2007). The ownership society idea, used to explain and defend the Social Security proposals, was also more than shallow rhetoric. Federal government power would be used to expand ownership of, for example, property and allow more people to experience the wealth and security borne of the country's economic success. The ownership society's political appeal was brought into question by the spectacular failure of Bush's Social Security reform to capture public imagination. Moreover, after the 2008 financial crash, ideas associated with stock market investments looked even less appealing. Despite its apparent electoral appeal in 2000, compassionate conservatism also failed to inspire public support. These two ideas have probably been stigmatised by their association with the unpopular Bush administration.

While the breadth of Bush's achievements in social policy was limited, the major reforms he did achieve in education and health care could look even more significant from a longer historical perspective, depending on students' educational achievement and future reform of Medicare. Bush also amassed high-profile legislative defeats, however, and passed major policy problems to the Obama administration. As Long and Ashbee each suggests (Chapters 4 and 13) Bush's greatest legacy in social policy may post-date his time in office. His appointment of two relatively young conservatives to the Supreme Court could shape judicial decisions for many years to come. In aggregate, though, Bush offered an experiment in conservative social policy-making that Washington was not willing to embrace. Notably, members of his own party were among his fiercest critics.

## 4. THE REPUBLICAN PARTY

Bush's ambition for the Republican Party was nothing less than long-term political dominance in the electorate and Congress. While he helped the party to electoral victories in 2002 and 2004, the number of people identifying themselves as Republicans, the volumes of Republican fund-raising and perceptions of the Republican brand had all weakened significantly by 2008 (Fullam and Gitelson, Chapter 15). Bush suffered disastrous opinion-poll ratings in his second term and weakened the party's standing on many issues, including national security and the economy. The Republican presidential candidate in 2008, Senator John McCain, tried to distance himself from the incumbent president, recognising that the association could only harm his chances of victory. Over the course of his presidency, Bush lost the trust of many within his own party, failed to reconstruct the party's image and divided his party while unifying the Democrats.

Bush's legislative strategy gradually alienated many politicians and activists within the Republican Party. In part, this alienation came from a breach between Congress and executive. Legislators resented the administration's assertive manner and refusal to acknowledge congressional prerogatives. Pfiffner describes in Chapter 3 a number of actions that riled legislators as the administration expanded executive power. Other examples, such as deceit over the potential cost of the

MMA and the presence or otherwise of weapons of mass destruction in Iraq, reduced Republican trust in Bush. More generally, however, policies Bush proposed were rarely what conservatives, the party's core, wanted. While he garnered Republican votes for his education and Medicare reforms, much of this support was offered reluctantly. Republicans in Congress would not take the substantial political risk of reforming the Social Security programme as Bush proposed. His "grand bargain" in immigration policy did much to mobilise conservative support, but mostly against the president. Frequently, and especially in the second term, Bush's proposals set him at loggerheads with elements in his party.

Most parts of the conservative movement found reasons to loathe the Bush administration, whether they were fiscal conservatives horrified by the increasing deficit and growth in federal spending or libertarians resistant to Bush's assertions of executive power. National security conservatives watched developments in Iraq with dismay. Ashbee (Chapter 13) outlines the disillusionment of the Christian right as the administration developed. While Bush offered a born-again biography and some appropriate rhetoric and sentiment, he delivered little in terms of policy. On abortion, he discussed a culture of life but only threw his weight behind the partial-birth ban. On same-sex marriage he failed to mobilise resources behind a constitutional amendment. He compromised on stem-cell research. However one classified Bush's conservatism, it seemed to drive key Republican constituencies away from the Bush presidency.

Repeatedly, Bush overestimated his party's willingness to support his unorthodox policy initiatives. The demise of his Social Security proposal and the temporary defeat of his $700 billion bail-out package for American banks, bookends to his second term, both exemplify Bush's limited capacity to convince his party to support his controversial proposals.

As Bush failed in his relations with established elements of his party, his attempt to widen the party's appeal also crumbled. The dream of a lasting realignment depended upon a change in the party's appeal, particularly drawing in racial and ethnic groups and women by quashing the Republicans' image as the uncaring party. Compassionate conservatism's legislative failure clearly hindered the realignment project, as did two particular incidents. First, the aftermath of Hurricane Katrina projected the image of an administration that was incompetent and indifferent to the flood victims' plight. Bush seemed not to be engaged by the disaster. Rap artist Kanye West caught the mood, saying simply: "George Bush doesn't care about black people." The failure of Bush's proposed immigration reform reinforced the impression. The proposal, intended to attract large swathes of the Latino population, triggered resistance that reaffirmed the Republicans as the White Anglo-Saxon Protestant (WASP) party of restrictionist immigration policy and cultural intolerance. Bush provided a lead that his party was not willing to follow, and his dream of reconstituting the party was dashed. Historians will have to decide whether to credit him with attempting to lead the change or to condemn him for failing to persuade his party to follow.

As Bush vacated his office, his party embarked upon a rancorous reassessment of its ideology and policies. The departing president left his party demoralised, divided and uncertain of its future direction. In contrast, he left the Democrats revitalised. Bush demonstrated a penchant for assisting Democratic progress. His strident partisanship late in his first term activated Democratic resentment and, with it, fund-raising. After his 2004 victory, Bush offered the downhearted Democrats an ideal rallying point by suggesting partial privatisation of Social Security. Unified, the Democrats resisted the reform. As Chorev details (Chapter 9) Bush's competitive liberalisation approach allowed Democrats to reconcile their perennial problem over the trade issue by advocating improved environment and labour standards without alienating crucial business constituencies. After 2005, an unpopular, failing but highly partisan Bush proved the Democrat's greatest asset.

The continuing partisanship in Washington and the nation was an integral part of the Bush legacy. Partisanship was present before Bush was elected, and it would be wrong to blame him for the partisan sentiment stirred up by the 2000 election controversy but Bush did much to augment partisan ill-feeling. Despite promises to act as a bipartisan leader, Bush rarely did so. Parker (Chapter 12) describes the bipartisan coalition developed to support NCLB but this proved to be the exception, not the rule. Politicising a national catastrophe, Bush consciously exploited the foreign policy crisis of 9/11 for partisan advantage, abandoning any pretence that partisan politics should stop at the water's edge. That partisanship was reflected in the fifty-plus-one electoral and legislative strategy detailed by Fullam and Gitelson, and did much to establish Bush as a "divider, not a uniter" (Jacobson

2008). Early exchanges in the Obama presidency over the new president's economic stimulus package suggested that the highly partisan environment in Washington had survived Bush's departure. The Texan's pledges to address the problem, made in 2000, seemed hollow as he passed this sour legacy to his successor.

As Bush left office, he had increased Republican influence in the Supreme Court but had overseen the loss of Republican power in the executive and legislative branches. He left his party in electoral and ideological disarray.

## CONCLUSION: THE END OF THE REAGAN ERA AND THE OBAMA OPPORTUNITY

Between 2001 and 2009, Bush weakened American power abroad, embarked upon two wars that had not concluded as he left office, took the country into a financial crisis and deep recession, failed to achieve many of his desired social policies, and oversaw the fragmenting of his political party and the abandonment of many of his core political values. While one may note the absence of further terror attacks on the United States homeland, some social policy successes and the electoral victories of 2002 and 2004, it is hard to describe Bush's overall record even as positively as "mixed".

The public reaction to Bush's record was negative, and contributed to Obama's triumph in 2008. The Obama presidency and Democratic control of the 111th Congress are important elements of Bush's legacy. Reactions to the 2008 result offered interesting commentary on the departing president. Obama won a mere 53 per cent of the vote, yet his victory was greeted by many as the beginning of a new era. Such analyses did not reflect the vote totals or changes in partisan representation in Congress but the ferocity of the nation's rejection of the incumbent Bush administration. As David Letterman put it within hours of polling booths closing: "Ladies and gentlemen, Barack Obama is our new president. And I think I speak for most Americans when I say, anybody mind if he starts a little early?"

Some even claimed that a realignment in American politics was underway, presenting the Bush presidency as the end of a conservative era that began with Ronald Reagan. Under Bush, many conservative ideas had been brought into disrepute across a range of policy areas, thus offering Obama extraordinary opportunities for presidential leadership. Yet it is premature to regard Bush's presidency as the end of a period of conservative dominance.

Bush's legacy also involved passing on to his successor extraordinary constraints. An enormous budget deficit in a time of recession both dictated that Obama made the economy his primary policy concern, and limited the options available to address the problem. Big spending programmes would confront the major obstacle of the federal deficit, as a starve-the-beast strategy would dictate. Addressing the deficit in the long term seemed likely to demand spending cuts. Inheriting two ongoing wars demanded immediate attention to Bush's primary strategic concerns in Iraq and Afghanistan. The desperate, and worsening, state of entitlements funding suggested that federal support for social services would be easier to cut than to sustain at existing levels. Obama was presented with federal ownership of numerous financial institutions and the long-term debate seemed likely to concern the means by which these institutions would be returned to the private sector. While commentators argued about whether the end of the Bush presidency marked a fundamental change in America's politics, a series of policy inheritances, largely derived from the Bush terms, appeared likely to limit Obama's options and, in some cases, push his administration towards distinctly conservative solutions, such as federal spending cuts and high-profile privatisations. Commentators arguing that the Obama administration could sweep all vestiges of conservative dominance away failed to recognise the nature of the new president's inheritance. The Bush legacy would constrain and direct his successor, maintaining a continuing influence rather than being consigned instantly to history.

## BIBLIOGRAPHY

Barnes, Fred (2003), "Big Government Conservatism", *Wall Street Journal,* 15 August

Barnes, Fred (2006), *Rebel-in-Chief: Inside the Bold and Controversial Presidency of George W. Bush,* New York: Three Rivers Press

*Economist* (2009), "George Bush's Legacy: The Frat Boy Ships Out", *The Economist,* 15 January

Gerson, Michael J. (2007), *Heroic Conservatism: Why Republicans Need To Embrace America's Ideals (And Why They Deserve To Fail If They Don't),* New York: HarperOne

Jacobson, Gary C. (2008), *A Divider Not A Uniter: George W. Bush and the American People*, London: Pearson Longman

Lynch, Timothy J. and Robert S. Singh (2008), *After Bush: The Case For Continuity in American Foreign Policy*, Cambridge: Cambridge University Press

Murphy, Cullen and Todd S. Purdum (2009), "Farewell To All That: An Oral History Of The Bush White House", *Vanity Fair*, February

Nye, Joseph S., Jr (2004) "The Decline of America's Soft Power", *Foreign Affairs*, May/June

Wines, Michael (2009), "China's Leader Says He is Worried Over U.S. Treasuries", *New York Times*, 13 March

# INDEX


AIG (insurance company), 161, 162, 163–4, 266
Aberbach, Joel, 170
abortion law, 50, 54, 70, 72, 203, 206, 211
Abramoff, Jack, 256
Abu Ghraib prison, 36, 53, 85, 87, 88, 122, 261–2
Addington, David, 31–2, 35
affirmative-action, 54–5
Afghanistan
  al-Qaeda and, 36
  Bush's policy in, 1, 9, 49, 51, 95, 127
  federal spending on, 63
  invasion, 224, 246
  and Middle East Free Trade Area, 136
  regime change, 93
  as threat to American security, 82–3
  war, 45, 84, 124, 152, 259, 260, 261, 275
Africa: cotton subsidies, 134; *see also* Morocco; Niger; Somalia
African Americans: civil rights, 61
agricultural subsidies, 133–4, 135–6, 139
aid: Hurricane Katrina victims, 69; *see also* conditional grants-in-aid; federal grants-in-aid; Medicaid
al-Libi, Ibn al-Shayk, 37
al-Qaeda
  Clinton's attack on, 80
  and 9/11 attack, 79
  perceived link with Saddam Hussein, 36–7, 42
  war on, 86, 260
Alito, Justice Samuel A. Jr, 49–52, 54, 57, 205
Allen, Senator George, 48
American Association of Retired Persons (AARP), 171–2
American Enterprise Institute, 94
*American Insurance Association* v. *Garamendi* (2003), 72
Americans with Disabilities Act (1990), 72
Anti-Ballistic Missile Treaty (1972), 18, 123
Arizona: same-sex marriage, 213
Arlington Group, 208–9
army *see* British army; United States forces
Article II *see* United States Constitution: Article II
Ashcroft, Attorney General John, 71
assisted suicide legislation, 71, 73
Atta, Mohamed, 37
Attorney General
  and assisted suicide legislation, 71
  and Foreign Intelligence Surveillance Act (1977), 39
Auletta, Ken, 233
Australia: trade with, 136
Aviation and Transport Security Act (2001), 102–3
axis of evil, 118
Aznar, Jose Maria, 119, 124

Baath Party (Iraq), 33
Bahrain: trade with, 136–7
Baker, Gerard, 124
Baker, James, 94
banks: and financial crash (2008), 162–3, 266
Barnes, Fred, 176
Baucus, Senator Max, 176
Bauer, Gary, 201
Bear Stearns, 161, 162
Bernanke, Ben, 153–4, 159
big government conservatism, 62–3
Bill of Rights, 61
Bin Laden, Osama, 83, 84, 87, 226
Blackmun, Justice Harry, 44, 71
Blair, Tony, 68, 119, 124

Blanco, Governor Kathleen, 69
Blix, Hans, 92
Blumenthal, Sidney, 216
Bolten, Josh, 160, 221
Border and Transportation Security directorate, 104
Born-Alive Infants Protection Act (2002), 206
Bosworth, Michael, 159
*Boumediene* v. *Bush* (2008), 52
Brazil
  and Group of 20 (G20), 134
  and trade, 139, 135
Bremer, Paul, 32, 33, 34
Britain *see* United Kingdom
British army, 125
Brown, Gordon, 23, 124–5
Brown, Michael, 251
*Brown* v. *Board of Education* (1954), 55
budget deficits, 151–2, 275
Bumiller, Elisabeth, 121
Bush, President George H. W.
  and campaigning, 219–21
  and centralisation, 62
  and education, 184
  and Iraq Study Group, 94
  and judicial appointments, 71
  minor speeches, 218
  press conferences, 221
  and taxation, 219–20
  and United States Congress, 233
Bush, President George W.
  and abortion, 54, 206, 209, 272
  and Afghanistan policy, 1, 9, 45, 49, 51, 95, 124, 275
  and Africa, 251
  and Alito nomination, 49, 51–2
  arrest for drink-driving, 201–2
  as a "big government conservative", 265
  and Brown, Gordon, 124–5
  and campaigning, 6–9, 216, 217, 219, 247, 254–5
  and centralisation, 72, 73
  character, 3, 7, 18, 160
  as Chief Executive Officer, 13, 26–7, 29–42
  and children's health insurance, 67
  and Christian right, 199–204
  and civil liberties, 53
  as "a compassionate conservative", 5, 21, 184–6, 210, 225–6, 240–1, 242, 258, 268
  and competitive liberalisation, 135, 273
  and conservatism, 4, 8, 24, 210, 268, 274
  and the courts, 203–6
  and decision-making process, 7, 23, 29, 30–4
  and Democrats, 13, 17, 18
  as "a divider, not a uniter", 13, 27, 273
  economic policy, 24, 149–64, 265–8
  and education, 64–5, 182–3, 184–6, 188, 189, 191, 192–4, 195
  relationship with Europe, 115–27
  European tour (February 2005), 121
  executive style, 7–8, 17
  use of federal mandates, 64
  "fifty-plus-one" strategy, 8, 247, 254
  fiscal policy, 151–3
  abandonment of Geneva Conventions, 36
  as governor of Texas, 7, 200
  "grand bargain" *see* Bush, President George W.: and immigration reform
  and Guantánamo Bay, 52–3
  and Hurricane Katrina, 250–1, 272–3
  and immigration reform, 4, 251, 269, 273
  objection to international laws, 117
  rejection of Kyoto Protocols, 118, 155
  non-compliance with the law, 38, 39–41
  and laws of war, 86–7
  legacy, 1, 57, 258–75
  at Marine Corps Air Station, 224
  and marriage law, 69, 207–8
  and Medicare, 166, 168, 169–70, 178, 269
  and Miers nomination to the Supreme Court, 49–52, 56, 206
  and military commissions order, 30–1, 32
  military record, 248
  and monetary policy, 153, 154
  at Mount Rushmore, 224
  and No Child Left Behind policy, 245, 268–9
  partisanship of, 18, 21, 25, 63, 234, 248, 251–6, 273
  and "the permanent campaign", 217, 219, 220–1, 227–8, 233, 234, 241, 246, 247–8, 250, 252
  personality *see* Bush, President George W.: character
  and polling data, 232
  popularity *see* Bush, President

George W.: and ratings
approval of pre-emptive statutes, 70
use of presidential veto, 21–2, 67
press conferences, 221–2
ignores professional advice, 35–8
and ratings, 22, 226, 227, 233, 234, 255
and regulation, 154–6
and Republican Party, 13, 239–5, 271–4
and Republican Primaries (2000), 200–1
and Roberts nomination to the Supreme Court, 45–7, 48
on Saddam Hussein, 229
and same-sex marriage, 272
and secrecy, 23, 32, 40, 41
and sex education, 209
and sexual morality, 201
use of signing statements, 40–1, 42
and Social Security reform, 172, 174–7, 178, 250, 258, 269
speeches, 13, 88, 219–20, 224, 229
and stagecraft, 222–3
State of the Union addresses: (2004), 175, 207–8; (2005), 175; (2007), 193
and stem-cell research, 272
strategic vision, 27, 239–55
support for post-9/11, 245–7
and taxation, 8, 151, 152, 157, 265
and Terrorist Surveillance Program, 38–40
and terrorist suspects, treatment of, 261–2
and travel, 219
and "triangulation", 225–6
trustworthiness, 233
lands on USS *Abraham Lincoln*, 223
as the "uncompassionate conservative", 18
and unilateralism, 25, 26, 27, 118
and United States Congress, 13–27, 63, 233, 254
and United States Supreme Court, 44–57, 271
as "a uniter, not a divider", 5, 13, 27, 182, 226, 242
accused of war crimes, 88
and World Trade Organization, 137–8, 267–8
Bush Doctrine, 78–9, 85, 90, 93, 94, 95, 96, 118, 264
*Bush* v. *Gore* (2000), 5, 13
business: lobbyists, 111, 156; *see also* financial crash (2008)

CIA
agents *see* Plame, Valerie
and Department of Defense, 109
and FBI, 109
and rendition, 123
and Saddam–al-Qaeda link, 37, 38
and Terrorist Threat Integration Center, 103
Caddell, Pat: "Initial Working Paper on Political Strategy", 216
California: same-sex marriage, 213; *see also* *American Insurance Association* v. *Garamendi*; Schwarzenegger, Governor Arnold
California, University of *see* *Regents of the University of California* v. *Bakke* (1978)
California Air Resources Board, 68
California Global Warming Solutions Act (2006), 68
campaign finance reform law *see* McCain–Feingold campaign finance reform law
campaigning, 6–7, 193, 216–17
"the permanent campaign", 216, 217, 219, 220–1, 227–8, 231–2, 233, 234–5, 240, 241, 246, 247–8, 250, 252, 254–5
Cancún trade negotiations, 133–4
car industry, 155, 162
carbon emissions, 73
Card, Andrew, 172, 219, 221, 227
Caribbean: cotton subsidies, 134
Carr, E. H., 77
Carter, President Jimmy, 80, 218, 219
Center for International and Security Studies, 231
Central America Free Trade Agreement (CAFTA), 135, 137, 139–40
centralisation: and federalism, 60–2, 72–3
Chambliss, Senator Saxby, 226–7
Chavez, President Hugo, 262
chemical industry, 106
Chemical Security Act, 106
Cheney, Vice President Dick
and conservatism, 18–19
and energy policy taskforce, 156
and promotion of goals and objectives, 218
and Iraqi weapon manufacture, 228

and military commissions order, 31–2
1 per cent doctrine, 90
power of, 29, 30
and pre-emption, 90
and presidential power, 70
on the press, 218
and prisoners, 122
and Republican control of the Senate, 5
and Saddam–al-Qaeda link, 37
and taxation, 151
and terrorism alerts, 229
and United States Congress, 18–19, 253
Chertoff, Michael, 103
children: health insurance for, 66–7; *see also* No Child Left Behind (NCLB) Act (2001)
Chile: trade with, 136, 144
China
and loans to USA, 150, 158, 265
rise of, 80, 263
trade with, 138, 142–3
and US treasury bonds, 267
Chirac, President Jacques, 124
Christian right, 199–204, 207–13
Chrysler (car makers), 162
Churchill, Winston, 95
Citizens Corps Program, 106
civil liberties, 52, 53
civil rights
African Americans, 61
and education, 185
Clarke, Richard, 37
Cleland, Senator Max, 226
Clinton, President Bill
and big government, 3, 14
and communication, 222
and counter-terrorism, 80–1
criticism of, 241
and defence, 80–1, 82
and education, 184
and federal courts, 205
and foreign policy, 80–1, 117
and Greenspan, Alan, 153
and Internet, state taxing of access to, 70
legacy of, 77
and Medicare, 168
and permanent campaigns, 217
and polling data, 232
assessment of presidency, 258–9
ratings, 22
and regulation, 154–5, 159
State of the Union address: (1996), 14; (1999), 168
and United States Congress, 233
co-operative federalism, 64
"coalition of the willing": trade negotiations, 134
Cold War, 78, 86, 96
Cole, Representative Tom, 244
Colombia: trade with, 125
Commission on Social Security Reform, 174
"compassionate conservatism", 240–1, 242, 248, 249, 270–1
"competitive liberalisation" strategy, 132, 134–5
Congress *see* United States Congress
*Congressional Quarterly* (CQ), 22
Connecticut: and No Child Left Behind Act, 189–90
conservatism
Bush and, 5, 21, 184–6, 210, 225–6, 240–1, 242, 258, 268, 274
Cheney and, 18–19
*see also* "big government conservatism"; "compassionate conservatism"
conservatives
and affirmative-action policies, 54–5
Bush and, 4, 8, 24
and centralisation, 72
congressional Republicans as, 24
economic, 14
and free-market principles, 24
and gay marriage, 70
and Medicare, 170
and No Child Left Behind Act, 185–6
and Supreme Court candidates, 44, 45, 46, 47, 49, 56
*see also* Christian right; neo-conservatives
consumer protection, 129
Corzine, Senator Jon, 106
cotton subsidies, 134, 139
Council of Economic Advisers (CEA), 159
counter-terrorism, 80–1, 103; *see also* terrorists
courts, 203
appeal, 204
federal, 52–3, 57, 166, 190, 199, 203–4, 205, 207

*see also* International Court of Justice; International Criminal Court; United States Supreme Court
Cox, Christopher, 159
Cuban missile crisis, 90, 91
Customs and Border Protection Bureau, 104

Daniels, Mitch, 159, 160
Davis, Representative Tom, 244
de-Baathification Coalition Provisional Authority Orders, 33, 34
Deaver, Michael, 222
Defense Authorization Act (2007), 69
Defense Intelligence Agency, 37
Defense of Marriage Act (1996) (DOMA), 207, 211
Deficit Reduction Act (2005), 67
DeLay, Tom, 27, 49, 51, 253, 256
democracy: Middle East, 92–4
Democrats
  Americans' view of, 13–14
  co-operation with Bush, 17, 18
  view of Bush, 13
  and centralisation, 73
  and chief justice's nomination, 46, 47
  and children's health insurance, 67
  and elections, 17, 122, 255
  and Executive Office of the President, 104
  and federal power, 62
  and financial crash (2008), 162
  and liberal internationalism, 127
  and Medicare, 171
  and Miers nomination to Supreme Court, 49
  and No Child Left Behind Act, 185, 188
  revitilisation of, 273
  and Social Security reform, 176, 177
  criticism of Terrorist Surveillance Program, 51
  and trade, 129, 130, 132, 133, 136–7, 138, 140, 144
  in United States Congress, 5, 9, 14, 18, 19, 20, 22, 23, 27, 94, 126, 192, 193, 242–4; House of Representatives, 126, 140, 142, 149, 242; Senate, 17, 226–7
Department of Defense (DOD), 101, 109
Department of Education, 19, 65
Department of Health and Human Services, 231
Department of Homeland Security (DHS)
  and bureaucracy, 109, 112
  creation of, 20, 65, 226, 246
  efficiency of, 100, 101
  Information Analysis and Infrastructure Protection (IAIP), 103, 108
  National Response Framework, 111
  Office of Personnel Management, 108
  transformation of, 103–4, 107–8
Department of Justice, 86
*Department of Revenue for Kentucky* v. *Davis*, 2008, 72
DeWine, Senator Mike, 242
Director of National Intelligence (DNI), 103
disaster planning, 68–9
discrimination
  education, 55
  race, 61
  *see also* affirmative-action
*District of Columbia* v. *Heller* (2008), 56
Dobson, Dr James, 201, 204, 210, 211
Dodd, Senator Christopher, 159
*Doe* v. *Bolton* (1973), 199
Doha Development Round of Multilateral Trade Negotiations, 133–4, 139, 145
dollar: and overseas borrowing, 150
Domestic Policy Council, 242
Donley, Michael B. and Pollard, Neal A., 107
Dooley, Cal, 140
Dow Jones index, 265
Draper, Roger, 34
driver's licences, 65–6
drugs *see* marijuana; prescription drugs
Dubai Ports World, 139
Duffy, Helen, 83

Eagleburger, Lawrence, 94
Economic Growth and Tax Relief Reconciliation Act (2001), 265
economic theory, Keynesian, 152–3
economy, 149–64
  fiscal policy, 151–3
  growth and equality, 156–7
  monetary policy, 153–4
  regulation, 154–6
education
  and coercive federalism, 64–5

sex education, 206
vouchers, 185, 186
*see also* Elementary and Secondary Education Act; Goals 2000: Educate America Act; No Child Left Behind Act
Edwards, George, 27, 176–7, 217
Eisenhower, President Dwight D., 62, 223
elderly: care of *see* Medicare; Social Security
Election Assistance Commission, 68
elections
congressional, 5–6; (1994), 240; (2002), 5, 17, 20, 169, 226–7, 234, 246–7, 248, 253, 274; (2006), 13, 14, 17, 27, 122, 138, 141, 144, 192, 242–4, 255, 274; (2008), 13, 126, 193, 239, 242–4, 274
and federal coercion, 67–8
Presidential Elections: (2000), 13, 67, 151, 168, 169, 184–5, 200–2, 217, 226, 234, 245; (2004), 14, 22, 202, 137, 161, 166, 167, 173, 178, 191, 208, 211, 248–9, 252, 253, 254, 255, 274; (2008), 162, 193, 205, 211, 239, 242–4, 255
Republican Primaries (2000), 200–1
and technology, 241
*see also* campaigning; Help America Vote Act
Elementary and Secondary Education Act (ESEA) (1965), 64–5, 184–5
Emergency Economic Stabilization Act (2008), 56
employment, 149; *see also* unemployment
"enemy combatants" *see* terrorist suspects
Energy Policy Act (2005), 70
Enron scandal, 156
environmental policy, 68, 123, 136; *see also* Kyoto Protocols; Kyoto Treaty
Environmental Protection Agency, 106
Estrada, Miguel, 204
Europe: relationship with United States, 115–27, 139, 263
European Union: trade with, 139
evangelicals: support for Bush, 199, 200, 201–2
*Ex Parte Milligan* (1866), 53
Executive Office of the President (EOP), 104

FBI
agents *see* Rowley, Colleen
and CIA, 109
and Department of Homeland Security, 108
expansion, 109
and Joint Terrorism Task Forces, 111
and Saddam–al-Qaeda link, 37
and Terrorist Threat Integration Center, 103
*FMC* v. *South Carolina Ports Authority* (2002), 71–2
Falwell, the Reverend Jerry, 210, 212
Family Research Council (FRC), 186, 203, 204, 208
Fannie Mae (mortgage traders), 3, 149, 154, 161, 266
farming *see* agricultural subsidies
federal courts, 52–3, 57, 166, 190, 199, 203–4, 205, 207
Federal Emergency Management Agency, 109
federal grants-in-aid, 60–1, 63–4
Federal Marriage Amendment, 70
Federal Reserve Board, 150, 153, 154, 266
federal spending, 63–4
federalism, 59–73
and big government conservatism, 62–3
and centralisation, 60–2, 72–3
co-operative, 64
coercive, 63–70; education, 64–5; elections, 67–8; environmental policy, 68; health care, 66–7; homeland security, 65–6; Hurricane Katrina, 68–9
and devolution, 60–2
"opportunistic", 73
and United States Supreme Court, 71–2
Federalist Society, 204
Feith, Douglas, 33
"fifty-plus-one" strategy, 8, 247, 251–4, 273
financial crash (2008), 2–3, 149–50, 158–64, 265–6, 270
financial institutions, 275; *see also* banks; Bear Stearns; Fannie May; Freddie Mac; Lehmann Brothers
Finn, Chester and Hess, Frederick, 194–5
firearms *see* National Rifle Association
First Amendment *see* United States Constitution: First Amendment
fiscal policy, 63–4, 151–3
Fleischer, Ari, 221, 223
Florida: same-sex marriage, 213

focus groups, 232
Focus on the Family, 204
Foley, Representative Mark, 256
Ford (car makers), 162
Foreign Intelligence Surveillance Act (1977) (FISA), 38, 39
foreign policy, 77–147, 259–65
  Bush and, 77–96, 116, 259–65
  impact of 9/11 on, 80
  realism in, 92, 94
Fourteenth Amendment *see* United States Constitution: Fourteenth Amendment
Fourth Amendment *see* United States Constitution: Fourth Amendment
France
  and invasion of Iraq, 120
  relationship with USA, 125
Freddie Mac (mortgage traders), 3, 149, 153, 154, 161, 266
Free Trade Agreement of the Americas (FTAA), 135
Friedman, Milton, 153
Friendly, Judge Henry J., 45

G20 coalition *see* Group of 20 (G20) coalition
Gallagher, Maggie, 231
Garcia, President Alan, 141
*Garcia* v. *San Antonio* (1985), 61, 71
Gates, Robert, 122
General Agreement on Tariffs and Trade (GATT), 131
General Motors, 162
Geneva Conventions
  and military commissions order, 32
  and detention of terrorist suspects, 85–6, 87
  US abandonment of, 35–6, 42
Germany *see* Merkel, Chancellor Angela; Schroeder, Chancellor Gerhard
Gerson, Michael: "smoking gun and mushroom cloud", 228
Gilmore Commission, 100
Gingrich, Newt, 171
Ginsburg, Justice Ruth Bader, 57
Giuliani, Mayor Rudi, 212
globalisation, 80, 81
Goals 2000: Educate America Act (1994), 184
Gonzales, Attorney General Alberto, 85–6
*Gonzales* v. *Carhart* (2007), 54, 72, 205
*Gonzales* v. *Oregon* (2006), 71
*Gonzales* v. *Planned Parenthood Federation of America* (2007), 54
*Gonzales* v. *Raich* (2005), 72
Gore, Al
  and Medicare, 168, 169
  and Presidential Election (2000), 13, 151, 201
  *see also Bush* v. *Gore*
governors *see* state governors
Graham, Bill, 261–2
Graham, Senator Bob, 262
Graham, Senator Lindsey, 142
Gramm, Senator Phil, 159
grants: children's health insurance, 66
grants-in-aid, 60–1, 63–4
Great Society programmes, 61
greenhouse gas emissions, 68
Greenspan, Alan, 153, 154, 159, 160, 161
*Griswold* ruling (1965), 203
Group of 20 (G20) coalition, 134, 143
*Grutter* v. *Bollinger* (2003), 55
Guantánamo Bay
  Americans' view of, 123
  terrorist suspects at, 36, 52–3, 85, 87, 122–3, 261–2
  United States Supreme Court and, 56
Gulf of Tonkin resolution (1964), 81
gun ownership, 55–6
Guter, Rear Admiral Donald J., 31

habeas corpus: terrorist suspects, 31, 52–3
Hacker, Jacob, 174
Hagel, Senator Chuck, 233
*Hamdan* v. *Rumsfeld* (2006), 32, 52, 87
Hastert, Dennis, 27, 168
Haynes, Jim, 31
health care, 4, 7, 61, 66–7, 166–72, 240, 270, 271
Health Savings Accounts (HSAs), 171
Heclo, Hugh, 217
Help America Vote Act (2002), 67–8
Hersh, Seymour, 230
Hess, Frederick *see* Finn, Chester and Hess, Frederick
Hildebrand, Steve, 234–5
Hobbs, David, 168
homeland security
  and bureaucracy, 102–4

and coercive federalism, 65–6
organisational challenges to, 107–11
partnerships, 110
politics of, 104–7
reform, 100–11
*see also* Department of Homeland Security
Homeland Security Act (2002), 103
Homeland Security Appropriations Act (2006), 105–6
Homeland Security Council (HSC), 110, 242
Homeland Security Grant Program, 105
homosexual rights, 203
Hoover, President Herbert, 218, 219
House of Representatives *see* United States House of Representatives
Huckabee, Governor Mike, 212
Hughes, Karen, 220, 221, 224, 225
human rights
Abu Ghraib prison, 122
Bush administration's approach to, 126
France and, 125
Taliban threat to, 82
Hume, Brit, 221
Hurricane Katrina, 3, 22, 68–9, 250–1, 272–3
Hussein, Saddam *see* Saddam Hussein

immigration reform, 4, 22, 251, 269
imports: steel, 137
income inequality, 156–7
India: trade with, 139
Inskeep, Steve, 234
Intelligence Reform and Terrorism Prevention Act (2004), 65, 103
interest groups: and homeland security, 106
International Court of Justice, 71
International Criminal Court, 18, 117, 118, 123, 126
International Labour Organization (ILO), 141
international trade policy, 129–45
bilateral and regional talks, 134–7, 139–42
Doha Development Round of Multilateral Trade Negotiations, 133–4, 139, 145
unilateral initiatives, 137–8, 142–3
Internet Tax Freedom Act Amendments Act (2007), 70
investment protection, 141
Iran, 2, 92–3, 94, 118, 123
and nuclear weapons, 92, 124, 263
Iraq
and Afghanistan, 85
disbandment of army, 32, 33–4
Baath Party, 32
invasion of, 90–1, 92, 119–20, 217, 227, 229, 230
regime change, 93–4
security forces, 34
Special Republican Guard, 34
and Weapons of Mass Destruction, 227, 229–31
*see also* Saddam Hussein
Iraq Study Group, 94
Iraq war, 41, 260
opposition to, 123–4, 263
United States Congress and, 20, 25–6, 246–8
Iraq War Resolution (2002), 24
Islamic fundamentalism, 124
Israel: trade with, 136
Israel–Palestine conflict, 1

Jacobson, Gary, 233–4
Jeffords, Senator James, 5, 17, 151, 186, 245
Johnson, President Lyndon B., 23, 61, 64
Joint Resolution 23, 81–2
Joint Terrorism Task Forces, 111
Jones, Charles O., 217, 241–2
Jordan: trade with, 136
Judge Advocate Generals, 35
judiciary, 16, 166, 204; *see also* courts
*jus in bello*: separation from *jus ad bellum*, 86

Kagan, Robert
and Europe, 117, 126
and invasion of Iraq, 120
*Of Paradise and Power*, 115–16
"The Benevolent Empire", 116
Kashmeri, Sarwar, 120
Keillor, Garrison: *Prairie Home Companion*, 195
Kennan, George, 95–6
Kennedy, Justice Anthony, 54, 55, 57, 205
Kennedy, Senator Edward, 18, 185, 186, 192

Kennedy, President John F., 90
Kentucky *see Department of Revenue for Kentucky* v. *Davis*
Kernell, Samuel, 252–4
Kerry, Senator John, 6, 175, 243, 248–9
Kettl, Donald F., 104
Keynesian economic theory, 152–3
Khalilzad, Zal, 33
Kissinger, Henry, 95
Knoller, Mark, 219
Kohut, Andrew, 213 n3
Korologos, Tom, 121
Krane, Dale, 63
Kristof, Nicolas, 230
Kumar, Martha Joynt, 220, 222, 225
Kuo, David, 210
Kyoto Protocols, 118, 155
Kyoto Treaty, 18, 117

labour laws, 136, 137, 141, 142
Lamy, Pascal, 139
Latino electorate, 212, 241, 251, 273
law and order: effect of Hurricane Katrina on, 69
law enforcement, 65, 81, 111
Law Enforcement Terrorism Prevention Program, 105
*Lawrence* v. *Texas* (2003), 70, 203
Lay, Kenneth, 156
Leahy, Senator Patrick, 50
Lee, Representative Barbara, 81
Lehman Brothers (investment bankers), 162, 163, 266
Letterman, David, 274
Levitt, Michael, 172
Libby, Lewis "Scooter", 92, 230
liberals, 62
  and centralisation, 73
  foreign policy, 78, 83
  and No Child Left Behind Act, 185–6
  and regulation, 154
  and the Supreme Court, 44–6, 48, 54, 55, 57
liberty: right to, 203
Lieberman, Senator Joseph, 104
Lincoln, President Abraham, 41
Lincoln Group (public relations firm), 231–2
Lindsey, Larry, 159, 160
Lizza, Ryan, 222
lobbyists, 106, 111, 156, 171–2, 208, 256
*Los Angeles Times*, 224
Lott, Senator Trent, 27, 48, 170
Louisiana: effects of Hurricane Katrina, 69
Luttwak, E., 77–8
Lynch, T. J. and Singh, R., 77–8, 79, 90, 95, 263

McCain, Senator John, 170, 200, 211, 213, 242, 271
McCain–Feingold campaign finance reform law, 20
McClellan, Scott, 217, 220–1, 227
McIntosh, David M., 204
McManus, Michael, 231
mandates: federal government, 64, 73
Mann, Thomas E. *see* Ornstein Norman J. and Mann, Thomas E.
marijuana, 72, 73
markets: and financial crash (2008), 159, 266–7
marriage: media promotion of, 231
marriage law, 69–70, 73, 203, 207–8; *see also* same-sex marriages
Marshall, Chief Justice John, 60
Massachusetts: same-sex marriages, 73
Massachusetts Supreme Judicial Court, 207
media
  Bush and, 216–36
  Iraq war coverage, 231
  *see also* press
Medicaid, 61, 66, 67
Medicare, 61, 66, 152, 166, 167, 251
Medicare Prescription Drug, Improvement and Modernization Act (2003), 7, 66, 166, 167–72, 178, 269
*Meredith* v. *Jefferson County Board of Education* (2007), 55
Merkel, Chancellor Angela, 125
Michaud, Congressman Mike, 140
Michelman, Kate, 46
Middle East
  democracy, 92–4
  United States–Middle East Free Trade Area, 136, 139, 144
  *see also* Afghanistan; Iran; Iraq; Israel; Jordan; Oman; Pakistan; Syria; Yemen
Miers, Harriet, 47–9, 56, 206
Military Commissions Act (2006), 52–3, 87

military commissions order (13 November 2001), 30–2
military tribunals, 53
Miller, Representative George, 185, 192
Minnesota: schools, 191
Mississippi: schools, 191
Moens, Alexander, 118
monetary policy, 153–4
Morocco: trade with, 136
Morris, Lawrence J., 31
mortgage crisis (2008), 149, 152, 158–9, 162
MoveOn.org, 45
Muasher, Marwan, 136
Muller, Harald, 117
Musharraf, President Pervez, 93
Myers, Richard, 34

National Assessment of Educational Progress (NAEP), 191, 195
National Commission on Excellence in Education: *A Nation at Risk*, 184
National Counterterrorism Center (NCTC), 103, 109
National Economic Council, 242
National Guard, 69
National Rifle Association, 56, 89
national security, 8, 20, 77–126
  and First Amendment, 53
  *see also* war on terror
National Security Agency (NSA): and Terrorist Surveillance Program, 38–40, 41–2
National Security Council (NSC), 33, 34, 242
National Security Strategy (NSS) (2002), 89–90, 103, 118
NATO: and Afghanistan, 85
Negroponte, John, 103, 109
neo-conservatives
  and big government, 62
  and invasion of Iraq, 120
  support for post-9/11, 245–7
  and US military capability, 261
  *see also* Kagan, Robert: *Of Paradise and Power*
Neustadt, Richard, 15
New Deal, 60
New Federalism, 62
New Orleans: effects of Hurricane Katrina, 68–9
New York Police Department: intelligence sharing, 111
*New York Times*
  and Bush's arrest for drink-driving, 201–2
  on Bush's speech at Mount Rushmore, 224
  on Iraqi nuclear weapon manufacture, 228
  investigation into Medicare, 172
  on uranium deal, 230
  *see also* Kristof, Nicolas; Lizza, Ryan; Stevenson, Richard
*Newsweek* magazine: poll on 2008 presidential campaign, 213
Niger: supply of uranium to Iraq, 229, 230
9/11
  aftermath, 8, 23, 65, 89, 263; *see also* war on terror
  American response to, 118–19
  Bush's response to, 245
  and Bush's strategic vision, 27
  and national unity, 19–20
  compared with Pearl Harbor, 79–80, 83
9/11 commission, 109
Nixon, President Richard, 23, 62, 218, 219
No Child Left Behind (NCLB) Act (2001), 7, 18, 64
  and academic standards, 65, 187
  funding for, 188
  implementation and future, 189–91
  passage into law, 184–6
  as political victory, 166
  reauthorisation of, 192–3
  and school sanctions, 191–2
  significance of, 182–3, 268–9
North American Free Trade Agreement (NAFTA), 135
North Korea, 92, 263
nuclear weapons, 228, 231; *see also* Weapons of Mass Destruction
Nussle, Jim, 160
Nye, Joseph, 261

Obama, President Barack
  and abortion, 211
  and Bush's presidential record, 274–6
  and courts, 205
  and the economy, 268, 274, 275

and Europe, 125, 127
and financial crash (2008), 152
and foreign policy, 263, 264, 265
and reduction of greenhouse gas emissions, 68
and Guantánamo Bay, 126–7
and No Child Left Behind Act, 193, 194
and the permanent campaign, 234–5
election to presidency, 242
and ratings, 234
and stem-cell research, 209
and resurgence of the Taliban, 84
and terrorism, 264
and trade, 145
O'Connor, Justice Sandra Day, 44–5, 46, 49, 50, 51, 205
Office of Information and Regulatory Affairs (OIRA), 155
Office of Management and Budget (OMB), 106, 155, 159
Oman: trade with, 140
1 per cent doctrine, 92
O'Neill, Paul, 159, 160
Operation Enduring Freedom, 82
Oregon: assisted suicide legislation, 71, 73
Ornstein Norman J. and Mann, Thomas E., *The Permanent Campaign and its Future*, 241, 254
overseas borrowing, 150, 158
ownership society, 270

Paige, Rod, 191
Pakistan: al-Qaeda in, 82; *see also* Musharraf, President Pervez
Palestine *see* Israel–Palestine conflict
Palin, Governor Sarah, 213
Panama: trade with, 141
*Parents Involved in Community Schools* v. *Seattle School District No.1* (2007), 55
Partial Birth Abortion Ban Act (2003), 54, 70, 72, 206
partisanship
Bush and, 18, 21, 25, 63, 234, 248, 251–6, 273
United States Congress, 233–4
Patriot Act *see* USA Patriot Act (2001)
Paulson, Henry, 3, 23, 24, 160
Pearl Harbor, 79–80, 83
Pelosi, Nancy, 27, 142, 163
Pennsylvania *see Planned Parenthood of Southeastern Pennsylvania* v. *Casey* (1992)
Pentagon: propaganda, 231–2
Perino, Dana, 225
Perkins, Tony, 210
"the permanent campaign", 216, 217, 219, 220–1, 227–8, 231–2, 233, 234–5, 240, 241, 246, 247–8, 250, 252, 254–5
Perrow, Charles, 107–8
Peru: trade with, 141
Peterson, Paul and West, Martin, 193–4
Pew Research Center, 202, 243, 249
Pharmaceuticals Research Manufacturers of America (PhRMA), 171, 172
Pillar, Paul, 37
Plame, Valerie, 91, 229
Planned Parenthood Federation of America *see Gonzales* v. *Planned Parenthood Federation of America*
*Planned Parenthood of Southeastern Pennsylvania* v. *Casey* (1992), 50
pluralism, 73
Poland: and rendition, 123
police *see* New York Police Department
Pollard, Neal A. *see* Donley, Michael B. and Pollard, Neal A.
Portman, Rob, 160
Powell, Colin
and abandonment of Geneva Conventions, 35–6
and Iraq War, 120, 262
and disbandment of Iraqi army, 34
marginalisation of, 41
and military commissions order, 31, 32, 33
and Weapons of Mass Destruction, 91
power: American and European view of, 115
pre-emption doctrine, 88, 119
prescription drugs, 66, 141, 168–9
presidents of the United States *see* entries for individual presidents
press
and information flow, 218
and Iraq, 231–2
White House and, 233
*see also Los Angeles Times*; media; *New York Times*; *Newsweek* magazine; *Time* magazine; *Washington Post*
"pressless presidency", 222

prisoner of war status
  terrorist suspects, 32
  US forces, 36
privacy: right to, 203
Prosper, Pierre, 31

race: and education, 55
racial discrimination, 61
Rangel, Charles B., 141
*Rasul* v. *Bush* (2004), 52
Reagan, President Ronald
  and centralisation, 62
  and communication, 222
  and Geneva Protocols, 86
  and judicial appointments, 71
  legacy of, 77
  minor speeches, 218
  and polling data, 232
  and *Roe* v. *Wade*, 201
  and Social Security, 173, 174, 254
  and Soviet threat, 89
  and United States Congress, 233
Real ID Act (2005), 65–6
realists: and invasion of Iraq, 120
recession *see* financial crash (2008)
Reed, Ralph, 210
Regan, Donald, 222
*Regents of the University of California* v. *Bakke* (1978), 55
regulation: economic policy, 154–6
regulatory agencies: political appointments, 156
Rehnquist, Chief Justice William H., 44, 45, 46, 54, 56, 205
Reid, Senator Harry, 27, 136–7
rendition: of terrorist suspects, 123, 126
Republican Primaries (2000), 200–1
Republicans
  Bush and, 13, 255, 271–4
  and centralisation, 72
  and Chemical Security Act, 106
  and nomination of chief justice, 47
  and children's health insurance, 66–7
  and Christian right, 211
  and defence, 79
  compared with Democrats, 13–14
  and education, 19, 185
  and elections, 242–4, 248, 255–6
  and federal power, 62–3
  and financial crash (2008), 162, 163
  in judiciary, 205
  and labour standards, 136, 141
  and Medicare, 166, 167–8, 169
  and Miers nomination to Supreme Court, 49
  and No Child Left Behind Act, 185, 186, 188
  and regulation, 155
  and Social Security reform, 173, 175, 177
  and trade, 129
  in United States Congress, 5–6, 13, 14, 17, 22–3, 202, 239, 242; House of Representatives, 4, 5–6, 20, 22–3, 24, 167–8, 192, 226, 248, 253, 255; Senate, 5, 6, 20, 63, 151, 226, 227
Rice, Condoleezza
  and foreign policy, 92–3, 94, 121
  and military commissions order, 31, 32
  and recovery of power, 263
  refutation of use of torture, 123
  and Weapons of Mass Destruction, 228–9
Ridge, Governor Tom, 102, 103, 104, 108
rights
  civil, 61, 185
  homosexual, 203
  to liberty, 203
  prisoners, 52–3
  to privacy, 203
  of self-defence, 89–90
  states, 62
  Taliban threat to, 82
  women, 82
  *see also* human rights
Ritter, Scott, 228–9
Roberts, Judge John Glover Jr, 45–7, 48, 49, 52, 54, 55, 57, 205
Robertson, Pat, 210
*Roe* v. *Wade* (1973), 48, 50, 54, 199, 200, 205, 211
Rollins, Ed, 243
Romania: and rendition, 123
Romig, Major General Thomas, 31
Romney, Governor Mitt, 212
Roosevelt, President Franklin
  minor speeches, 218
  and New Deal, 60–1
  and polling data, 232
  and post-war order, 86
  and travel, 219

Rose, Richard, 219
Ross, Fiona, 175
*Rostker* v. *Goldberg* (1981), 53
Rove, Karl
  and electoral strategy, 212
  and immigration reform, 4
  influence of, 220–1, 239–40, 242
  investigation into conduct, 49, 51
  and mid-term elections (2002), 247, 248
  power of, 253
  and Presidential Election (2000), 201–2
  and Social Security reform, 176
Rowley, Colleen, 105
Rubin, Robert, 159
Rumsfeld, Donald
  replacement by Robert Gates, 122
  and "old Europe", 9, 121–2
  and Saddam's link to al-Qaeda, 37
  vision for a new US military, 260
  and war on terror, 84
  *see also Hamdan* v. *Rumsfeld*
Russia: relations with USA, 80, 263; *see also* Soviet Union

Saddam Hussein
  perceived link with al Qaeda, 36–7, 42
  and uranium, 229–30
  and Weapons of Mass Destruction, 90–1, 228–9
  *see also* Iraq
salaries: executives, 164
same-sex marriages, 69, 73, 199, 203, 207–8, 211, 213, 249, 272
Santorum, Senator Rick, 242
Sarbanes–Oxley corporate accountability regulations, 20, 156
Sarkozy, President Nicolas, 125
Scalia, Justice Antonin, 45, 54–5, 56, 205
Schiavo, Terri, 206–7, 212, 250
schools
  Adequate Yearly Progress (AYP), 187, 190–1
  and discrimination, 55
  funding, 187
  performance, 187
  impact of sanctions, 191–2
  students, 187, 189, 194–5
  teachers, 187, 190
  *see also* No Child Left Behind (NCLB) Act (2001)
Schroeder, Chancellor Gerhard, 120, 124
Schumer, Senator Charles, 51, 142, 159
Schwarzenegger, Governor Arnold, 68
Scowcroft, Brent, 92, 120
Second Amendment *see* United States Constitution: Second Amendment
Securities and Exchange Commission (SEC), 159
security: and Weapons of Mass Destruction, 89; *see also* Center for International and Security Studies; homeland security; national security
segregation *see* discrimination
self-defence: right to, 89–90
Senate *see* United States Senate
Senate Homeland Security Appropriations Subcommittee, 105
Senior Executive Service (SES), 156
sex education, 206, 209
sexual morality, 199–213
Sforza, Scott, 222–3, 224, 228
Sherwood, Representative Don, 256
shipping, 155
signing statements: Bush's use of, 40–1, 42
Singapore: trade with, 136
Singh, R. *see* Lynch, T. J. and Singh, R.
Sixteenth Amendment *see* United States Constitution: Sixteenth Amendment
"smoking gun and mushroom cloud", 228, 229
Snow, John, 160
Social Security, 166–7, 172–7, 250–1
Social Security Act (1935), 60–1
Social Security Act (1965), 66
Somalia: al-Qaeda in, 82
Souter, Justice David, 48, 206
South Korea: trade with, 142
Soviet Union, 79, 96
Spain: and Iraq war, 92, 119
Specter, Senator Arlen, 48
Spellings, Margaret, 191
State Children's Health Insurance Program Act (1997), 66–7
State Department: Office of Intelligence and Research, 38
state governors: co-operation with presidents, 63; *see also* Blanco, Governor Kathleen; Huckabee, Governor Mike; Palin, Governor Sarah; Ridge, Governor Tom; Romney,

Governor Mitt; Schwarzenegger, Governor Arnold
State of the Union addresses, 218
  Bush, President George W.: (2003), 229; (2004), 175, 207–8; (2005), 175, 250; (2007), 193
  Clinton, President Bill: (1996), 14; (1999), 168
states: rights, 62
steel imports: tariffs, 137
stem-cell research, 206, 209
*Stenberg* v. *Carhart* (2000), 54
Stevens, Justice John Paul, 57
Stevenson, Richard, 220
stock market, 162
*Strengthening Social Security and Creating Wealth for all Americans* (The President's Commission to Strengthen Social Security 2001), 174
Supreme Court *see* United States Supreme Court
surveillance *see* National Security Agency
Sweeney, John, 142
Swift Boat Veterans for Truth, 249
Syria: al-Qaeda in, 82

Taguba, Major General Anthony, 88
Taliban, 82, 83, 84, 85
taxation
  discriminatory *see Department of Revenue for Kentucky* v. *Davis*
  and Internet access, 70
  reforms, 206
  tax cuts, 18, 19, 151–3, 157, 158, 160, 164, 166, 219–20, 265
Teles, Steven, 178
Tenet, George, 33, 34, 90
*Tennessee* v. *Lane* (2004), 72
Tenpas, Kathryn Dunn, 232
Tenth Amendment *see* United States Constitution: Tenth Amendment
terrorism, 229, 263; *see also* al-Qaeda; axis of evil; counter-terrorism; homeland security
Terrorism Prevention Act (2004), 65
terrorist suspects
  Abu Ghraib prison, 36, 53, 85, 87, 122
  civil liberties, 52
  habeas corpus, 31, 52–3
  Guantánamo Bay, 52, 85, 122–3
  prisoner of war status, 32
  rendition, 123, 126
  torture, 31, 32, 35, 36, 37, 42, 85–6, 87, 122–3, 261–2
  trial of *see* military commissions order
Terrorist Threat Integration Center (TTIC), 103, 108
terrorists: surveillance of *see* National Security Agency
Texas
  Bush as governor of, 7, 200
  school students, 190
Thomas, Justice Clarence, 45, 55, 71–2, 205
Thompson, Tommy, 168
*Time* magazine: poll on the Terri Schiavo case, 212
torture *see* terrorist suspects: torture
trade *see* international trade policy
Transportation Security Administration (TSA), 103, 104
Treasury Department, 138, 150, 154, 159
Truman, President Harry S.
  administration compared with Bush's, 77–8
  minor speeches, 218
  ratings, 233
  reputation, 259
  and travel, 219

UN *see* United Nations
*US* v. *Curtiss-Wright Export Corporation* (1936), 53
*US* v. *Miller* (1939), 56
*US* v. *US District Court* (1972), 53
USA Patriot Act (2001), 20, 52, 65, 102
USS *Abraham Lincoln*, 223
unemployment, 157, 265; *see also* employment
Uniform Code of Military Justice, 31, 32, 87
United Kingdom: support for Iraq war, 92, 119
United Nations
  attack on headquarters in Iraq (August 2003), 92
  US support for, 118
United Nations Security Council resolution 1441, 119
United States
  and Europe, 115–27, 139, 263
  image abroad, 262

power, 261, 262–3
United States Comptroller General, 101
United States Congress
and Bush, President George H. W., 233
and Bush, President George W., 13–27, 63, 233, 254
and Bush administration, 271–2
and Cheney, Vice President Dick, 18–19, 253
and Clinton, President Bill, 233
and Executive Office of the President, 104
ratification of international trade agreements, 136
partisanship in, 233–4
and pre-emption of state power, 70
and trade, 130–2, 139, 140–1, 143–5
relationship with the White House, 25, 130, 216
*see also* United States House Senate; United States House of Representatives
United States Constitution, 38
First Amendment, 53
Second Amendment, 55–6
Fourth Amendment, 38–9
Tenth Amendment, 60
Fourteenth Amendment, 61, 203
Sixteenth Amendment, 60
Article II, 19, 39
Bush administration's subversion of, 15
and discrimination, 55
United States General Accounting Office (GAO), 100, 101
United States House of Representatives
Democrats in, 126, 140, 142, 149, 242
and education, 185–6
and financial crisis (2008), 162–3
and Medicare reform, 167, 177
Republicans in, 4, 5–6, 20, 22–3, 24, 167–8, 192, 226, 248, 253, 255
and tax cuts, 220
United States–Middle East Free Trade Area, 136, 139, 144
United States Senate, 15
Democrats in, 17, 226–7
filibustering in, 204
Homeland Security Appropriations Subcommittee, 105
judiciary hearings (13–16 September 2005), 46–7
Republicans in, 5, 6, 20, 63, 151, 226, 227
Senatorial Campaign Committee, 226
United States Special Operations Command, 231–2
United States Supreme Court
Bush and, 44–57, 271
cases *see* entries for individual cases
and federalism, 61, 71–2
and military commissions order, 41
and moral issues, 205
and prisoner abuse, 87
Republican influence in, 274
and Terri Schiavo case, 207
and war, 9
United States war crimes statute, 35
universities: and discrimination, 55
Urban Areas Security Initiative, 106
Utah: and No Child Left Behind Act, 190

Vietnam *see* Gulf of Tonkin resolution
"Vietnam Syndrome", 261

war
European view of, 116
laws of, 86–7
on terror, 1, 18, 20, 52, 78, 79–92, 246, 263–4
Vietnam, 81
*see also* Cold War; "war on terror"
war crimes: Bush accused of, 88; *see also* United States war crimes statute
"war on terror", 1, 18, 20, 52, 78, 79–92, 246, 263–4
Warren, Pastor Rick, 211
Washington consensus, 3, 161, 267
Washington, DC: risk of terrorist attack, 105
*Washington Post*
on No Child Left Behind bill, 231
and vote on Iraq, 246–7
Weapons of Mass Destruction (WMD), 88–9, 91–2, 119, 227, 229–31, 262; *see also* nuclear weapons
Weiner, T., 177
West, Kanye, 273
West, Martin *see* Peterson, Paul and West, Martin
Wheeler, Russell, 204, 205

White House
  Brown, Gordon at, 125
  and Christian right, 199, 202, 207, 208, 210, 212, 213
  Coalition Information Center (CIC) (later Office of Global Communications), 224–5
  communication strategies in, 216–35
  and Department of Homeland Security, 104, 105, 106, 108
  and International Labour Organization, 141
  key actors under Bush, 159–60
  and Military Commissions Order, 30, 31–2
  Office of Communications, 216, 224
  Office of Global Communications (formerly Coalition Information Center), 225
  Office of Media Affairs, 221, 224
  and pollsters, 232
  and marginalisation of Powell, Colin, 41
  press briefings, 225
  Press Office, 221, 222, 224
  staff, 242
  and taxation, 18
  relationship with United States Congress, 25, 130, 216
Wilkinson, Jim, 225
Wilson, Joseph, 91, 230
Wolfowitz, Paul, 120, 124
women's rights: Afghanistan, 82
Woodward, Bob, 119
World Trade Organization (WTO), 131, 132, 133, 137, 267–8

Yemen: al-Qaeda in, 82

Zoellick, Robert, 134, 136